JOURNALISM
COMMUNICATION
AND THE LAW

JOURNALISM
COMMUNICATION
AND THE LAW

G. STUART ADAM, Editor

PRENTICE-HALL OF CANADA, LTD.
SCARBOROUGH, ONTARIO

Canadian Shared Cataloguing in Publication Data

Journalism, communication and the law /
G. Stuart Adam, ed. —

Bibliography: p.
ISBN 0-13-51118-8-9; 0-13-51117-0-6 (pa.)

1. Journalism — Canada.   2. Journalism —
Social aspects — Canada.   3. Press law —
Canada.   I. Adam, G   Stuart.

PN4903.J   071'.1

Published by Prentice-Hall of Canada, Ltd.
Scarborough, Ontario

Prentice-Hall, Inc., Englewood Cliffs, New Jersey
Prentice-Hall International, Inc., London
Prentice-Hall of Australia, Pty., Ltd., Sydney
Prentice-Hall of India, Pvt., Ltd., New Delhi
Prentice-Hall of Japan, Inc., Tokyo

BOOK DESIGN: William Fox/Associates

ISBN 0-13-51118-8-9
ISBN 0-13-51117-0-6 (pa.)

Printed and bound in Canada.

1 2 3 4 5 80 79 78 77 76

contents

To the Memory of
Dorothy and Alex Adam, Sam and Sara Wallack,
and Irwin Tradburks

Introduction

The primary goal of education in journalism is to prepare students for careers in newspapers, magazines and broadcasting. Although there is some variation from institution to institution, the strategy for achieving this goal normally entails study in three basic areas.

First, in such subjects as reporting, editing and production techniques, students are introduced to and required to face the analytical and practical problems of the working journalist. The role of such courses is so fundamental as to be obvious. Secondly, courses in the humanities and social sciences provide a broad intellectual backdrop for such practical problems. In the conviction that an advanced education and standards of writing and thought are intimately connected, however mysteriously, students are typically introduced to some of the facts of social, political, intellectual and cultural history, and to some of the contemporary methods for interpreting modern society and its important institutions. Wedged between these two areas is a third area—Journalism Studies—with which this book is concerned.

Journalism Studies refers to the growing body of knowledge on journalism, its history, its practitioners and institutions, its issues and qualities, the various functions it performs in society, and the social, economic and legal setting within which it operates. It is an interdisciplinary field, relying for its substance on the contributions of historians, scholars of law, literature and communications, sociologists, political scientists, philosophers, economists and journalists. Journalism Studies borrows almost equally from each. Accordingly, it combines the study of things which are as remote from one another as the literary analysis of journalistic writing is from the discussion of the economic basis of publishing and broadcasting. But they are combined in the conviction that when such analyses are done in an orderly and detailed manner, the potential for professional development is increased. The examination of the context and limits of journalism, intellectual and social, is both of practical importance—journalists, for example, should recognize libellous writing when they see it — and an academic study in its own right.

This book represents a preliminary attempt at giving form and some substance to Canadian Journalism Studies. The articles and bibliography are unified by the concern the authors have with journalism and the relationship between it, on the one hand, and society, its institutions, communication systems and other forms of writing and thought, on the other. In the cases where the research base of the articles is only partially developed, they have been included because they establish either important concepts or promising lines of inquiry. In this respect, the book should be regarded as a scouting of the terrain of Journalism Studies in Canada with highlights on problem areas rather than an exhaustive inventory of problems and research. It will be a long time before such an exhaustive inventory can be published in this country.

Part I is devoted to an examination of the internal character of journalism, some of its functions, and, more important, the relationship between journalism and other forms of knowledge and literature. The first three articles in Part II are concerned with the relationship between journalism, on the one hand, and politics, government, and national consensus, on the other. The final article in the section is an illustration of the fact that the news communication system in Canadian society is not coterminous with the news media. The news media are the institutionalized means for circulating news and commentary, a process which also takes place informally on a face-to-face basis. Part III is concerned with the common law, constitutional and statutory controls which define the rights, privileges and obligations of the journalist.

The law is quite obviously the most manifest and easily-described form of control. Those who have already begun the study of journalism will note that there is no article dealing with the control exercised through the economic system. The reason for this omission is that John Porter's theoretical discussion of the relationship between the organization of economic power and the mass media in *The Vertical Mosaic*[1] is already widely circulated and accessible and the documentation of the structure of ownership which Porter initiated is contained in the equally accessible *Report of the Special Senate Committee on Mass Media.*[2] As relevant as these companion studies are to the outlook of this book, there is no need to reprint them.

Part IV includes a bibliography which exemplifies a major purpose of the book — to stimulate the systematic study of journalism in this country. It and the book as a whole have been prepared with students and teachers of journalism in mind. Hopefully, however, the book will find an audience among students and teachers of communication, political science, sociology and even law where questions bearing on the nature and functions of journalism arise.

All but three of the articles have been prepared for this text. The reprints — all of them in Part III — are identified by the acknowledgments which appear on the first page of each.

NOTES TO INTRODUCTION

1/ *The Vertical Mosaic,* (Toronto: University of Toronto Press, 1964); see Chapter XV, "The Ideological System: The Mass Media".

2/In 3 volumes, (Ottawa: Queen's Printer, 1970).

ACKNOWLEDGMENTS A sabbatical leave from the School of Journalism at Carleton University taken to do other research enabled me to spend extra time on the preparation of this manuscript. I would like to thank the officers of Carleton University, particularly the now-retired Dean of Arts, Trevor Tolley, who arranged the leave and who in the time of our association supported and encouraged me in this and other enterprises. Furthermore, I would like to acknowledge the contribution of my colleagues to whom I owe thanks for their advice and criticism and to whom I owe the idea that Journalism Studies is a viable field of inquiry. Particularly, I would like to thank the former director of the School of Journalism, Joe Scanlon, to whom I am indebted for his continuing encouragement, advice and support.

Most of all, I would like to thank my secretary, Carol Ramkerrysingh, who helped to prepare and edit the manuscript, typed all of it and who, while I was away, kept the project moving. Only her wise counsel and competence enabled the completion of the work.

G. Stuart Adam
Director, School of Journalism
Carleton University
Ottawa

PART ONE

The Nature
of Journalism

EDITOR'S NOTE: The three essays in this section are devoted to defining journalism and locating it in the domain of culture.

In Chapter One, journalism is defined broadly. There are four major points of discussion: a) twentieth-century journalism is a reflection of styles and subject matter evolved over a period of more than two centuries; b) it is a form of thought which may be compared to other forms, such as philosophy, history and literature; c) its primary function is to locate members of society in a world of real events and things; but, d) the bias of journalism is to point members of society toward political events and things, even when there is a substantial amount of economic and social matter in the public media. To highlight this latter point, two types of journalism are identified—"literary" and "civic". It is "civic" journalism which ties members of society into the democratic political process.

In the second essay the focus is narrower, as Phyllis Wilson examines "news", the dominant mode of contemporary journalism. She surveys some definitions of news, but concentrates on an analysis of the five elements—timeliness, proximity, prominence, consequence, and human interest—on which it is traditionally based. She concludes with a discussion of some criticisms of news which have been made by thoughtful journalists and reporters who believe that news is too concerned with limited events and not concerned sufficiently with broader social and political currents.

The theme of Chapter Three is the close alliance between journalism and fiction which, according to Roger Bird, are two branches of the single cultural movement "social realism". The primary difference between these two modes of expression is that journalism is a record of "reality" while fiction is a vision of it. Such a difference notwithstanding, it is the points of convergence on which Dr. Bird concentrates, through an examination of some eighteenth- and twentieth-century examples. He begins by showing that writers work as both journalists and novelists and concludes with some observations on the "New Journalism" in which the "impulses of journalism and fiction co-exist in such a way as to prevent their falling neatly into either category".

chapter one

The Journalistic Imagination

G. STUART ADAM

The professional journalist is caught between the admiration of those who believe him to be the custodian of the democratic order and the disdain of those who see him as a threat to decency, order and standards in culture. On the one hand, he is the agent of the press which provides "the breath of life for parliamentary institutions"[1] and, on the other, he is the author of "journalese", a "facile" style of writing, "with hackneyed expressions or effects".[2]

The reasons for this ambiguity are many and they include the fact that there have always been bad journalists giving good ones bad reputations. In the seventeenth century, for example, it could be said (by another journalist no doubt) that one of the first of the breed "was an infamous and unclean person next to the hangman".[3] Indeed the seventeenth- and eighteenth-century journalists, by their venal extravagance, contributed permanently to the journalist's reputation. A press historian notes: "If one adds up the names supplied by various polemical papers of those allegedly suffering from venereal diseases he would expect most middle and upper-class Englishmen of the next generation to be born idiots."[4]

In a brief aside in one of his most famous essays, the sociologist Max Weber focussed on yet another reason. He wrote: "In common with all demagogues, the journalist shares the fate of lacking a fixed social classification . . . . The journalist belongs to a sort of pariah caste, which is always estimated by society in terms of its ethically lowest representative."[5]

Weber was writing before the mass media had acquired their modern dimensions. In the late twentieth century he probably would have regarded the journalist in much the same way as contemporary social scientists view him—with a certain malevolence—as an information bureaucrat, a gatekeeper or communicator rather than as a free-floating cosmopolitan. But he noted rightly that the attitudes toward the journalist were more a result of the journalist's relationship to social structure than a comment on his work.

Indeed, Weber was complimentary about the quality of some journalism.

3

"Not everybody," he wrote, "realizes that a really good journalistic achievement requires at least as much genius as any scholarly accomplishment, especially because of the necessity of producing at once "on order" and because of the necessity of being effective . . . under quite different conditions of production."[6]

Such compliments notwithstanding, it was neither journalistic excellence nor virtuous behavior that secured for the journalist the better half of his reputation. Despite the fact that the fathers of the craft were little more than party hacks, they played a vital role in forging democratic politics. The liberal theorists acknowledged this and there has not been a friend of liberal democracy who has not been at the same time a friend of the journalist.

None of this is new. We are taught to despise and admire the journalist with equal enthusiasm for getting things wrong, for distorting the truth, for being shallow or, alternatively, for saving the American people from Richard Nixon or the people of Ontario from the government's police bill. God bless-damn the press! But we have not tried to explain the ambiguities of the journalist's image by exploring the nature of journalism itself. In what follows I have tried to do this in an examination of what may be called the journalistic imagination.

In adopting the term "imagination", I am guided by the example of C. Wright Mills who in one of his best books described the properties of the "sociological imagination". He said that it was a quality of mind which helps men "to achieve lucid summations of what is going on in the world and what may be happening within themselves".[7] The journalistic imagination is perhaps less of an imagination—perhaps at its best a fragment of the sociological imagination. But it is nevertheless a distinctive approach to understanding and representing the affairs of the world.

Its venue is the public media. Historically such media have included newspapers, magazines and pamphlets—especially newspapers—but in this century they include the public affairs and news channels of the broadcast media which command at least as much attention as the newspaper. Furthermore, it reflects the concerns of society as a whole rather than its specialized branches.

Constructing a portrait of this journalistic imagination will entail an examination of some of its sources in the traditions and history of journalism followed by a profile of some of its qualities and a description of its relationship to other forms of knowledge and to literature. It will conclude with an examination of the way in which the functions it performs in the larger social system dominate its content. If there is a bias in the discussion it is toward that kind of journalism which sharpens our conception of the world or, as Mills would have it, "achieves lucid summations of what is going on . . .".

I

Journalism is a living tradition with a history in the English-speaking world which dates roughly from the third decade of the seventeenth century when *corantos* first appeared in the streets of London. Of Dutch inspiration, the *corantos* were for the most part skimpy productions containing only foreign news of a sort that did not upset the authorities. Except for two years during the Long Parliament, printing was subject to licensing in the seventeenth century and it was not until after the Licensing Act was suspended in 1695 that journalism began to shed its basically official and cautious character.

While this is not the place for a comprehensive review of the histories of British, U.S. and Canadian journalism it is of interest to note that the craft's traditions on both sides of the Atlantic took root in the eighteenth and nineteenth centuries. A few examples can be usefully cited. The polemical essay, precursor of the modern editorial, was typical of the party papers of the reign of Anne and, later, of Walpole's ministry. While it is true that the passion (and even the sedition) of the essays of those days is unlikely to be found in the editorials of modern dailies, it is equally true that the opinion function earned its footing in the journalistic tradition in the first half of the eighteenth century. In a broader sense, it can be argued that whatever adversary elements survive in journalism—and some such as Richard Nixon and Spiro Agnew would argue that they do—they acquired their foundations in the party journalism of the eighteenth century in both Britain and the colonies.

As the eighteenth century progressed, reporting of domestic news became increasingly important. Domestic subject matter included tales of the court, coffeehouses and the streets. But no subject was more important after the 1770s than Parliament. The history of parliamentary reporting begins much earlier but it would be impossible to deny that the affairs of the legislature have dominated the news imaginations of British and North American journalists since that time.

The century also witnessed a turn in news values toward sensationalism. Dr. Johnson observed in the *Idler:* "Scarcely anything awakens attention like a tale of cruelty. The writer of news never fails in the intermission of action to tell how the enemies murdered children and ravished virgins; and, if the scene of action is somewhat distant, scalps half the inhabitants of a province".[8] Dr. Johnson's news writers had discovered that to the serious business of politics and war one could add bits which were exciting, titillating and shocking.

The sensationalism exemplified by Dr. Johnson's writers was even more prominent in the nineteenth century, the golden age of the human interest story. Perfected in the penny papers of New York in the first half of that century, it has since remained a staple of journalism. Even now a story by James Gordon Bennett for his *New York Herald* in 1836 has a familiar ring to it, if not in style at least in the morbid preoccupation with the spectacle of death. Bennett was covering the murder of a prostitute called Helen Jewett:

> "Here," said the Police Officer, "here is the poor creature." He half uncovered the ghastly corpse. I could scarcely look at it for a second or two. Slowly I began to discover the lineaments of the corpse as one would the beauties of a statue of marble. It was the most remarkable sight I ever beheld. I never would have and never expect to see such another. "My God," I exclaimed, "How like a statue! I can scarcely conceive that form to be a corpse." Not a vein was to be seen. The body looked as white, as full, as polished, as the purest Parian marble. The perfect figure, the exquisite limbs, the fine face, the full arms, the beautiful bust, all, all surpassed in every respect the Venus de Medici, according to the casts generally given of her.[9]

The editors of Bennett's time began to give content to their papers by having their reporters investigate the previously unspeakable realm of the poor and dispossessed as it was revealed in such institutions as the police courts. The lore of the streets and the common man had been appropriated to the journalistic imagination.

But it was left to such men as Joseph Pulitzer and William Randolph Hearst to perfect the sensationalism which was anticipated in the eighteenth century and the early part of the nineteenth century. The "yellow journalism" associated with their papers was highly sensational, reckless, and, in some cases, completely irresponsible. Journalism histories inevitably note the role Hearst played in stirring up public opinion during the Spanish-American War by citing his response to an artist-reporter's telegram from Cuba that he wanted to come home because there was no action. Hearst replied: "Please remain. You furnish the pictures. I'll furnish the war."[10]

Yellow journalism reminiscent of that age has disappeared from all but a very few of the major newspapers, although the display techniques which it fostered survive to some extent. However, its opposite, the "objective" news story, which can be traced to the development of wire services in the middle of the nineteenth century, has survived and flourished. Because of the need to appeal to a clientele of newspaper editors whose political convictions were different, the wire service managers perfected the mode of journalistic writing in which facts were supreme and opinions absent. Today this spare and unembellished form of writing is dominant.

A further observation might properly be made. In tracing the career of journalism in the English-speaking world, it becomes clear that it is intimately connected with the growth of democratic and urban culture. It is impossible to conceive of a modern democratic society without at the same time conceiving of the journalist enmeshed in its political events. Equally, the city has been the creative center of journalism. The newspaper has been the domain within which public discourse of the city has taken place and it is impossible to separate journalism's history from the histories of Britain's and North America's great cities, especially London and New York.

But this is not the major point that is being made. Even a cursory examination of the history of journalism reveals that there were stages of development in which certain styles and certain objects became appropriated to the tradition. The result has been a mosaic of subjects, qualities, and styles unified by a common function—to provide a continuing picture and, to a certain extent, values by which to judge the social, economic, political and cultural environment within which we live. Accordingly, as Robert Park once said of the newspaper, but here applied more broadly to journalism, "it is not the willful product of any . . . group of living human beings".[11] The fact that it is a tradition implies that the modern journalist labors in the shadow of his professional forebears. In other words, the present forms of journalism are guided by past performances and are the outcome, in short, "of an historic process in which many individuals participated without foreseeing what the ultimate product of their labors was to be".[12] With this lean portrait of journalism's past in view, we can turn now to an examination of some of its more basic properties.

II

John Porter wrote of Canadian newspapermen that although they have "no disciplined training in any particular sphere . . . they seem prepared to write about anything".[13] As contemptuous as the phrase may be, it is close to the truth. Journalists are writers first and specialists second. How then to define what they produce?

To begin with, theorists have associated the practice of journalism with the natural habit of human beings to speak of things they have seen or felt. From this point of view local gossip and the sagas of itinerant balladeers in the days prior to the development of the press were precursors of modern journalism as they, like newspapers after them, conveyed to individuals opinions and information about a world which was not experienced directly. Such functions were absorbed by journalism when the invention of the press and the rise of literacy made it possible. In this formulation, journalism is cast as a functional equivalent to conversation in which the contingencies of daily existence are foremost. The importance of this formulation is that it distinguishes journalism from other forms of knowledge in which there is a formal universe of discourse and a highly technical method for acquiring and evaluating such knowledge. Although it is true that the values journalists use to judge the importance of the phenomena about which they write may be derived from a structure of thought such as Marxism or liberalism, it is also true that journalism is "talk", not science or philosophy.

More precisely, journalism is the record of and comment in the public media on ideas and events as they occur. It is necessary to stress the obvious point that journalism is concerned with real events. Even where fantasy invades writing that is conventionally thought of as journalism or where layers of argument obscure the facts, it is the concern with facts that distinguishes journalism from the novel or some forms of philosophy. To borrow a point Alfred Kazin made in a discussion of the New Journalism, the novel is an invention while journalism is fundamentally a report.[14] If it is not itself a report, it is at least dependent on one.

Furthermore, the facts journalists dwell on are contemporary ones. One could say that unlike history or some other branches of the social sciences it is a first attempt at cutting through the opaqueness which clouds our perception of the external world. Historians and other scholars may provide much clearer pictures of the phenomena journalists have described—but only much later with research devices and hindsight unavailable to the journalist.

As much as journalism is concerned with contemporary facts, it is written for immediate consumption. In this respect, it tends to be perishable, although occasionally the achievements of individual journalists are highly durable and thereby become part of a culture's permanent inventory of aesthetic and intellectual artifacts. When they become part of this inventory, they are examined just as great scholarly, literary or artistic achievements are examined long after being produced—for their beauty, for the way in which they capture human experience or for their insight. For the most part, however, individual pieces of journalism are most important on the day they are published to be succeeded quickly by new events and new productions.

In other words, durability is a primary virtue in art and scholarship; it is only a secondary virtue in journalism. Self-evidently, the slimmest, most uncomplicated and perishable three-paragraph news brief announcing the fall of a government or a dam is of enormous importance, even when it is written in "journalese" which, as noted in the introduction, is defined in such a way as to reflect the disrespect in which some of journalism is held. But such a story alerts members of society to the business at hand and it is important that it does. Accordingly, journalism's primary functions—to convey and analyze information about the contemporary world—dominate its organization and substance.

Still, the distinctions between journalism and other forms of knowledge are not always clear. Before proceeding to a more careful examination of these functions and their sources, it is expedient to examine the relationship of journalism to these other forms of knowledge and then to use some of the criteria by which they are assessed to assess individual pieces of journalism. Such an examination will provide a sharper impression of the journalistic imagination.

Robert Park's essay entitled "News as a Form of Knowledge"[15] is one basic reference for this enterprise. In this essay, published first in the forties, Park proposed to examine the news by first imagining a continuum representing degrees of precision in knowledge. Nothing very complex was at stake. Park was simply arguing that there is a kind of knowing which is superficial, fragmentary and, in a scientific sense, incommunicable. It is the "sort of knowledge one inevitably acquires in the course of one's personal and firsthand encounters with the world about him. It is the knowledge that comes with use and wont rather than through any formal or systematic investigation".[16] Such knowledge, he said, is "acquaintance with". At the other end of the continuum he put "knowledge about", that is to say, knowledge that is formal, exact, tagged, regimented and verified. Such knowledge, Park argued, is typical of science. By such a word he meant more than the natural sciences. He meant philosophy and history as well, the first dealing with ideas and the second with events.

Somewhere between these two ends of the continuum Park located news. He said, for example, that it was subject to verification, an attribute it has in common with forms of knowledge which are more substantial. But he also said news is usually concerned with events which are viewed in isolation. News normally comes as an independent communication rather than in a logical and analytical frame in which events are explained or tied to others. The capacity to view events in a broader context obviously increases the substance of journalism.

To follow Park's argument but substitute the broader concept of journalism for his concept of news, it is possible to imagine individual pieces of journalism at a number of stations along this imagined continuum, each station representing increasing descriptive richness, increasing complexity in the relations between phenomena described and increasing explanatory power. At one end of the continuum one would find journalism which would approximate mere gossip and rumor. Other pieces would be closer on the continuum, although never the equivalent, to exact pieces of scholarly knowledge derived from historical, philosophical or scientific investigation. The reason for this latter limitation is simple enough. Journalists stand on the frontiers of public knowledge but not on the frontiers of knowledge itself. The latter is not their business. However, reportorial care and depth as well as explanatory and analytical rigor are for journalists, as well as for scholars, criteria which may be used to assess the quality of their productions. A few examples may help illustrate the point.

In *The Globe and Mail* of Thursday, November 14, 1974, the following story appeared on page 3:

> PARIS (Reuter) - Tens of thousands of striking workers demonstrated in Paris and other major cities yesterday in protest against the Government's anti-inflation program.
>
> Civil servants, postmen, printers—who stopped publication of nationally circulated newspapers—and sympathetic journalists took part.
>
> Hospital, customs and social security employees went on strike for 24 hours as gas and electricity workers prepared for a campaign of sporadic stoppages to bring power cuts today and Friday.
>
> A settlement of the four-week-old postal strike, which triggered the wave of disputes, seemed as far off as ever.
>
> Postmen are asking for a minimum wage of about $350 a month plus better working conditions and a $41-a-month advance against pay raises due in 1975.

It's probably superfluous to point out that the story is very low on content and explanatory power. Although it is useful to have an "acquaintance with" such facts—the story is functional—it is self-evident that it simply skims the surface of events.

Such reporting can be compared with the remarkable achievements of the two *Washington Post* writers who, over a period of a year, discovered and pasted together the fragments of the Watergate story which led finally to the resignation of the President of the United States.[17] Since the story of this reporting achievement is related in a book the two reporters wrote when their assignment ended, there is no need to examine it here. But it may be noted that just as in many scholarly achievements, it was investigative stamina and careful documentation that distinguished the work of the *Post* writers. Many stories of that kind—perhaps not as many as there could be—inhabit the pages of our daily newspapers and magazines.

The Watergate story, its reportorial achievement notwithstanding, was fundamentally descriptive in its rhetorical purpose. For an example of an explanatory achievement, it is more useful to turn to yet another story, this one by Ron Haggart, a former Toronto columnist who wrote a piece called

"How the Tories Hold Power in Ontario" for *Saturday Night* in January 1972.

Haggart set the tone in the opening paragraphs:

> When Leslie Frost thought of urban transportation, he thought of the railways, and when he thought of the railways he thought of the marvelously grotesque old CNR station in his home town of Lindsay, the tracks running down the residential streets, and the one train a day which lumbered into Toronto, occasionally carrying the Premier of Ontario himself, always an event to be remarked upon by the other three passengers.
>
> It was an article of faith with Leslie Frost that he would never subsidize the railways and that, by extension, meant he would never give money to the Toronto subway. And he never did, for if there was one black devil in the politics of Leslie Frost larger than the railways, it was, of course, Toronto.

The problem Haggart was unravelling was one which belonged as much to history and political science as to journalism. For his theme was built out of an event that had at that time lasted 28 years—the period of the Tory supremacy in Ontario—and had embraced four premiers. What may have appeared at first blush to have been the achievement of a distinctive political philosophy was in Haggart's view the achievement of barely-noticed reversals such as Robarts' "urbanization" of government which "found expression not only in the new attitude toward city transportation with massive highways for the workday and summer cottage commuter, but also in the complete reversal of the government attitude toward consumer legislation".

Haggart described the metamorphosis of the Tory governments by examining some of the major policies and issues of the period. It is impossible to assess the substance of his achievement without knowing the reliability of the evidence. But the scope of the argument based on events which seem remote from one another shows analytical depth which is possible but not very common in journalism. It may still be read for insight. It may be noted in passing that unlike scholars working in the social sciences, Haggart was not using a technical vocabulary or manipulating an esoteric set of concepts to develop his argument. As rich and as imaginative as the analysis was, it sprang from ordinary as opposed to technical discourse.

Haggart's story also reflected an aesthetic dimension which is unlikely to be found in the spare and simple news story. If logic and evidence are two criteria by which journalistic pieces are judged, so too is there an aesthetic criterion. A sentence such as this one was one of several examples: "One of Frost's earlier ministers of education occupied himself with speeches eulogizing the one-room schoolhouse (on the eve of Sputnik) while Frost himself (undoubtedly the most charming man in the politics of his time) comforted the people with a syrup of cracker-barrel political yarns, plus the aphorisms which pass for rural values and a most embarrassingly straightforward and frontier brand of promised patronage." Haggart's writing reflects both a vocabulary and an imagination which are subtle and interesting. Although it is far from extraordinary, the article on the Tories was written carefully and skilfully.

In passing judgment on such writing an aesthetic standard is at stake. Journalists, like novelists and poets, sometimes exploit the language to build impressions of people or events or things. Sometimes they are successful. One is reminded of the description of Miami in Norman Mailer's account of the Republican convention in the summer of 1968:

> Of course it could have been the air conditioning; natural climate transmogrified by technological climate. They say that in Miami Beach the air conditioning is pushed to that icy point where women wear fur coats over their diamonds in the tropics. For ten miles, from the Diplomat to the di Lido, above Hollandale Beach Boulevard down to Lincoln Mall, all the white refrigerators six and eight and twelve stories high, twenty stories high, shaped like sugar cubes and ice-cube trays on edge, like mosques and palaces, shaped like matched white luggage and portable radios, stereos, plastic compacts and plastic rings, Moorish castles shaped like waffle irons . . . .[18]

There is no need to present a brief on behalf of Mailer. I do not think he is a very good political reporter. But at the very least, the attempt to develop a conception of a civilization built on technology is strenuous. It demonstrates that aesthetic devices are not off limits. One can go further. The discussion of the New Journalism—a movement with which Mailer is associated—is concerned very largely with the use in the report of devices familiar to students of literature.[19] To the extent these devices are used successfully, the aesthetic substance and, it may be added, the uniqueness and durability of individual pieces of journalism appreciate.

In sum, the criteria by which journalism may be judged are similar in kind to the criteria we use to judge history, social science and literature. Clearly, the functions journalism is required to perform and the conditions under which it is produced tend to diminish its evidential, analytical and aesthetic substance. Accordingly, it is not at all surprising that journalism is viewed sometimes with disdain. But there have been many remarkable journalistic achievements over the years nevertheless.

In short, Weber was right when he noted that some journalistic achievements are worthy of profound respect. Such achievements show that the mind has been tested in a way which approximates the tests in literature and scholarship. We can now return to the questions raised by the functions of journalism, particularly the way in which these functions impress themselves on the journalistic imagination.

III

It is a long-established convention of the social sciences to explain the significance of various social stuctures by showing the functions they perform in the overall social system. The mass media compose one such social structure and, accordingly, it is commonplace to find in the literature of the social sciences propositions referring to the functions they perform and, where distinctions are carefully made, the functions journalism performs.

For example, the political scientist Harold Lasswell once postulated that the three major functions of the mass media—journalism may be considered a central activity of the mass media—were the surveillance of the environment, the correlation of its parts, and the transmission of the social heritage.[20] The first referred to an information service through which events of significance were noted and communicated to members of society. Lasswell conceived it to be essential because individual and collective responses to such things as threats must be based on an understanding of facts. The second referred to the perspective achieved on these events through their display in newspapers or the way in which they were discussed in editorials and columns. The sense of proportion achieved in such ways was conceived as a prophylactic against unwarranted or exaggerated responses. The third referred to passing on the basic values of society by expressing and repeating them in the context of judging and interpreting events. This final function was no less critical for being third. It is axiomatic in social theory that without a core system of values which is shared by all members of society there can be no society.

Lasswell's formulations are typical of that part of social science in which society is conceived as an organism with a rational organization. Propositions are developed in a way which stresses the dependancy of the organism for its very existence on the co-ordination of activities such as the production of newspapers and the writing of journalism. In modern social theory it is also axiomatic that the mass media through which journalism is circulated constitute the basic communications infrastructure which makes modern societies possible.

Canadian sociologist John Porter also works within the traditions of functional analysis, although in his discussion of the mass media the focus is much narrower. Porter's interest in the organization of power in Canadian society led him to argue in *The Vertical Mosaic* that the function of the press is basically a conservative one—that is to say, the function of journalism is to preserve the complex of power in Canadian society.[21]

Porter's proposition is not in conflict with those of Lasswell. The social heritage could very well include a reverence for a power structure of the sort Porter described. If there is a conflict, it would be between Porter and journalists who, unaccustomed to thinking of themselves as instruments of social control, would likely reject the proposition in light of their manifest aims, some of which would include reporting the news, exposing corruption, entertaining the people, or acting as watchdogs on government. In other words, even if journalism serves to maintain the structure of power, it is not the intention of journalists to do so.

To secure a more satisfactory link between the function of journalism in society and the intentions of journalists, it is expedient to broaden the focus to capture much of what was intended in Lasswell's categories but to state the proposition in a more efficient way. To do this it is necessary to rely once again on Robert Park who said of news that its function is "to orient man and society in a real world. Insofar as it succeeds it tends to preserve the sanity of the individual and the permanence of society".[22] By the preservation of the sanity of the individual, Park meant that an individual's sanity may be in part measured by his capacity to operate in the real world. The conception of the existential field or the world "out there" provided by journalism is a guarantee that social reality is embedded in individual consciousness. As much as the individual needs journalism, so too does society. For a society exists only to the extent that its individual members have a shared conception of its parts and its values. Thus the empirical basis intrinsic to journalism and the value orientation of much of it are highly functional both in a sociological and psychological sense.

Before going on, it is necessary to digress briefly. Park's formulation is useful because it expresses at a very high level of generalization just what it is that journalism does. But it may be noted that the formulation is not without problems. Journalism can equally be seen to be dysfunctional from the point of view of society and the individual. It matters greatly the vantage point from which it is viewed. For example, it is not hard to imagine journalism providing intellectual justifications and information to revolutionaries whose aims would be to destroy specific social systems. Nor would it be hard to imagine journalism without any basic change in its present character, driving the fragile or simply the sensitive among us stark, raving mad. The shape of the modern apocalypse is visible daily on the front pages of the newspaper. If that portrait of impending nuclear, ecological and international disaster doesn't drive one mad, what will? Park would no doubt answer that we do not make ourselves more sane by substituting happy illusions. If Park wouldn't say it, newspapermen certainly would. It may be noted, however, that the problem demonstrates the limits of theory.

Still, the basic proposition is sensible, even if it should be used cautiously. The point is that it secures the link between the aims of journalists, on the one hand, and some of the outcomes of journalism practice on the other. If journalists do not actually intend to "orient man and society in an actual world", the sum of their intentions approximates that aim. Accordingly, the functions implied by Park's proposition must be read back into the journalistic imagination itself.

Just as reportorial, analytical, explanatory and aesthetic substance is represented in degrees in journalism, so too is function. These degrees of functional substance can be imagined by locating stories on yet another continuum. At one end would be human interest stories similar in kind to James Gordon Bennett's description of Helen Jewett's cadaver and at the other end political stories such as the one announcing the fall of a government. The choice of non-political human interest stories and explicitly political news stories is deliberate. It provides a final opportunity to add dimensions to the journalistic imagination.

The Helen Jewett story was based on real events. It provided a fragment of the real world. But those who read it in its time probably read it, as they would a popular novel or short story, for its own sake. It is not hard to imagine them talking about it at great length, weeping for the wretched soul or emitting what editors of the old school imagined to be a hearty "gee whiz". In a primitive way Bennett's story exploited the elements with which the writer of fiction is often concerned—mystery, beauty and tragedy. In this sense the story was a form of popular literature.

The human interest story is always of that character. Its functional character is limited by the literary ambitions which are also basic to it. Its aim is to entertain as much as it is to inform, although it is worth noting here that sometimes the human interest story is freighted with a strongly moralistic undertone. The balance of the Helen Jewett story was about the man Robinson who murdered her. The scenario of his descent from upper class privilege to degradation was a lesson in the perils of debauchery and high living. But for all that it was just a story.

Accordingly, one end of this second continuum may be properly labelled "literary" (not aesthetic) so that pieces on the stations approaching it represent the literary tradition in journalism. Most of the time such pieces reflect a limited imagination, especially when they are written as police stories often are—according to an explicit formula. Sometimes, of course, they reflect a reportorial and descriptive imagination of considerable depth. When they do, their relationship to literature is clearer.

In February 1972, Barnard Collier published an article in *Esquire* called "On Chuck Hughes, Dying Young". It started abruptly with the disclosure that on a Sunday afternoon in 1971 "a twenty-eight-year-old Detroit Lion named Chuck Hughes dropped dead of a heart attack on the fifteen-yard line in front of a gathering of millions of Americans" who were either in the Detroit stadium or watching on television.

Collier wrote:

> You did not know right away he was dead, but you knew something was wrong. The cameras showed a close-up of Dick Butkus of the Chicago Bears standing over him and waving in a scared and frantic way for the referees and then for the doctors on the Lions' bench. A player must wave for the referees before the doctors can come out on the field or it is a violation of the National Football League rules. A player might be lying there faking an injury to stop the clock. The Lions were behind by five points and they needed a touchdown before the clock ran out in order to win. But an incomplete pass had already stopped the clock, so Chuck Hughes had no reason to fake. He must have looked very bad off to Dick Butkus because you knew that Butkus is mean and ornery when he is out there on the football field and doesn't normally come to the aid of an injured man who is not on his team.

After this spare description of the action on the field, Collier provided a detailed portrait of Chuck Hughes's love affair with football and his wife. Of his love affair with football, Collier reported that as a boy Hughes had "loved to catch the football. He loved to catch it and feel it in his hands . . . . He was too small and skinny to catch the ball and run over people so his coaches all told him: 'Chuck, you must never try to run over people. You get the ball in your hands and run away from them' ". According to Collier he ran away from them with increasing success. With remarkable dedication he overcame his physical limitations to become a competent professional and he was helped in his great cause by the support he had received from his wife, who on that grim day sat with the fans in the Detroit stadium as the medics tried frantically to arouse him. They had met when he was a sophomore, married when she was twenty-one. The detail of the story included a portrait of this loving relationship. And it included the unhappy intelligence that there had been a history of heart attacks in the Hughes family. The story ended: "They turned the TV cameras on him for us until the spirit left him, and then they turned away. For millions of Americans to intrude on the unfortunate death of a football player was no longer appropriate".

Short of publishing the complete text it would be impossible to do justice to Collier's reporting and writing accomplishment. Its character can best be understood in light of the analytic criteria elaborated earlier. But that is not the manner in which it should be understood here. It is a human interest story. It captures human experience and conveys it as much for its own sake as it does for the sake of the information it contains. Its functional character is limited. It stands in obvious contrast to a straightforward political story in which function is primary.

Self-evidently, not all stories of instrumental value are political. The intelligence that inhabits the business pages is useful to businessmen as they assess the prospects of their own and their competitor's businesses. Weather reports are non-political, but they are manifestly useful. However, in a society such as our own in which politics is conceived as the chief business, no story is more highly valued, no source is more carefully cultivated than political ones even though the political arena is no richer than any other for stories of intelligence, stupidity, venality, lechery, cowardice or, for that matter, human virtue.

Accordingly, despite the potential for attending to uncountable numbers of events and ideas that occur on any given day, city editors consistently and predictably note and assign reporters to the meetings of local governments, school boards and legislatures. Reporters report the business of such bodies with remarkable zeal.

Evidence for this is not difficult to accumulate. The great newspapers and magazines have secured their reputations not simply because of a general dedication to truth and its elegant presentation. The source of their reputation has been rather a consequence of their dedication to political truth. The coverage given to Washington and to New York state and city politics by *The New York Times* is a case in point. It commits resources to political coverage that dwarf those of most other papers and its editors see to it that the political news is displayed prominently. For example, in the edition circulated on November 19, 1974, four of the front-page stories were political stories originating in Washington. They dealt with the message President Ford sent to Congress urging it to deal efficiently and expeditiously with the legislation before it, with the revelations at the Watergate trial that former President Richard Nixon had planned to grant clemency to one of the men convicted for his part in the raid on the Democratic Party's headquarters, with Vice-President-designate Nelson Rockefeller's spending and lending habits which were then under the review of a Congressional committee, and with President Ford's reception in Tokyo by the Emperor of Japan. The latter story had a Tokyo dateline, but it was a national political story just the same.

The fate of a New York state narcotics law providing for mandatory life sentences for the possession for sale of certain kinds of drugs was the subject of yet another story. The state's appellate court had upheld the law even though the justices were reported to have agreed with the appellant's attorney that the law was unduly harsh. A city story dealt with the actions and justifications of the police commissioner who on the previous day had dismissed nineteen police officers for their alleged collaboration with Brooklyn gamblers. The remaining four stories dealt with a nationwide bus strike, the events in Washington surrounding a gunman's attempt to use the Philippine ambassador as a hostage, an Arab riot in Jerusalem and (of all things) the Canadian government's budget which had been just brought before Parliament. Six of the ten stories were on domestic politics or government.

Needless to say, individual journalists and individual papers engage the problems of governance with unequal degrees of competence and vigor. But even the smaller dailies encumber themselves with the responsibility of looking more carefully at political institutions and events than at any other kind. On November 26, 1974, for example, seven of the nine front-page stories in *The Ottawa Journal* were based on events that were associated with federal, provincial or municipal governments. The lead story reported in a straightforward manner the Economic Council of Canada's eleventh annual report, the main recommendation of which was that provincial and federal governments should permit the oil prices to rise in order to encourage exploration and discourage excess consumption. The second story dealt with warnings that tax rises in the Ottawa-Carleton region were coming. Yet another dealt with a federal government commission of inquiry into the Royal Canadian Mounted Police. The two subjects which did not impinge on domestic public authorities of one kind or another, at least not directly, were an international story dealing with British legislation to outlaw the Irish Republican Army and a report that a convict serving time for murder at the Joyceville prison near Kingston in eastern Ontario had escaped. All were written in that spare, unembellished style in which facts are efficiently ordered so that they may be easily digested.

The journalism originating on Parliament Hill in Ottawa comes in a variety of styles. Columns, backgrounders, analyses and features are almost, but not quite as common as the straight news story which is perfectly suited to the circulation of political business. Such a story is exemplified by the following, written by a Canadian Press reporter and displayed on the front page of *The Ottawa Citizen,* October 1, 1974.

> Parliament opened Monday with a government promise to restrain its spending and tackle the "serious and urgent" problem of inflation. Housing, transportation and consumer protection received most of the emphasis in the outline of government plans for the new session.

But the pledge to restrain spending was the keynote of the throne speech, read by Chief Justice Bora Laskin. The speech left no doubt that the battle against inflation will be the Liberal government's priority in the immediate future.

While the speech was the first government acknowledgement in Parliament of the magnitude of current economic problems, opposition leaders found little to praise.

Aside from recognition of the scope of the inflationary problem, Conservative Leader Stanfield said "there was really nothing surprising in the speech from the throne".

Ed Broadbent, New Democratic Party parliamentary leader, saw indications of the government following a deflationary policy, despite the explicit promise to not deliberately "generate slack in the economy in order to combat inflation".

The story goes on to provide further detail of the action inside and outside Parliament as various spokesmen reacted to the government plans. It and several collateral stories appearing on the inside pages dealt with the record of the events on the Hill on that day.

It is easy to underestimate the skill required to construct stories of this kind. The efficient and speedy ordering of such facts requires considerable training and intelligence. But such considerations notwithstanding, it is easy to see that they provide small fragments of reality and provide bare facts without much of an analytical dimension. They are important nevertheless. They convey some part of the business of politics to the nation at large. Needless to say their importance increases in proportion to the analytical and explanatory dimensions that are added and their importance increases further as they direct attention to issues and events that are of major significance. But even where they are slim and formula-like, they are a reflection of that part of the journalistic imagination that is based on the functions democratic theory ordains.

The primary mandate of political journalists is to maintain the domain within which public discourse takes place. It is to bridge the gap between public institutions and the public so that the exercise of the rights of citizenship are based on the facts of political life. To amend Robert Park's formulation slightly, the political role of the press is to locate the citizen in the political world and to activate his civic responsibilities. To this end politics is inscribed on the journalistic imagination. The end of the second continuum may be properly labelled "civic".

IV

The journalistic imagination is heterogenous, embracing a wide variety of styles, subjects and qualities. The styles are as remote from one another as the spare and unembellished news communication on the Paris strike is from the richly-documented feature on the Tory power in Ontario. The subjects are as remote from one another as deaths on football fields are from parliamentary business. When journalistic writing is examined critically it becomes evident that within the limits set by these styles and subjects there is much that is qualitatively exceptional even if standards used to judge other forms of knowledge and literature are applied to it.

Such qualitative achievements notwithstanding, it is not purely accidental that the term "journalese" is used to refer to "a facile style of writing, etc". So much of journalism must be constructed according to a strict formula and must be shallow in order to meet the functional requirements which circumscribe its production. Members of society would not be informed of anything if they were to wait for artistic or analytical genius to be born, even though the benefits to society increase in proportion to the art and genius with which journalism is written.

Where journalism imitates the literary tradition, achievements are harder to come by. The law plays a role in this. It is not possible to draw portraits of living human beings in the frank and exhaustive way in which writers of fiction do without running afoul of the laws of libel. But the main reason is that the literary journalism exemplified by the human interest story does not require the reader to respond in a direct and purposeful manner. Its functional value is limited and, therefore, the appreciation of its quality depends largely on other factors.

Other types of journalism, especially political journalism, are not like that. Designed to stimulate a civic response such as a vote or a petition, political journalism is manifestly instrumental. Accordingly, it matters less that the writing is insightful or elevated. It is functional or instrumental even where it is pedestrian. Cumulatively, it delivers news and analysis to the citizen who in our tradition is the source of whatever legitimacy individual governments have. That the citizen is informed even in bits and pieces is so fundamental that disciples of the democratic tradition can do nothing but applaud when the journalist writes political news.

We feel so strongly about this function that the maintenance of press freedom—that is to say, the freedom of the journalist from the direct supervision by organized political power operating through the state—is seen to be an essential condition for democratic life. James Mill summed up our faith in the following words:

So true it is ... that the discontent of the people is the only means of removing the defects of vicious governments, that the freedom of the press, the main instrument of creating discontent, is, in all civilized countries, among all but the advocates of misgovernments, regarded as indispensable security, and the greatest safeguard of the interests of mankind.[23]

It is the civic, not the literary dimension of the journalistic imagination to which the journalist owes his modestly happy reputation.

NOTES TO CHAPTER ONE

1/Chief Justice Lyman Duff in the Alberta Press Bill decision, *Dominion Law Reports,* Vol. 2, 1938, p. 106.

2/ *Webster's New World Dictionary of the American Language* (New York: World Publishing, 1953), p. 791.

3/R.V. SYMONDS, *The Rise of English Journalism* (Exeter: A. Wheaton and Co., 1952), p. 18.

4/JOSEPH FRANK, *The Beginning of the English Newspaper, 1620-1660* (Cambridge: Harvard University Press, 1961), p. 272.

5/"Politics as a Vocation", *From Max Weber: Essays in Sociology,* H.H. GERTH AND C. WRIGHT MILLS, eds. (New York: Oxford University Press, 1968), p. 96.

6/ *Ibid.*

7/ *The Sociological Imagination* (New York: Oxford University Press, 1959), p. 5.

8/No. 30, 1758; cited in R.L. HAIG, *The Gazetteer: 1735-1797* (Carbondale: Southern Illinois University Press, 1960), p. 144.

9/Cited in HELEN MACGILL HUGHES, *News and the Human Interest Story* (New York: Greenwood Press, 1968), p. 12.

10/Cited in SIDNEY KOBRE, *Development of American Journalism* (Dubuque: Wm. C. Brown Co., 1969), p. 495.

11/"The Natural History of the Newspaper", *Mass Communications,* 2nd ed., WILBUR SCHRAMM, ed. (Urbana: University of Illinois Press, 1960), p. 8.

12/*Ibid.*

13/*The Vertical Mosaic* (Toronto: University of Toronto Press, 1964), p. 485.

14/"The World as a Novel: From Capote to Mailer", *The New York Review of Books,* Vol. XVI, No. 6 (April 8, 1971), pp. 26-30.

15/In RALPH TURNER, ed., *Robert Park on Social Control and Collective Behaviour: Selected Papers* (Chicago: University of Chicago Press, 1967), pp. 33-52.

16/*Ibid.* p. 34.

17/CARL BERNSTEIN AND BOB WOODWARD, *All The President's Men* (New York: Simon and Schuster, 1974).

18/*Miami and the Siege of Chicago* (London: Weidenfeld and Nicolson, 1968), pp. 4-5.

19/Cf. TOM WOLFE, "The Birth of the New Journalism. . . ", *New York,* Vol. 5, No. 7 (Feb. 14, 1972) and "Why They Aren't Writing the Great American Novel Anymore", *Esquire,* Vol. LXXVIII, No. 6 (December 1972).

20/"The Structure and Function of Communication in Society", *Reader in Public Opinion and Communication,* 2nd ed., eds. BERNARD BERELSON AND MORRIS JANOWITZ (New York: The Free Press, 1966), p. 179.

21/Ch. XV, "The Ideological System: The Mass Media", pp. 457-489.

22/TURNER, *op. cit.* p. 50.

23/*Essays on Government Jurisprudence, Liberty of the Press and Law of Nations [1825]* (New York: Augustus M. Kelley, 1967), p. 18.

chapter two

The Nature of News

PHYLLIS WILSON

A president of the United States, caught in the quicksands of a scandal, resigns in mid-term. In the long run, he assures himself of a page in American history books as the first president to do so. In the short run, he pre-empts prime time television and radio entertainment on domestic and foreign networks and commands headlines around the world.

Even the least knowledgeable listener or reader found little reason to dispute the media's judgment of the presidential resignation as a great, in the qualitative sense, news story—a momentous event, unique, controversial, dramatic, a climax to a lengthy real-life whodunit, and burdened with human tragedy. Still, many less momentous events are reported on television and in the papers as news and only an infinitesimal fraction of the flood of information now threatening to engulf the world is similarly tagged. The line dividing information and news would seem to be, like the equator, imaginary.

The concept of news is considered difficult to grasp. There is a belief, widespread in the news world, that the recognition of news is intuitive, that it is a faculty with which the select are born not bred, that a Geiger counter clicks in the heads of a gifted few in proximity to the uranium of news. Does this mean that the eyewitness who phones the newsroom with a tip, or the official who hands out information to reporters with the conviction it is news is similarly equipped? Or does it mean that both have gone to school on a lifetime of reading the papers and listening to the newscasts?

Journalism scholars and practising journalists have labored to define and to describe news and to identify those elements on which news is judged and which are the focus of criticism today.

Mitchell Charnley, for example, has written: "News is the timely report of facts or opinion that hold interest or importance, or both, for a considerable number of people."[1] In examining that definition, no one quarrels with the emphasis on news as an account of something. Nothing is news until it is reported—on paper, on videotape or film, or over the air. However, thoughtful journalists today argue that, in a world so swiftly changing, any definition of news is too narrow if it omits the "timely report" of that currency of the mind, ideas. Further, veterans in the news business claim that, in skilful hands, any information can be made interesting. As for importance, it may lie, like beauty, in the eye of the beholder. Nevertheless, implicit in the judgments journalists make on the information they present as news is the faith they know what is of interest and/or of importance to their audience. Complicating their judgments, of course, is the fact that their audience is seldom, if ever, homogeneous, but is made up of innumerable groups, each with its own interests and needs.

"News . . . is what the city editor says is news."[2] That definition has been tottering around newsrooms of the country for many years. It may be cynical, but it is also realistic. In deciding to which geographical or institutional beats they will post their reporters, and in assigning them to specific stories for coverage, the city editor and his counterparts in the electronic media do define what news is. If they also play the role of what sociologists call gatekeepers, that is, if theirs is the decision on whether a story will be published and where and how it will be packaged, they further define what news is. As realistic as the definition is it may be misleading because it fails to account for the role of the reporter. In the first analysis, the determinant of news is the reporter's perception of which facts, opinions and ideas he gathers are interesting or important. On that perception reporters often disagree, among themselves, and with their editors.

A couple of examples may serve to illustrate the point. Carman Cumming, a former reporter for The Canadian Press covering the 1968 federal election campaign, filed a detailed story on the Liberals' agricultural policy. The same week the new Liberal leader relieved the fatigue of campaigning with a swim in an Oakville motel pool, exchanging witticisms with the pretty girls and reporters on hand. Cumming dictated a light piece by phone. He was chagrined to find that the agricultural policy story appeared to be ignored while the pool story got front-page play across the country. Most reporters have a record of similar frustration in their notebooks. The obverse of the coin is the story, perhaps apocryphal, of Deems Taylor, American composer and critic, assigned to review a Metropolitan Opera performance. He was awakened by an irate editor demanding the review. Taylor explained he had filed no review since the performance was cancelled because of the leading singer's sudden illness, or, depending on the version told, attempted suicide.[3] The point of the story is, of course, that although no review could be written, an interesting news story could and should have been filed.

In descriptions of news, the use of adjectives like "clear", "concise", "accurate", "balanced", "fair", "objective" and their synonyms before the noun "report" or "account", is almost mandatory. Certainly consumers of news feel no obligation to wrestle with the meaning of a foggy story. And reporters for any medium learn the first day on the job that their greatest enemies are space and time.

As descriptive qualities of news, "accuracy" and "objectivity" are traditionally given primacy. Accuracy is taken to cover not only simple facts such as names, ages, addresses and direct quotations, but the general impression conveyed by the news account as well. (Obviously the former are easier to correct than the latter.) The American publisher Joseph Pulitzer once said that accuracy is to a newspaper what virtue is to a woman.[4] Of course, he was not addressing a permissive society. The new morality notwithstanding, gross errors in the media are grounds for dismissal. Lesser errors can lead to demotions and reprimands, severely damaging to a journalist's self-esteem.

Some media are providing an example in their open admission of error other institutions of society might follow. The standing head "Our Mistake", which frequently appears on page 2 of *The Globe and Mail,* is a case in point. In a somewhat broader approach, the *Toronto Star* has had a senior editor, "Your Man at The Star", serve as its readers' ombudsman. He writes a weekly column reviewing the paper's performance and sees that errors caught by staff and readers are acknowledged and corrected day by day. Monthly statistics of errors are analyzed as to their origin—reporters, rewrite men, copy editors, head writers—and posted in the newsroom. Periodically the *Star* mails clippings of its account of some local event to people who were also there and invites comments on the accuracy of the facts and general flavor of the printed story. At the very least such measures ensure that journalists make no appeal to the doctrine of infallibility.

The claim of objectivity has stimulated more controversy among journalists and their critics than any other. The controversy has spilled into studies, seminars, speeches and articles with no sign of abating. While disavowing an only-the-facts-please concept as too much of a strait jacket, reputable news organizations and journalists profess objectivity as their goal. They agree that reporters and editors are no less laden with biases and prejudices accumulated in their upbringing, education and environment than other human beings. They contend, however, that the training and experience of newsmen promote awareness of these flaws and thus awareness becomes a prophylactic. Proponents of the recent "advocacy" or "participatory" journalism ridicule the argument and objectivity itself. They say the audience is little served by reporters who heed the news desk's traditional order to "give the other side", even if all six sides of a hexagonal story are given, unless the reporter is free to rule on the best. Seeing themselves as movers and shakers, urgent to create a new and better society, they come down hard in favor of subjective news. In describing the stand of what is now known as the "alternate" press, Robert Glessing notes:

> Subjectivity is a journalistic principle among underground press staffers and they care much more about opinion than fact . . . . Objectivity is assumed to imply a lack of involvement with the subject, and noninvolvement is a cardinal underground sin . . . .[5]

Possibly the most perplexed are the youngsters on their first assignment who conscientiously collect more facts than they can use and, in sifting out those for which they have time or space, realize they have already compromised their objectivity.

Thomas Griffith, former editor of *Life,* believes bias shows up prior to the sifting of facts:

> . . . the real question of bias begins earlier, in what is pursued, or not pursued, as news. A news story originates in a collision of fact with an interested mind, and what makes one journalist "see" a story and another not has much to do with his own imagination, curiosity, and temperament. Other craftsmen, the copy editors, can later deprive the writer's words of any hint of feeling so that an article reads as if the reporter were as impersonally fashioned of metal as his typewriter. But the reader who thinks that the news can be delivered untouched by human hands and uncorrupted by human minds is living in a state of vincible ignorance.[6]

Assuredly, consumers of news who complain of bias or the lack of objectivity in the media are free to view the news from the perspective of their own prejudices. After all, a charge of bias in a report of a confrontation between police and demonstrators may rest on whether the consumer is a law-and-order man or regards all policemen as pigs.

Perhaps the nature of news can be illuminated by consideration of the major elements or values on which it is commonly assessed and on which the most important editorial decision—what items are to go on the front page or in what order on the newscast—is based. As Ivan and Carol Doig point out:

> News values weren't developed in the light of a smoky fire as neolithic newsmen pondered what to chisel into stone for their first issue. News developed to serve informational needs, and thoughtful people later looked at the product and, to try to understand it better, searched for its elements so that they could talk about it with greater precision.[7]

One such thoughtful person, journalism professor Curtis MacDougall, has identified five elements on which news is assessed: timeliness, proximity, prominence, consequence and human interest.[8]

Newspapers have taught generations of readers to equate the latest news with the best—to the ultimate profit of radio and television. Use of such technological marvels as computers and photocomposition, the testing of facsimile transmission to homes under way and talk of lasers as the magic on the horizon, has done little so far to right the time imbalance for newspapers. To deliver their news they must fight urban traffic tie-ups and accommodate themselves to the school hours of their paper persons. Newspapers whose editions may go to press shortly before noon or shortly after and are delivered four or five hours later are still classified as afternoon papers. The idea that newspapers should concentrate on being best and stop worrying about being first in an unequal race is apparently heretical. The desire to see "today" in all the front-page news is compulsive, even while radio is updating its half-hourly bulletins and television is seating its viewers behind the camera lens at news-in-the-making. Such is the testimony to the value of timeliness. Yet however uneven the battle of the clock has become, newspapermen everywhere take comfort in reflecting that the unravelling of the Watergate skein was largely a print enterprise.

In evaluating news, the geographic location of its origin plays a role, though that role may be diminishing. In a world where a decision of the Organization of Petroleum Exporting Countries may lower thermostats in Halifax, it could be harder to maintain that nearest is dearest in future news stories. Traditionally, the relative proximity of the news consumer to the event or situation reported has been regarded as some sort of index to its relevance for him. Thus, reports of drought in southern Ontario or too much rain on the Prairies are assessed to be of more concern to Canadians than reports of drought in the sub-Sahara or floods in far off Bangladesh. Accounts of public transit strikes in Toronto and Montreal are of limited interest to Vancouverites unless they plan to visit either city. Other values being equal among several news reports, the local story will be given preferential treatment.

Geographic location may be an indirect influence in the case of media which post reporters across the country or abroad. There is an inclination to use their accounts, if for no other reason than to justify the cost. On the other hand, media whose self-image, by ambition or directive, is national, may virtually ignore proximity as a news value. CBC television's nightly news package, "The National", makes an effort to represent every region of the country with a news item. Still, the importance given proximity as a news value helps to explain specifically local newscasts and the growth of suburban and community newspapers.

Prominence, or personality, may be decisive in the judgment of whether to cover or how to use a news story. Prominence is the dividend from the office or position an individual holds and from the individual's news past. In an era of fast-disappearing wedding write-ups, a Vancouver wedding made headlines. The bridegroom was Canada's Prime Minister. The views of Hank Aaron on racial discrimination in the United States may be news, but not because he is an expert or has been a victim. He beat Babe Ruth's home run record. The public utterances of Dr. Hans Selye are newsworthy because he is the Canadian authority on the problems of stress. How else to explain photographers' continuing pursuit of Jacqueline Onassis into stores and concert halls save that she was the wife of an assassinated president? There seems to be a kind of reinforcement principle operating here. The more times a prominent individual figures in the news, the more prominent, and thus newsworthy, he becomes.

The element of consequence is variously interpreted by practising journalists as relating to numbers, to size, to the breadth and depth of impact on the people affected, to significance. In simplistic and macabre terms, an air crash that kills 120 people is a better (qualitatively) news story than one that kills 12. Accounts of a convention that attracts 2,000 delegates are likely to be judged more newsworthy than those of a constituency meeting. The results of a federal election, regardless of whether the government is defeated, are unlikely to be upstaged by any other news that day—so many Canadians are affected and so many Canadians had a pencil in the outcome. The media view the bringing down of the federal budget as a red letter news day because it affects more Canadians in such a vulnerable spot, their pocketbooks. Journalists have speculated that the ultimate discovery of the basic cause of cancer will rank with the splitting of the atom as the most significant news of this century.

Human interest is perhaps the most pervasive of all the elements on which news is evaluated, particularly the news that is merely interesting. An entire book[9] has been devoted to a scholarly analysis of the history and development of the human interest story. Its heroes or villains are often ordinary people who may figure in the news but once in their lives. Human interest is considered a major element in accounts of conflict, controversy, sports, crime, natural disasters, accidents, adventure, achievement, children, animals. It is also present in accounts whose themes are either self-interest or self-improvement, pathos or humor, the odd or unusual. The list is endless and as varied as the human beings to whom such stories appeal. And the appeal is thought to be to the emotions rather than to the intellect. About the poorest bets in the human interest stakes are the middle-aged of either sex and the plain female, of any age.

Samples of the human interest story are easily mustered by anyone who follows the news. Older people could cite the kidnapping of the Lindbergh baby, the Moose River mine disaster, the birth of the Dionne quintuplets. The conquest of Mount Everest and the lonely voyage of Sir Francis Chichester in his Gipsy Moth are classic examples. More recently, there were the stories of pianist Vladimir Horowitz's dugout visit prior to a Mets' baseball game, the airlift of polar bears threatened with execution for raiding the Churchill dump, the duck muzzled by the ring off a soft drink can, the mysterious career of Patricia Hearst and in the late summer of 1974, the success and failure of two teenagers' attempts to swim Lake Ontario. Then, of course, the winner of the $1,000,000 lottery prize, the person who celebrates a 100th birthday and the one who paddles, bicycles or walks from Halifax to Vancouver are perennial human interest fare.

However, it must be clear that Professor MacDougall's five elements most often appear in combination in highly rated news reports. In reports rated the highest of the day, even of the year, all five are usually present. Certainly that was the case in the resignation of Richard Nixon, even for Canadians, for whom Washington is closer geographically and culturally than either Peking or Moscow. The assessment of the hundreds of news reports that pour into newsrooms daily demands their constant weighing, each against the others, on the basis of these elements. This constant weighing explains why one report is rated "good" in one community and not in another, why similar stories are played up one day and down another, why the judgment of the top story of the day is frequently unanimous.

Dissatisfaction with traditional concepts of news has been growing, particularly among journalists themselves. For example, newsroom insistence that news reports must answer the questions as to "who, what, when, where, how and why" is under attack. The critics argue neither for ignoring nor for substituting the five W's and H, but claim primacy for "why". They believe that answers to "why" are pursued less frequently and less vigorously than responsible journalism demands today. The discovery of causes is seen at least as important as effects for the public's understanding of events and situations in the news. For instance, it might be interesting to know how many media which covered the story of armed conflict in Cyprus during the summer of 1974 and/or of the "settlement" a decade earlier had a reporter on the island in the interval.

The exploration of "why" in news reports has come to be known as interpretative or in-depth reporting and, whatever the critics say, has been practised by the best reporters for a long time. The major obstacles to more interpretative reporting are that it is both difficult and time-consuming. It has its own critics, who object to it mainly on the grounds that its practitioners too often stray across the hairline separating explaining from editorializing. And in news reports, editorializing has traditionally been judged to be the second blackest crime after outright error.

Closely allied to those who seek more emphasis on causes and on the "why" in news are others who see news as too event-oriented, too dominated by happenings. They advocate greater attention to situations and issues. Taking the notion a step farther, the report of a study conducted in Britain has suggested that "events will be selected for news reporting in terms of their fit or consonance with pre-existing images—the news of the event will confirm earlier ideas" and moreover, that a reporter, uncertain about how to report an event, is disposed to report it "within a general framework already established".[10] The implication is that in reporting events reporters grasp at the similarities to the past rather than the differences.

Related to a preoccupation with events as news is what Toronto journalist Robert Fulford, in reference to Canadian newspapers, has described as a built-in bias towards authority "and in this case Authority means anything which is organized, what has a name, and which gives speeches."[11]

James Reston of *The New York Times,* a long-time advocate of broadening the news concept, has partially explained the news media's concentration on national and international events: "It takes some thumping crisis to startle a vast continental nation out of its normal preoccupation with family and work."[12] Erwin D. Canham, editor emeritus of *The Christian Science Monitor,* thinks the corrective process is already under way:

> News in the past has been event-oriented. It is getting to be more and more situation-oriented. We have been the slaves of the event, the servants of time alone, and we have wasted a lot of time just waiting around for things to happen. Investigative reporting about situations is much more rewarding, gets much deeper into significance and validity than merely covering an event . . . .[13]

A television special report on strip mining and a documented piece on the situation of Canadian women under the law are two examples that suggest Canham is justified in his optimism.

Yet William Johnson, a political reporter for *The Globe and Mail,* mused during the 1974 federal election campaign, "The mass media have their own imperatives: the news must somehow conform to the dynamics of the theatre. What is not new is not news. What is not paradoxical, dramatic, incongruous, shocking or momentous has little news value".[14]

Years earlier, Max Ways, in a provocative *Fortune* article, complained that the real trouble is that news is not new enough:

> News today can concentrate with tremendous impact on a few great stories: a moon landing, a war, a series of civil disorders. But mean-

while, outside the spotlight, other great advances in science and technology, other international tensions, other causes of social unrest are
in motion. Yet today's inadequately reported trends will shape to-
morrow's reality.[15]

Reston was making the same point when he said, "Things don't have to
'happen' to be news. They can just be going on quietly . . .".[16]

Ways assailed American journalism for its failure to report adequately
on "the economic and social implications" of the computer and to alert
white society to the growing frustrations of the almost invisible black society.[17] Measured against the admonition in the *Report of the Special Senate
Committee on Mass Media* that the media's "prime job is to prepare the
people for the shock of change",[18] Canadian journalism has had its failures
too. In fact, Quebec's "quiet revolution" was virtually inaudible outside that
province. In retrospect, journalism on both sides of the 49th parallel seems
to have been slow off the mark after William Vogt's *Road to Survival* and
Rachel Carson's *Silent Spring* to find news in the population explosion,
ecology and the environment. Ralph Nader's battle royal with the General
Motors colossus seems to have been a delayed charge, eventually setting
off the avalanche of news which has identified the consumer's changing role
in the market place.

Hindsight is easy of course. From the viewpoint of the reporter, required
to explain to a society in flux what its changes mean, Theodore White has
offered a wry comment: "One of the occupational hazards of reporting is
that it takes so long for the reporter to recognize the importance of what
he learns while he is learning."[19]

In 1959, a police reporter for *The Herald* in Miami told Philip Meyer,
then on rewrite duty, that police were dealing with a new form of drug
abuse—teenagers sniffing model airplane glue from paper bags. Meyer had
not heard of it before and thought it unimportant. He did not turn in the
story.[20] Hindsight permits us to say that the story was very important. Many
deaths have been caused by glue sniffing.

As Thomas Griffith says, "Some news 'happens,' the rest is discerned.
And it is this process of discovery of the news that is most mysterious, and
most creative."[21]

NOTES TO CHAPTER TWO

1/*Reporting* (Toronto: Holt, Rinehart and Winston, Inc., 1966), p. 31.

2/CHRISTOPHER YOUNG, LUCIEN BRAULT, JEAN-LOUIS GAGNON, WILFRED KESTERTON, D.C. MCARTHUR, FRANK UNDERHILL, eds., "Introduction" to *A Century of Reporting* (Toronto: Clarke Irwin & Company Limited, 1967), p. ix.

3/CURTIS D. MACDOUGALL, *Interpretative Reporting* (New York: The Macmillan Company, 1972), p. 10.

4/CHARNLEY, *Reporting*, p. 20.

5/*The Underground Press in America* (Don Mills, Ontario: Fitzhenry & Whiteside Limited, 1971), p. 99.

6/"A Few Frank Words about Bias", *The Atlantic Monthly*, 233, No. 4 (April 1974), p. 47.

7/*NEWS: A Consumer's Guide* (Englewood Cliffs, N.J.: Prentice-Hall, Inc., 1972), p. 9.

8/*Interpretative Reporting*, pp. 59-65.

9/HELEN MACGILL HUGHES, *News and the Human Interest Story* (New York: Greenwood Press, 1968).

10/JAMES D. HALLORAN, PHILIP ELLIOTT, GRAHAM MURDOCK, *Demonstrations and Communication: A Case Study* (Harmondsworth, Middlesex, England: Penguin Books Ltd., 1970), p. 27.

11/"The Built-in Bias of the Press". *Reporting the News*, ed. Louis M. Lyons (Cambridge, Massachusetts: Belknap Press of Harvard University Press, 1965), p. 154.

12/*The Artillery of the Press* (New York: Harper & Row, 1966), p. 70.

13/From an address to Lovejoy Convocation, Colby College, May 5, 1972, quoted on back cover, *Columbia Journalism Review* (November/December 1972).

14/"The real David vs Goliath (Canada) Ltd.", *The Globe and Mail* (Toronto), May 30, 1974, p. 8.

15/"What's Wrong with News? It isn't New Enough", *Fortune* (October 1969), p. 110.

16/JAMES RESTON, *Sketches in the Sand* (New York: Alfred A. Knopf, 1967), p. 230.

17/WAYS, *Fortune*, (October 1969), p. 110.

18/Canada, *Report of the Special Senate Committee on Mass Media*, Vol. I (Ottawa: Queen's Printer, 1970), p. 258.

19/ *The Making of the President 1960* (New York: The New American Library, Inc., 1967), p. 245.

20/"The limits of intuition", *Columbia Journalism Review* (July/August 1971), p. 18.

21/ *The Atlantic Monthly,* Vol. 233, p. 48.

chapter three

Journalism, Fiction and Other Alliances

ROGER BIRD

Teachers of literature and teachers of journalism stress the great divide between the craft of journalism and the art of literature, but writers of journalism and writers of fiction show more of an alliance than an aloofness. The reason for the alliance goes beyond the fact that both journalist and writer of fiction work with words. The journalist works primarily with an *observation* of current, objective, external phenomena; the writer of fiction works primarily with a *vision* of reality or truth. But for any writer of fiction, the vision of reality begins with an observation of life itself,[1] and journalists are not exempt from the human necessity of directing and ordering their observation of the objective world by some vision of what it all means.

This tendency to share skills and cognitions is observable in the English-speaking tradition from that time in the first half of the eighteenth century when regular journalism and extended prose fiction appeared almost simultaneously. It may be recalled that the generation to witness the foundation of the first successful daily newspaper in 1704 was reading novels such as *Robinson Crusoe* fifteen years later. *Gulliver's Travels* was published several years before the foundation of the *Gentleman's Magazine*, a monthly which is regarded traditionally as the first magazine.

It would be possible to argue that journalism and fiction, rather than representing opposing tendencies in writing, are two parts of a single cultural movement, which may be called social realism, with its origins in eighteenth-century publishing and urban commercial culture. The movement has lasted these 250 years.

As interesting as it would be to explore such a thesis, I propose a more limited task here. I propose to explore some of the features of the alliance between journalism and fiction with special attention to eighteenth and twentieth century examples. Specifically, I will show, first, that writers of fiction and journalism have very often been the same persons. Second, I will examine the two genres along a spectrum of writing with a view to showing how the relationship between external phenomena and the writer's structure of meaning may be altered to produce either one type or the other.

Finally, I conclude with some observations on writing in which the impulses of journalism and fiction coexist in such a way as to prevent their falling neatly into either category. The evidence seems to suggest that writings of this sort are especially useful for communicating information about social change.

I

Most extended narrative up until the year 1700 was written in verse. Until that time most prose was reflective or directly persuasive—it did not set out to tell a story. Regular newspapers and realistic prose fiction were established over the years 1700-1750 by writers who were working in a generic vacuum and with a social landscape which in recent history had been abruptly transformed. They often wrote both forms simultaneously. Not surprisingly, their works showed a mixture of fact and fantasy and demonstrated the finished product of both the reporter's notebook and the artist's vision. Approach the early eighteenth century either from the direction of fiction or the direction of journalism, and the same names are inescapable: Daniel Defoe (1659-1731), Jonathan Swift (1667-1745), Henry Fielding (1707-1754), Tobias Smollet (1721-1771), Samuel Richardson (1689-1761). These are the writers who founded the novel in English, and all of them wrote for and edited newspapers (except Richardson, who was a printer and publisher). Substitute social drama for prose fiction, and the group expands to include Joseph Addison (1672-1719) and Richard Steele (1672-1729), editors of *The Spectator,* England's most famous tri-weekly journal.

Daniel Defoe is one of the most striking examples. He edited *The Review* (1704-13) as a government propagandist and seemed to care equally for what he wrote whether the government was Whig or Tory. He edited and wrote for many other journals and produced an astonishing number of reviews, polemics, satires, proposals for public enterprises, and speculative essays. He fell into fiction only when he reached the age of 59, and his fiction—though it makes him remembered in our time—seems almost an afterthought in the career of a great journalist.

Defoe's conception of fiction was typical of his time in its apparent willingness to scramble fact with fiction. The titles themselves have the diction of reality. Starting in 1719 he published *The Life and Strange Surprizing Adventures of Robinson Crusoe,* then the *Memoires of a Cavalier, The Life, Adventures and Pyracies of The Famous Captain Singleton* (1720), *The Fortunes and Misfortunes of The Famous Moll Flanders, A Journal of the Plague Year, The History and Remarkable Life of the truly Honourable Col.*

Jacque, (1722), *The Fortunate Mistress: Or, Roxana, The History of the Remarkable Life of John Sheppard* (1724), and *The True and Genuine Account of The Life and Actions of the Late Jonathan Wild* (1725).

Only two of these narratives have any basis for claiming to be "true and genuine" accounts of anything—John Sheppard and Jonathan Wild were real criminals. Not only is the diction of the titles—words like "history", "journal", "famous"—an attempt to convey the flavor of reality, but Defoe took considerable care to convince his readers that all these works were factual. They came upon the reader disguised as autobiographies or biographies, and most had a prefatory framework that authenticated the record to follow. It is doubtful whether Defoe himself thought the distinction between the "real" accounts and the fictional ones was particularly important. To him and to his readers, they were "lives", useful for pointing a moral, and of engrossing interest because they dealt with a class of people that had not been visible in literature, or even in journalism much, until then—criminals, businessmen and servants.

The accounts of Jonathan Wild and John Sheppard were expansions of Defoe's reports of their executions that had appeared in a weekly newspaper, *Applebee's Weekly Journal.* The Wild report appeared May 29, 1725, and the Sheppard report November 21, 1724. Even here fiction and fact were deliberately confused. The factual report of the Sheppard execution was accompanied in *Applebee's* by a fictional and rather funny letter written by a lovelorn lady pickpocket, lamenting Sheppard's death and protesting her devotion to his memory.[2]

Journalism and fiction lived cheek by jowl in this and many periodicals of the time. The reason was neither dishonesty nor naïveté on the part of writers or readers. This journalistic fiction, or fictional journalism, was not only presenting a new class of people and its attached social reality in print for the first time, it was attempting to make sense out of that social reality. Facts alone were not equal to the task. Some fictive, artistic imagination—and licence—was also necessary.

Jonathan Swift was a journalist, something like a public relations counsellor to the Tory government of his time, before he came to anything that looked like fiction. *Gulliver's Travels* (1726) shared Defoe's pretence at fact. An elaborate apparatus of prefatory letters (between Gulliver and his "cousin Simpson" and from Simpson, as publisher, to the reader) established in a farcical way the actuality of the voyages about to be described. The original title page reinforced this sense of reality:

> *Travels into Several Remote Nations of the World.*
>   *In Four Parts.*
> *By Lemuel Gulliver, First a Surgeon,*
> *and then a Captain of several ships.*

This book was clearly mimicking the popular and factual (well, mostly factual) accounts of travels being published by opportunistic sailors during the 1720s. Yet it was a combination of fiction and political satire that incorporated the wildest fantasies in order that Swift could make philosophical comments on the human race in general. The book was written during the same years that Swift produced the *Drapier's Letters* and *A Modest Proposal*, brief tracts by a skilled journalist aiming to correct economic and social conditions in Ireland at the time. One way or another in all these works Swift was delineating something new, a new economic man stripped of the humanistic tradition and pledged to commerce and empirical facts as a basis for life. Swift despised this new man and evolved his blend of fiction and journalism to mount the attack. Factual reporting was inadequate.

Many writers have worked on both sides of the great divide. Even a list confined to outstanding writers of fiction reveals journalism as an intermittent or continuing part of the writer's career. Charles Dickens began as a Parliamentary Press Gallery reporter; Stephen Crane was a war correspondent for the Hearst newspapers; George Orwell was for many years a reporter on the London *Tribune,* writing his novels when he could. Sometimes their writing was purely journalistic, sometimes purely fictional: Dickens in the Parliamentary Press Gallery was doing work different in kind from the work that appeared as *Oliver Twist;* Orwell of *1984* was performing a different function than he was in *Homage to Catalonia.* But often aspects of one genre can be found in the other, and this combination is a natural outgrowth of the history of both journalism and prose fiction that goes back to the early eighteenth century.

II

The historical record, then, shows no sharp distinction between journalist and writer of fiction. It seems reasonable therefore to expect no great divide between the products of their writing and the tasks faced in producing that writing. Journalism and fiction are and ought to be distinguished, but their compartments are not watertight, once they escape the categories of literary criticism or journalistic evaluation. A sociologist posits a spectrum of writing:

> At one pole we have the creative artist with a vision, a vocation, represented, let us say, by someone like Henry James. At the other

we have the technician of words, the scribbler preoccupied with the immediate, the evanescent, the surface . . . But the reality is much more like a continuum. The moment we leave the extremes, the distinctions become blurred. At the higher ranges of journalism the journalist stops being a mere reporter and becomes a commentator, essayist, propagandist—a "writer". The writer who leaves pure fiction becomes a commentator or essayist, thus meeting the journalist moving in the other direction.[3]

The adjectives "higher" and "purer" for fiction could well be avoided, but the idea of a spectrum of functions is useful. There are many genres available for the writer—of journalism or fiction—who attempts to deal with the external world. The archetypal news story, "Dog Bites Man", can serve as illustration for these generic possibilities, but for convenience and allusiveness it will be modified here to "Horse Kicks Man".

A straight news story describes the incident, identifies horse and man, says where and when. Such a story will always be necessary, will always be the main part of what we call news. It occurs most often when the event (in this case the kick) is of a reasonably familiar type. Reports of such events reinforce standard conceptions of reality. The event is totally in the foreground and the writer is rhetorically invisible and anonymous, even if the story has a by-line. But sometimes the journalist cannot rest content with this approach, particularly if "Horse Kicks Man" is a story dealing with a complex social, economic or political circumstance. Here, with a shift along the spectrum away from straight news report, the reader is involved in analysis, comment, interpretation: "Horse Kicks Man Because . . ." The qualities of horse and man are scrutinized to show the inevitability or the destructiveness or the calamity of the kick. Or, the scene is given in more detail in order that the reader feel the quality, mood or tone of the kicking. The reader's attention is being directed about equally to the event and to the processing of that event through the writer's cognitive machinery. Notice too at this stage, both writers (or both writings) are using techniques common to fiction and journalism—observation of reality, selection of detail, and, in the interpretative piece, scrutiny and cognition.

A further shift away from straight news, further along toward the interpretative end of the spectrum, brings the writer into judgments about the worth of the event or the participants. Here the writer works with praise or blame, with the generic descendants of encomium—a set piece of exaggerated praise—satire or sermon, genres considered to be mainly literary in their effects. In satire or encomium the reader senses a literary quality (apart from the skill or ineptitude of the actual writing) because in these genres the focus falls upon the value judgment of the writer, rather than on the factual outline of the event *per se*. The reader finds he must deal with the writer's interpretation of reality, his "vision" if you will.

In much satire and secular sermon-making the factual basis is often a given, a set of facts or an abstraction of facts assumed by the writer to be known to his audience. English-Irish politics was such a basis in Jonathan Swift's *A Modest Proposal* (1729); the Second World War was equally a basis in Joseph Heller's *Catch-22* (1961). Swift never mentioned his main target, the commercial policies of the English government of Sir Robert Walpole; Heller never mentioned Adolph Hitler. This is Swift opening his attack:

> It is a melancholly Object to those, who walk through this great Town [Dublin], or travel in the Country; when they see the *Streets,* the *Roads,* and *Cabbin-doors* crowded with *Beggars* of the Female Sex, followed by three, four, or six Children, *all in Rags,* and importuning every Passenger for an Alms.

This passage is warm with familiarity as the writer insinuates his point of view upon the reader. As the passage develops, the reader is happy to carry the implication that he is civic-minded, concerned about the economy, and patriotic:

> These *Mothers,* instead of being able to work for their honest Lively-hood, are forced to employ all their Time in stroling to beg Suste-nance for their *helpless Infants;* who, as they grow up, either turn *Thieves* for want of Work; or leave their *dear Native Country, to fight for the Pretender in Spain,* or sell themselves to the *Barbadoes.*[4]

The reader was assumed to know about unemployment, the abysmal gross national product in Ireland, the Roman Catholic threat in the person of James Stuart, claimant to the throne lost by his father, James II, in 1688. In this pamphlet, Swift demolished the personality-type, and the politics, represented by the *persona* writing the modest proposal. That is, his tasks were satire and the making of a moral judgment. He had no space to move ponderously through the political background; instead, he was urgent to communicate his attitude. But notice, combined with these tools of the fiction writer—exaggeration, persuasion, what used to be called rhetoric—was the eye of the journalist. The scenario of the routine for effective begging—ragged mothers and equally ragged children with hollow eyes standing in cabin doors—was the result of accurate journalistic observation. Yet the focus in this pamphlet fell as much upon Swift's own internal structures of morality and meaning as it did upon the external reality. Swift forced his reader to focus on both. "Horse Kicks Man" became an attack on man's brutality or stupidity, an attack on social or political structures that make certain elements of the population vulnerable to injury in stables while others were immune.

Fiction is another point on the spectrum. Here the focus is almost entirely upon the internal structures of the writer's own vision and not at all upon any current, on-going event or persons in the real world. "Horse Kicks Man" may evaporate, to be replaced by a fiction about violence, animal passion, senseless destruction, murderous innocence, or whatever theme preoccupies the author enough to set him typing. This is not to say that the writer of fiction pays no attention to the external world; fiction is art, at least when it succeeds, and there have been few lasting disputes with Aristotle's concept that art is an imitation of nature. The writer of fiction must be skilled in all the techniques mentioned so far. He must observe, select detail, evaluate, and convince the reader of the worth of his view of life. Further, his work must ring true, it must, curiously, be at least as convincing as the straight news story. This is the clog at the heels of artistic freedom. The writer may wish to expand upon the possibilities of "Horse Kicks Man", and he is no longer bound by the limits of the actual or even the possible. He can create a world in which horses not only kick men but rule them. Lemuel Gulliver encountered just such a world in his fourth voyage, but Swift had to cast enough reality into that world to make his reader follow.

Gulliver's Travels is, literally, a fantastic extension of the "Horse Kicks Man" event. But Swift, as much as the writer of the straight news story, had the obligation to make his narrative believable at some level. To do so, in the neoclassical age as well as in the twentieth century, required observation of horses and men—their size, the structure of their muscles, the color of their skins, the length and location of their hair, their general demeanor. Even here, in this extreme fantasy, journalist and writer of fiction were sharing skills:

> Their Heads and Breasts were covered with a thick Hair, some friz-
> zled and others lank; they had Beards like Goats, and a long Ridge
> of Hair down their Backs, and the fore Parts of their Legs and Feet;
> but the rest of their Bodies were bare, so that I might see their Skins,
> which were of a brown Buff Colour. They had no Tails, nor any Hair
> at all on their Buttocks, except about the Anus; which, I presume
> Nature had placed there to defend them as they sat on the Ground;
> for this Posture they used, as well as lying down, and often stood on
> their hind Feet.[5]

The extreme shock value of this section of *Gulliver's Travels* resulted from the reader's slowly-growing realization that Swift was writing an accurate description of a herd of human beings, stripped only of their clothes, their rationality and their bathtubs. The accuracy gave the fantasy its power. In other terms, the journalist's skills were reinforcing those of the writer of fiction; and the fiction was thus able to reveal a truth about men and their animal nature that could never be revealed by means of plain description or through the simple news story, "Horse Kicks Man".

Consider one more example. This time, a modern novelist working with an equally extreme fantasy, the soldier in white from *Catch-22:*

> The soldier in white was encased from head to toe in plaster and gauze. He had two useless legs and two useless arms. He had been smuggled into the ward during the night, and the men had no idea he was among them until they awoke in the morning and saw the two strange legs hoisted from the hips, the two strange arms anchored up perpendicularly, all four limbs pinioned strangely in air by lead weights suspended darkly above him that never moved. Sewn into the bandages over the insides of both elbows were zippered lips through which he was fed clear fluid from a clear jar. A silent zinc pipe rose from the cement of his groin and was coupled to a slim rubber hose that carried waste from his kidneys and dripped it efficiently into a clear, stoppered jar on the floor.[6]

So far, completely accurate observation, as accurate in Heller's measure of the horror of a wartime casualty ward as Swift's was of raw human nature in the fourth book of *Gulliver's Travels.* But both writers went forward, past mere observation, into the darkness of their vision of what it all meant. Here is Heller's next sentence:

> When the jar on the floor was full, the jar feeding his elbow was empty, and the two were simply switched quickly so that stuff could drip back into him.

No observation of even the most callous medical malpractice produced that sentence; it derives from Heller's vision of what it means to be involved as an anonymous soldier in a great war. Similarly Swift's description of the vile and savage Yahoo species resulted from a vision of humankind stripped of its rationality (and its language, bathtubs, clothes, etc.). But the vision of both writers is rendered acceptable by means of the empirical observation upon which they are based: European men do have buff skins and hair around the anus; some soldiers' bodies are so broken in combat that they are encased in plaster and gauze with tubes for vital fluids.

Fiction and journalism are allied though they stand at extreme ends of a spectrum of written forms attempting to deal with reality coherently. Equally allied are the other forms along that spectrum—satire, commentary, analysis. This is not to deny to fiction its greater creative glory, its power to go beyond the events of the day and make meaning out of the flux. But both journalist and story-teller aim at truth, both imitate life in words, and both are subject to the limitations, even distortions, inherent in words as a medium for imitation.

III

Fiction and journalism, then, are allied in their genesis and history, and in at least some of the skills required to produce them. Works that share the two impulses equally have been (and still are) particularly useful in dealing with shifts in the social landscape that might be disconcerting or just plain incomprehensible if reported as straight news. Confronted with a social reality too hot or too hazy, fiction appears that is structured by generous amounts of factual data, and journalists produce descriptions of day-to-day reality informed by fantasy and some of the licences of a writer of fiction. Convenient illustrations would include Richard Rohmer's *Exxoneration*,[7] dealing with the energy crisis between Canada and the United States, or the handful of other bad novels that followed the October crisis in Quebec. Such fiction is often condemned as "journalistic", but the journalism has the flavor and power built in to literary realism and is currently enjoying great favor under the name "new journalism". Tom Wolfe's version of its occurrence in the early 1960s is notorious:

> . . . in the early 1960's a curious new notion, just hot enough to inflame the ego, had begun to intrude into the tiny confines of the feature status-sphere. It was in the nature of a discovery. This discovery, modest at first, humble in fact, deferential, you might say, was that it just might be possible to write journalism that would . . . read like a novel.[8]

This modern blend of the fabulous with the realistic can cause confusion and resentment. Hunter Thompson's *Fear and Loathing: On the Campaign Trail '72* stimulated comment like this:

> The "new journalism" is thus, in his hands, a form of fiction: "Fear and Loathing, or how Sir Gawain observed the White Knight's armor slowly tarnish before his pure yet troubled gaze." I will believe noth-

ing Thompson tells me, unless I have corroboration. Since he tells me of many times when he has gleefully lied and watched his auditors squirm under his deceptions, I must stand back a bit and doubt even his deepest claim of all: to tell his feelings as he felt them. Did he really take all those drugs? Did he really almost crack up? Did he really crash the Nixon Youth demonstration and carry a Nixon sign?[9]

One of the passages being questioned in this review of Thompson's report on the 1972 American presidential election campaign begins like this:

I was just idling around in the hallway, trying to go north for a beer, when I got swept up in a fast-moving mob of about two thousand people heading south at good speed, so instead of fighting the tide I let myself be carried along to wherever they were going . . . .[10]

The people were young Republicans and they were hurrying toward a staging area for a "spontaneous" demonstration for their presidential candidate. Thompson was using a device from fiction—comic hero interrupted by unexpected violence—and it didn't much matter whether it happened that way. The spontaneous demonstration of Republican youth is corroborated plentifully by reports at the time in the more conventional press. Thompson was trying to convey the tone or flavor of that demonstration, and a fictional device was a convenient way into it.

An educated reading public, like the one represented by the reviewer of Thompson's book, is exposed to some ideas of literary criticism and to journalism's claim to objectivity. Such a public expects sharper distinctions between journalism and fiction than apparently exist for those who write the stuff. This reading public is apt to regard as inauthentic any journalism colored by fantasy, or fiction overly-burdened by fact. But if we remove for a moment the arbitrary division of fiction and journalism, if we agree that a spectrum of writing exists, then many good works, like Defoe's *Journal of the Plague Year* (1722) or Norman Mailer's *The Armies of the Night,* can be better appreciated. Admittedly, the confusion between the two genres puts the reader off balance and casts the burden of figuring things out equally upon him and the writer. But being off balance and burdened is a posture that often produces good insight.

Such insight arises when the journalist is constrained to pursue meaning as well as facts, and when the writer of fiction finds he must provide more factual data to justify his vision. The eighteenth-century writers examined earlier confronted a world in which a new social class was not only emerging but beginning to dominate the economics, religion and habits of thought of the whole country. A news report of the marriage of a male member of the merchant class to the daughter of a lord would not convey that complex reality. Nor would a thousand such reports. A similarly large social change occurred in North America in the late 1950s and early 1960s. A new class of people—teen-agers—were becoming powerful in the United States, and habits of thought, ideology, economics, and mundane behavior were changing. An attempt to chronicle this change, and to comment on its importance, can be read in Tom Wolfe's *The Kandy-Kolored Tangerine-Flake Streamline Baby.*[11] Both Defoe and Wolfe were clear-eyed and strident about the new reality that surrounded them. Both were fascinated by that reality.

An obvious problem arises when the journalist moves along the spectrum toward fiction, or when the writer of fiction moves toward journalism. It becomes possible for either of them to lie. In defence of this kind of writing, it can be said that lies in such circumstances are possible but not probable. There is too much conventional journalism around for corroboration. Conventional journalists have also been known to lie, and have been caught by other conventional journalists who were quick to dispute the lie.

The operative word is "fantasy", not "lie". Fantasies are valid in this kind of writing as an efficient method of approaching and describing some kinds of problems. Defoe's *Journal of the Plague Year* was mainly factual— he used recent historical records to construct the London plague of 1665. The narrative itself was a result of a fantasy—the story of the plague was told in the first person by a man who said he was there. He wasn't. The narrator was a fiction. Defoe told the story. But the narrator brought us into the circumstances quicker, with more immediacy, with more conviction. And this method is no distortion of reality. It is no lie.

Defoe's *Moll Flanders* is packed with the results of a reporter's work. The reader discovered what life was like for a sexy woman in a London jail, found out how a team of pickpockets worked, was instructed in fencing stolen goods, and was made aware of what our own century would call the sociology of the criminal class that was growing up around the edges of a new economic order. But the narrator again was Defoe, not Moll Flanders, and Moll was a fiction though her crimes were not. An instance of almost exactly the same exposition occurred in Truman Capote's *In Cold Blood,* the difference being that the criminals were real. Crime and criminals are antennae of social change, and in any age a mixture of fiction and factual report is a powerful way of looking at the data.

Eighteenth-century English writers of fiction wrote for an audience that was slowly getting out of the habit of reading only religious works. As Ian Watt points out:

By far the greatest single category of books published in the eighteenth century, as in previous centuries, was that composed of religious works. An average of over two hundred such works was published annually throughout the century. *The Pilgrim's Progress*—although little noted by polite authors, and then usually with derision—went through one hundred and sixty editions by 1792; while at least ten devotional manuals had sales of over thirty editions during the eighteenth century, and many other religious and didactic works were equally popular.[12]

Writing for this audience presented other aspects of the fact-fantasy problem. The normal commercial or working-class Englishman, particularly if he was a Dissenter, a Protestant Christian outside the Church of England, was inclined for a long time to consider any fiction as a pack of lies. John Bunyan himself, whose Dissenting credentials couldn't have been more in order (he wrote *The Pilgrim's Progress* while serving a 12-year jail sentence for religious dissent), was constrained to preface his allegory with "The Author's Apology" (in verse) to defend his use of fiction:

> Solidity, indeed, becomes the pen
> Of him that writeth things divine to men;
> But must I needs want solidness, because
> By metaphors I speak? Was not God's laws,
> His gospel laws, in olden time held forth
> By types, shadows, and metaphors? Yet loth
> Will any sober man be to find fault
> With them, lest he be found for to assault
> The highest wisdom . . . .[13]

Writers like Defoe, less scrupulous than Bunyan, got around the difficulty by pretending to fact—in effect they compounded the lie of fiction with a further lie. The trick was easy because English prose was breaking away from baroque ornamentation, and the techniques of literary realism were becoming familiar. Prose was able for the first time to give detailed and convincing descriptions of everyday life.

Samuel Richardson was another writer less scrupulous than Bunyan. He wrote and published *Pamela* (1740) considered generally to be the first psychological novel. *Pamela* was written in the form of a series of letters between a sixteen-year-old servant girl, Pamela, and her parents. In his preface Richardson claimed that he was merely editing and printing a packet of letters written by a real adolescent girl named Pamela: he called himself "the Editor of the following letters which have their Foundation in *Truth* and Nature". He argued the morality of the work on the basis of his own reaction to the letters "because an *Editor* may reasonably be supposed to judge with an Impartiality which is rarely to be met within an *Author* towards his own Works".[14] This was a stark denial of the existence of Richardson's rich fictive imagination, but useful for reaching a new class of reader. In this passage from Richardson's novel, Pamela is under guard and trying secretly to pick up a hidden letter:

> When I came near the Place, as I had been devising, I said, Pray, step to the Gardner, and ask him to gather a Sallad for me to Dinner. She called out *Jacob!* - Said I, he can't hear you so far off; and pray tell him, I should like a Cucumber too, if he has one. When she had stept about a Bow-shot from me, I popt down, and whipt my Fingers under the upper Tile, and pulled out a little Letter, without Direction, and thrust it in my Bosom, trembling for Joy.[15]

The impressive effect here is not just the naturalness of Pamela's ruse, but her realistic servant-class diction—"sallad for me to dinner", "popt", "whipt". This is fiction packed with factual observation of a new class of servant girl—vain, literate, with social ambitions. Richardson was explaining that class to itself. Swift came so close to the diction and thought patterns of the merchant class in *A Modest Proposal,* and provided enough workaday details of butchering, packaging and marketing, that some early readers were outraged, believing the author to be a real merchant who wanted to solve Irish poverty by encouraging the rich to eat the fattened babies of the poor.

It was not until Henry Fielding wrote *Joseph Andrews* (1742), partly by way of a satiric reply to *Pamela,* that fiction was able to stand on its own with no apologies for being un-factual, even though Fielding's novel, like Richardson's, was full of the results of empirical observation. Fielding claimed the generalized truth for fiction, a truth that went beyond specific facts, and beyond many elements of journalism. With Fielding's explanation of one of his characters, a heartless lawyer in a stagecoach, a theoretical basis for factual-sounding fiction was established:

> I declare here, once for all, I describe not men, but manners; not an individual, but a species . . . . The lawyer is not only alive, but hath been so these four thousand years; and I hope God will indulge his life as many yet to come. He hath not indeed confined himself to one confession, one religion, or one country; but when the first mean selfish creature appeared on the human stage, who made self the centre of the whole creation, would give himself no pain, incur no danger, advance no money, to assist or preserve his fellow creatures; then was our lawyer born.[16]

Fielding set the custom. It was long after that, not until quite recently in fact, before novelists felt easy about using "real" people as characters in fiction. By 1742 the new social and economic realities of the eighteenth century were becoming understandable enough to allow both journalism and fiction to pull back to their own more exclusive tasks.

In the twentieth century, fiction, even outrageous fiction, is acceptable to most readers; Bible-belt resistance to books such as *Catcher in the Rye* is enough of a curiosity to be reported in the newspapers. Straight reporting, however, sometimes encounters as much reader resistance as prose fiction used to suffer. The response by many writers has been similar to what happened in the eighteenth century, only instead of fiction disguised as fact, there is a lot of fact infused with the fictive imagination. The reason for this reader resistance is not completely clear, but straight facts may be either too raw and jarring, or too dull.

A useful fictive pattern was visible in Hunter Thompson's *Fear and Loathing: On the Campaign Trail '72*. The pattern, dimly in the background, was the picaresque novel: the narration was in the first person, the narrator was something of a *pícaro* or rogue because he drank heavily, took drugs, lied a lot, and was careless of private property—at least as he told it. Like the picaresque hero, Thompson moved warily through a hostile world and was continually surprised by violent accident and the treachery of people he once trusted. The message that emerged is that the world is full of scoundrels. Don Quixote worked similarly in a similar world. There is little question of the authenticity of Thompson's record of an outrageous and unbelievable presidential campaign. He counted noses, named names, and chronicled the cities travelled by the politicians. But a fictional framework was a convenient way to handle the material.

Social and political change has been considerable in North America since 1962. Ethics have been adjusted in everything from retail credit to sexual behavior. Canada and the United States have witnessed political terrorism, assassination and military rule. Economic certainties have been replaced by phenomena that leave the professionals grasping for labels like "stagflation". The inadequate term "new journalism" has emerged as an attempt to define the kind of writing that recorded these changes. But this writing represents the long-standing alliance of fiction and journalism; it is merely a convenient way of dealing with the unusual.

It is a tricky form to write honestly. It requires readers more enlightened than the naive crowd getting its first taste of prose fiction in the early decades of the eighteenth century, but surely that is not too much to ask. This journalism allies itself with literary forms, and it can use the resources of the fictive imagination without being dishonest.

The tendency to blur the line between fiction and fact is deeply imbedded in our culture. In general it is a happy tendency. Fiction is often more illuminating than fact, and facts are sometimes so dull the reader won't pay attention, or so bizarre that the reader won't believe them if he does. The trick is to recognize the distinction even when the writer is deliberately blurring it. Events themselves often make the distinction difficult:

> Hernia, hernia, hernia, hernia, hernia, hernia, hernia,
> hernia, hernia, hernia, hernia, hernia, hernia, HERNia;
> hernia, HERNia, hernia, hernia, hernia, hernia, HERNia,
> HERNia, HERNia, hernia, hernia, hernia, hernia, hernia,
> hernia, hernia, eight is the point, the point is eight;
> hernia, hernia, HERNia; hernia, hernia, hernia, hernia,
> all right, hernia, hernia, hernia, hernia.[17]

This, it turns out, is factual, or at least Tom Wolfe gives enough plausible surroundings to convince the reader it is. The "hernia's" are being spoken—like an auctioneer's sing-song—by a dealer at a Las Vegas crap table. But it sounds, upon first encounter, like the wildest kind of fantasy. The truth is stranger than fiction often; life does imitate art as well as the other way around. The Hearst kidnapping was close to the plot outline of a really bad novel: it was crude, it exploited sex and violence, it lacked plain verisimilitude. But it was fact. It was human suffering and pain on an appalling level, and somewhere in it lies a truth about human nature and the year 1974. But that truth never emerged in the straight news reports—only the facts did.

We live in a time of extremes when facts seem to be sliding toward fiction. Fiction is performing a complementary function by taking on the structuring that fact can offer. In skilled and honest writers, the results of both processes can be illuminating.

NOTES TO CHAPTER THREE

1/The concept was first recorded by Aristotle in his *Poetics.*

2/DANIEL DEFOE, *Selected Poetry and Prose of Daniel Defoe,* ed. Michael F. Shugrue (New York: Holt, Rinehart, 1968), pp. 225-27.

3/HERBERT PASSIN, "Writer and Journalist in the Transitional Society", *Communications and Political Development,* ed. Lucian W. Pye (Princeton: Princeton University Press, 1963), p. 85.

4/JONATHAN SWIFT, *A Modest Proposal, The Writings of Jonathan Swift,* ed. Robert A. Greenberg (New York: Norton, 1973), p. 502.

5/JONATHAN SWIFT, *Gulliver's Travels,* ed. Robert A. Greenberg (New York: Norton, 1970), p. 193.

6/JOSEPH HELLER, *Catch-22* (New York: Dell, 1961), p. 10.

7/RICHARD ROHMER, *Exxoneration* (Toronto: McClelland and Stewart, 1974).

8/"The Birth of 'The New Journalism'; Eyewitness Report by Tom Wolfe", *New York,* February 14, 1974, p. 34.

9/WAYNE C. BOOTH, "Loathing and Ignorance on the Campaign Trail: 1972". *Columbia Journalism Review* (November/December 1973), p. 10.

10/HUNTER S. THOMPSON, *Fear and Loathing: On the Campaign Trail '72* (New York: Popular Library, 1973), pp. 353-54.

11/TOM WOLFE, *The Kandy-Kolored Tangerine-Flake Streamline Baby* (New York: Farrar, Straus and Giroux, 1965).

12/*The Rise of the Novel* (Berkeley: University of California Press, 1965), pp. 50-51.

13/*The Pilgrim's Progress and Grace Abounding,* ed. JAMES THORPE (Boston: Houghton, Mifflin, 1969), p. 89. It must be emphasized that Bunyan was writing for an audience completely ignorant of humanist defences of the literary art, like Sidney's *The Defence of Poesie,* which would be familiar to the educated aristocracy.

14/SAMUEL RICHARDSON, *Pamela* (Boston: Houghton, Mifflin, 1971), p. 3.

15/*Ibid.* p. 117.

16/HENRY FIELDING, *Joseph Andrews* (Boston: Houghton, Mifflin, 1961), p. 159.

17/WOLFE, *op. cit.* p. 3.

PART TWO

Politics, Media and Communication

EDITOR'S NOTE: The articles in this section are tied together by an underlying concern for the process of journalistic communication in Canadian society.

The starting point is the federal government. In Chapter Four, Anthony Westell assesses and finds wanting the performance of the news media in Ottawa. Westell observes, for example, that the tremendous growth in the size of government in the postwar years has not been matched by a parallel growth in the number of reporters despatched to cover it. Nor are there sufficient numbers of correspondents in Ottawa specializing in vital areas such as external affairs, economic policy or the Supreme Court. Westell says, however, that additions of general and specialized reporters will not help unless news organizations revise their news judgment away from the drama of politics to the substance of it.

Spliced into this critique is a discussion of additional sources of conformity in Ottawa news reporting. Westell argues that the social life of the Press Gallery leads to consensus journalism and, further, that the parliamentary system of government narrows the focus of political reportage to the House of Commons and its Question Period.

While Westell concentrates on the activities of journalists in the Press Gallery, T. Joseph Scanlon directs attention in Chapter Five to the communication activities of the federal government. Four publicity campaigns—each different in kind—are analyzed.

The first was an open campaign with a purpose acknowledged by everyone who participated in it. The second had an unacknowledged purpose. Newsmen were invited to report an event, but they were not told that they were being used to improve the image of a federal department. In campaign number three, news media personnel were unaware of its dimensions even though they participated in it. And the fourth stands on its own, according to Scanlon, as the most ambitious peacetime mass merchandising campaign ever undertaken by government. He concludes with the comment that journalists sometimes stand ready "to assist government in its attempts to manipulate public opinion".

The focus in Chapter Six is changed from government to society as a whole. Carman Cumming analyzes Canadian Press, our major wire service. He questions the standard view that CP is a conduit through which neutral information flows, and he argues that the importance of CP is that it plays an important role in determining which events and issues will become topics for public discussion. After a careful analysis of the structural and performance characteristics of the wire service, Cumming concludes that "CP's role in agenda-setting is to keep the national perspective focussed on the known and accepted at the expense of the new and different".

The last chapter in this section is based on original research conducted by Scanlon and a group of journalism students who were interested in the flow of communications in crisis situations. The analysis of their findings provides an opportunity to sharpen our conception of the ways in which individuals receive and use communications which originate in the news media. A major point is that parallel to and intertwined with the news media are networks of human communication based on face-to-face meetings or telephone conversations. Thus the news communication system in Canada is not limited by the formal media, but includes networks such as those revealed by Scanlon. With such an understanding in view, it is possible to modify the implication sometimes contained in mass media analyses that audiences are homogeneous. The extent to which they are heterogeneous is partially revealed by the different ways in which communication takes place.

chapter four

Reporting the Nation's Business

ANTHONY WESTELL

The importance of the mass media in the democratic process is so well recognized that the familiar descriptions have become clichés. In Britain the press was described as the Fourth Estate, more powerful than the three estates represented in Parliament, the Lords Spiritual, the Lords Temporal, and the Commons. In the United States Thomas Jefferson said he would prefer newspapers without government to government without newspapers.[1] In Canada Prime Minister William Lyon Mackenzie King described the Parliamentary Press Gallery as an "adjunct of Parliament",[2] and Prime Minister Pierre Trudeau's Task Force on Government Information said flatly in 1969, "The Gallery is unquestionably the most important instrument of political communication in the country".[3]

Common sense confirms this view of the importance of the press.[4] The average Canadian never meets the Prime Minister or a member of the Cabinet, hardly knows his MP, is not a member of a political party and does not attend election meetings. He forms his opinions about politics and government from information received through the news media, reading or hearing it himself or hearing it at second or third hand from someone else who has received it through the media. What he reads in his daily paper is selected and angled by the reporter and then edited and displayed by an editor. The TV film he sees or the radio tape he hears is clipped from context to convey the information the journalist thinks is important. And even when he sees a politician on TV, the great man is probably being interviewed by journalists who choose the subjects and ask questions designed to produce preconceived answers.

So while the mass media are not the only channels of communication between the governors and those they govern, they are the most important. When the media do their job well, people have the information to form intelligent opinions and make wise decisions at elections; when they fail to provide information, or supply incorrect information, the democratic process is damaged.

The contention in this article is that the media in Canada are not doing a good job of providing to the public information about federal government and politics. This is not to say that the media are utterly failing, but to argue a personal judgment that they are not doing as well as they could and should.

It is notoriously hard to prove a negative. To say that the needle is not in the haystack is not proof; you may not have looked in the right straw. The difficulty here is to prove that there is a great deal of relevant information which is not reported to the public and that a significant part of the information which is reported is incomplete or misleading.

It would be dramatic to be able to produce examples of important stories which the media have missed. But if one could do that, the place to put the stories would not be in this article but on the front pages of the papers. The fact is that if they have not been reported, we don't know about them and we can only suspect their hidden presence.

Another way to approach the subject would be by methodical analysis of what the media do report about federal affairs. From experience and casual observation, one suspects that research would show overwhelming emphasis on personalities, trivialities and one-day crises and very little in the way of serious investigative reporting and policy analysis. Unfortunately little or none of that sort of content research has been attempted in Canada.

It would be possible to focus on a few incidents and situations and to criticize the performance of the media. There was, for example, little reporting of the spirited debate within the government in 1972 about whether Canada should participate in the international commission being organized to supervise the peace settlement in Vietnam. As the issue involved questions about whether to send Canadian forces abroad, whether Canada could sensibly refuse a U.S. request, whether in fact Canada could continue in the role of international "helpful fixer" which was so popular with public opinion, the lack of interest by most reporters was surprising.

To take another example, one could ask whatever happened to the energy supply crisis in Canada the news media spent much of the winter of 1973/74 reporting. Obviously it hardly existed beyond political speeches and scare stories. There were no lines at the gasoline stations, as there were in the United States and in Europe; no shortages of hydro power to dim lights and slow industry. There was not even a problem in the balance of payments because Canada sold as much oil at world prices as it imported. Far from being a critical threat to Canada, the rise in oil prices has possibly worked to national advantage, and certainly to the advantage of the oil-producing provinces. The myth of a shortage of energy in 1973–74 seems to have been imported from the United States and Europe where there were serious problems, and applied to different circumstances in Canada. The politicians, for their own reasons, promoted it in public. In private, they took a different view. At one of the closed federal-provincial conferences on energy, there was a discussion about whether to follow the U.S. example of reducing highway speed limits to save gasoline. It was decided it would be too much trouble to change all the road signs! So much for the energy crisis. But it produced a lot of exciting copy.

Or one could look again at Larry Zolf's engaging book, *Dance of the Dialectic*,[5] in which he describes relations between the Press Gallery and Prime Minister Pierre Trudeau in the period 1968-72. Even allowing for literary licence—that is, exaggerations, distortions and downright errors— it is a penetrating account of how the Gallery operates and rates a politician essentially by his entertainment value. One might say that the media behavior described by Zolf was extraordinary, except that it was probably very ordinary, very much in character and tradition. Ask John Diefenbaker.

Alternatively, one could take an example of an important continuing story on which the press, with few exceptions, has been wrong from start to finish. For example, starting in 1970 and continuing for several years, most media reported that the powers of the Auditor General were being curbed by the government to prevent him from exposing waste. It was said, first, that the government had introduced a bill which restricted the powers of the Auditor General. In fact, the bill was recommended by the all-party Commons committee on Public Accounts to strengthen the independence of the Auditor General and made no significant change in the scope of his duties. It was said, second, that the government had prevented the Auditor General from hiring adequate staff, but the public records show this allegation also was unfounded. Nevertheless, the idea that the government did try to hobble the Auditor General is still being repeated by the press, a myth masquerading as fact.[6] What happened? Reporters took their version of events from the Auditor General and from his supporters in the Opposition in the House of Commons instead of doing their homework in the dusty records of the Public Accounts committee. Besides, a scandal—"Government gags AG"—was a better story than no scandal.

But what is proved by such examples? Only that mistakes are sometimes made, that reporters and even editors are human, that under the pressure of competition and the desire to interest the reader, facts are sometimes sensationalized. One cannot draw sweeping conclusions from a few examples of where things went wrong.

So instead of producing direct evidence that the press is failing to report a great deal of significant news about government, one has to rely on indirect evidence. One has to establish that there is at least a very high probability that the press is not doing a good job of communicating information. One way to do this is to show that machinery of government and politics—Parliament, Cabinet executive, bureaucracy and party organizations—has grown at a much greater rate than the number of reporters assigned to cover it.

A quarter century ago, the federal budget forecast expenditure of $2.4 billion; the current budget is more than 10 times that amount. Between 1952 and 1969, the number of federal employees rose by more than 50 per cent, and it is still rising. The proceedings of the House of Commons in 1950 filled 5,225 pages of *Hansard;* the proceedings in 1969, a comparable year of majority government immediately following an election, filled 9,393 pages. But that is not the full story of how the work of Parliament has expanded. Prior to the reforms of the 1960s, there were few committees of the Commons; in the period 1970-72, for which I have statistics, 21 committees held 900 meetings to hear 2,751 witnesses and fill 30,000 pages with their proceedings.

Prime Minister Louis St. Laurent had a Cabinet of 21 members in 1949, running 18 departments of government. In 1969, Prime Minister Trudeau had a Cabinet of 29 running 24 departments. The Cabinet secretariat grew from 10 officers in 1945 to almost 70 in 1971. National political parties hardly existed as functioning organizations between elections until the 1960s; now with the growth of party democracy, they are full-time institutions with substantial staffs which organize frequent national policy conferences.

One could go on spinning out statistics to demonstrate the growth of government, the way in which programs have multiplied and now reach into every corner of national life in a way which would have been unthinkable 25 years ago.

Who is in Ottawa reporting and analysing the activities of government? In 1949 there were 75 members of the Press Gallery. By recent count there were 159 members. The increase does not parallel the growth in the size of the Ottawa beat, and in any event, the numbers are misleading.

It was not until 1961 that print reporters gave way after stubborn resistance and admitted radio and TV journalists to the Gallery.[7] It is this which has contributed most to the rise in membership. In 1949, all 75 members represented daily papers, news services and the occasional magazine. Recently there were still only 100 print journalists. The other 59 members were radio and TV journalists, and while some are excellent reporters, most are required by their media to provide only the most perfunctory news coverage in the form of a dramatic visual image or instant recorded quote. TV does, however, specialize in actually questioning politicians on the various interview shows, a form of reporting almost lost in the press. It is probably true also that broadcast journalists are allowed more freedom to interpret and analyse in their reports than print journalists.

In any event, the increase in the number of reporters in the Gallery, whether print or broadcast, does not necessarily mean that more stories are covered. Often it is simply a case of more reporters representing more news organizations covering the same story.

There is a chance that more stories will be covered, more byways of bureaucracy explored and more policies analysed, when a news organization enlarges its reporting team in Ottawa. While one or two are covering the routine news, others can dig for news that is not routine. But little of that has occurred. The Canadian Press had nine reporters in the Gallery in 1949 and now has 29, of whom 17 are English-language print reporters—not enough to staff all Parliamentary committees on a busy day. The *Toronto Star* had three, now five or six; Southam News Services four, now six; *The Globe and Mail,* one or two, now five or six. But most papers have not significantly enlarged their bureaus. The Task Force on Information reported in 1969: "Only about 20 daily papers in Canada have their own men in the Canadian Parliamentary Press Gallery and nearly half the newspapermen there are working for papers in Toronto, Montreal and Ottawa".[8] On a recent gallery list, there were 18 daily papers, but also some agencies representing groups of dailies, and of course weeklies and magazines.

It is fair, therefore, to say that while the number of reporters in the Gallery has more than doubled in 25 years, the ability to cover news in breadth and depth is far from twice as good. More reporters are covering the main news events of the day for many more outlets and are probably covering them better. But when measured against the enormous expansion of government, it seems obvious that journalistic resources are stretched thinner than ever.

It is worth noting also that while numbers of newsmen on the Hill have increased, space to accommodate them has not. Facilities and communications have declined.

Even if one is prepared to make the generous assumption that reporting of federal affairs was adequate 25 years ago, one has to accept the probability that it is less than adequate today.

There is another way to assess the quality of journalism in Ottawa. There are very few specialists among the reporters. The U.S. State Department is covered by newsmen specializing in foreign affairs. The Foreign Office in London has its diplomatic correspondents. But in Ottawa, there are only one or two reporters who try to cover the External Affairs Department on a continuing basis. Only a handful of members of the Press Gallery have more than a passing interest in foreign affairs or make any effort to cover the beat except when it becomes a top story source for a day. For the rest of the time, information pours into the department from more than 100 countries with which Canada maintains relations and almost nobody tries to tap it for public consumption.

There is now a sizeable economic establishment in Ottawa, in the Finance Department, the Bank of Canada, the Economic Council of Canada and many other departments and agencies. Yet there are probably no more than a dozen Gallery reporters with the formal training or the acquired experience to ask intelligent questions about economic policy.

The Supreme Court of Canada is not as important in our scheme of government as the Supreme Court is in the United States. But it does from time to time make important decisions about the meaning of the constitution and about the application of laws passed by Parliament. One recalls in recent years, for example, judgments about the ownership of offshore mineral resources, the scope of provincial marketing legislation, rights of Indians, the Official Languages Act and sex discrimination.

Yet who covers the Supreme Court on a regular basis? Nobody. Canadian Press has a man who keeps his eye on pending judgments and the Toronto papers have legal correspondents who occasionally visit Ottawa or write about the court. But there is no reporter working the court as a regular beat, listening to legal arguments before the courts, seeking to establish contacts with the judges and to analyse trends of judgments, backgrounding and explaining major decisions. Indeed, there is often an appalling ignorance about the court and its duties. When one of our best known magazine writers was in Ottawa fairly recently and inquiring angrily why the court was not more "progressive" in its views on women's rights under the law, one of the judges had to take her into his office and explain quietly that under the Canadian system, Parliament and not the court writes the law.

Chief Justice Bora Laskin has been buttonholing editors and other journalists for years complaining about the lack of attention which the court receives and offering co-operation. Little has happened.

From time to time a reporter appears with particular interest in science and works that beat. There is the occasional military buff with contacts in the Defence Department. But in the main, Ottawa reporters are generalists confronting a growing array of experts in government. Only The Canadian Press agency has made a serious effort to develop a beat system.

Most newsmen are also unilingualists reporting a government striving to become bilingual. Groups of English-speaking members of the Gallery have tried from time to time to take French courses offered to civil servants, but few if any have had the time and determination to become bilingual. Life in the Gallery is hectic enough without committing evenings and weekends for years to come to instruction in French. Nor are editors quite as willing as government departments to give their employees a few months at a time to be immersed. The hope must be that editors will require reporters to have a working knowledge of French before posting them to Ottawa.

But meantime, few English media men in the Gallery are bilingual. It goes without saying that French media men can work in English.

In summary, the facts suggest that large areas of the federal government are not covered at all, and that other areas are covered on a casual, uninformed, hit-or-miss basis. It is so likely as to be almost a certainty that much significant information is not reported, and that much other information is badly reported. This means that the media are not doing as well as they could and should and that accordingly, the democratic process is not functioning as well as it should.

In establishing these probabilities, I have indicated where one of the main weaknesses lies: shortage of competent reporters in Ottawa. Although daily newspapers are highly profitable, as the Senate Committee on Mass Media documented,[9] they simply do not assign enough reporters to Ottawa to find out what is really going on beneath the most superficial level of observation.

But that is not the whole story, as I can illustrate by a personal digression. In 1972, I put some of this analysis and criticism into a memo to the Publisher and Editor in Chief of the *Toronto Star*.

I suggested that what was needed to do a much better job in Ottawa was to double the size of the *Star's* bureau to 10 journalists, and to transfer from Toronto to an editor on the spot in Ottawa much of the authority to decide what news to cover, how to cover it and how to write the story.

The ideal bureau, I proposed, would consist of an Ottawa Editor with the status, approximately, of an assistant managing editor and the responsibility for planning and directing all Ottawa coverage; a bureau chief in day-to-day charge of coverage, assigning reporters and approving their copy for transmission to Toronto; three experienced general reporters to respond to fast-breaking news and to handle the routine daily queries; plus reporters specializing in economic affairs, science and the environment, social policy, consumer affairs and the regulatory agencies, foreign affairs and defence; and a free-ranging Ottawa columnist to focus mainly on the politics behind the scenes of major news events.

The Publisher and the Editor in Chief responded with enthusiasm. They made me Ottawa Editor and gave me the staff and the budget for which I asked. After a year, the experiment failed.

I was too closely involved to have a clear view of what went wrong, and certainly I bear a share of the blame. But what I think happened was this. We in Ottawa wanted to put less emphasis on the daily trivia from the question period in the Commons, the trumped-up "Cabinet crises", the Ottawa reaction to some remote and half-understood event, and the other staples of the regular Ottawa news budget. We wanted to put more effort into digging into the government departments and agencies to develop stories and features about policy alternatives, internal debates, and those pre-parliamentary occasions when decisions are really made. We were interested also in getting a story right rather than just exciting, and that meant very often putting the facts in a cool perspective rather than stretching them to the limit to get a dramatic lead and a big headline.

To achieve all this, the Ottawa Editor and the bureau chief had to have the authority to decide what to cover and what to ignore or leave to CP, what was old news and what fresh, what was significant about a story and how it should be written. But while the editors in Toronto were not opposed to depth reporting and careful features, their first priority was to compete with other media, and that meant basically covering the same stories in the same way with the same sense of news values. Some middle-level editors also held firmly to the traditional view that, sitting at the center of the news organization with information flowing in from many sources in addition to Ottawa, they were in a better position than the Ottawa staff to assess what was really happening and to assemble a complete account for the paper. There was, of course, merit in this view and it was always understood—or should have been—that news desks in Toronto could contribute much to the Ottawa file. The difficulty was in devising an effective system of communication and co-operation and in deciding how to resolve disputes. The Managing Editor in Toronto, of course, had final authority; there was never any quarrel about that. But I took the view that the Managing Editor ought normally to accept the Ottawa judgment, from the men on the spot, and should overturn it, or allow his Toronto staff to overturn it, only occasionally and in unusual circumstances. In practice, however, when it came to clash of news judgment and priorities, the editors in Toronto at all levels were extremely reluctant to yield any of their traditional authority to Ottawa.

When the conflict of authority finally came to a head over how to use the Ottawa staff during the 1974 election and I realized that I could not enjoy the degree of autonomy on which I had planned, I resigned. Some other members of the bureau quit at the same time.[10]

For most of us, it was a disappointing rather than a bitter parting. We had not been able to achieve what we had hoped for, and as I had planned and set up the bureau, the failure to foresee the difficulties was partly mine.

The lesson, I think, is that it is not enough for a news organization to increase the number of reporters in Ottawa and to encourage them to specialize. The organization also has to be prepared to change its ideas about what makes news, bucking the conventional competition where necessary to set its own standards about what is honest, important and interesting. That's hard enough for us reporters raised in the popular press traditions of news judgment and news writing; it is much harder for editors responsible for putting out day by day a paper which at least matches its competitors in popular appeal. Conformity is usually the better part of innovation.

Competition leads to conformity in the Press Gallery also. A Gallery man, like any other reporter, desires a scoop, but even more he desires not to be scooped. It is easier and safer to do the story that everybody else is doing than to seek a totally different story. In fact, most of the one- and two- and three-man bureaus on Parliament Hill have little option. Their editors may tell them when they are assigned to Ottawa to leave routine to CP and to seek original material—all editors say that—but they know that in practice they are expected to earn their place in the paper by covering the big news of the day, the main story treated in the conventional way. The editor, of course, wants features and backgrounders and news-in-depth, but only after he has his own man's bylined story of the day for his front page. When the daily story or stories have been done in Ottawa, there is time only for a few independent news checks or for a quick and flimsy news feature.

The atmosphere in the Press Gallery and the organization of Parliament both tend to encourage and reinforce this conformity.

The members of the Gallery elect every year an executive committee to administer their affairs and they also hold occasional and interminable general meetings at which they prove they are better critics than actors: the discussions bog down in a parody of parliamentary procedure, records are lost and, on a recent occasion, it was discovered that the treasurer had departed leaving no books, but a desk full of unpaid bills and uncashed cheques. Somehow or other, the Gallery does its main business of admitting members who meet the tests prescribed in the constitution, reproving those who break embargoes or otherwise infringe on the unwritten rules of proper conduct, and negotiating with the Speaker and other officers of Parliament for better facilities.

The Gallery, however, is much more than a service organization. It is also a social club. Formally, the Gallery holds an annual dinner for the Governor General, the party leaders, several hundred lesser politicians and civil servants, publishers and editors and even the occasional business tycoons, such as the presidents of the Canadian Pacific Railway and Canadian National Railways.

The proceedings are strictly off-the-record, not, one suspects, because the Prime Minister and the other speakers are likely to say anything of importance, but because members and guests sometimes get drunk—much more in the past than nowadays, it should be said.

The Gallery—over the objections of some members—also gives parties for backbench MPs and wives, and seems to be in the custom of giving farewell dinners to retiring Prime Ministers.

Informally, Gallery members drink together at the famous Blind Pig just behind the hot-room, so called, where the work is done, play cards together in the lounge, eat together in the parliamentary restaurant and cafeterias, write side by side in the crowded workroom, curl or play hockey together outside working hours, entertain each other as friends as well as colleagues, meet constantly at embassy receptions, and talk, talk, talk together about the news of the day.

There used to be acknowledged syndicates of reporters from non-competing papers who routinely swapped carbon copies of their stories. It is doubtful if that happens much anymore, but the Gallery is such a close community that communication occurs by other means. The herd instinct becomes strongest during an election campaign, when reporters share not only planes and buses but also ideas and conventional wisdom. As one member remarked, during a campaign the reporters share everything but a salt lick.

A collective wisdom based upon a shared idea of news values and some pooling of information and interpretations decides what the story of the day is—for example, what angle to take out of a report by the Economic Council, what quote to highlight from the daily question period or the scrum outside the chamber when the politicians repeat their performance for the cameras, what gossip about Cabinet debates and decisions is reliable. It is tough for an individual to reject the majority view which will be on the CP wire, on the 11 o'clock news and in all the papers the next day, and to take his own line on events. Genuine scoops are extremely rare.

The parliamentary system reinforces the tendency to conformity and superficial reporting by being, on the one hand, closed and guarded against prying reporters, while, on the other hand, offering a daily theatrical performance for the benefit of the media in search of what can pass as news.

This is not the place for an extended criticism of parliamentary government. It is enough to point out that all the real decisions about public policy are made in private: in the bureaucracy with its passion for secrecy; in the Cabinet where ministers are bound by oath not to disclose details of proceedings to outsiders; and in the party caucuses where members seek to reconcile their differences so that they can offer in public at least the appearance of unity.

A diligent reporter can penetrate all these private places, but it takes time and effort. It is a great deal easier and more practical for the small bureau to focus instead on the House of Commons where there is a daily pretense of public debate and decision-making. The question period, in fact, is almost a perfect media event—a sort of guerrilla theatre. *Public personalities* come into *Conflict* over current *Controversies,* providing in one neat package the basic ingredients for a good news story.

Take for example the subject of unemployment. Statistics Canada publishes each month not only the percentage of the labor force out of work, but a mass of material about changes in the labor force, the ages, sexes and localities of the unemployed, the duration of their unemployment and much other information.

Economists in the Department of Finance seek to relate the figures to the state of the economy, and the Department of Manpower analyses the figures to discover why its programs are not as effective as they might be. In addition, there are numerous other agencies, private and public, concerned with the question of unemployment, doing research or generating ideas.

Few reporters have the time to try to tap all this material and analyse it for readers. If they did, few editors would welcome a long story. It is much simpler and more colorful to report the exchange in the House. *Unemployment up—opposition leader charges—Prime Minister replies—bitter words—House in uproar.* The issue of unemployment has been *personalized* in the shape of political leaders, *simplified* into a conflict of charges and insults, *dramatized* in the theater of Parliament, and *capsulized* into an exchange which occupies perhaps seven or eight minutes and fits nicely into a column. Very little of substance, of course, has been said or reported about unemployment.

Day after day, the question period provides the Gallery with much of its raw material. It is such "good copy" that reporters dare not ignore it, but it serves in fact as a substitute for real news which is made in private.

One should note in passing that there has recently been a significant refinement of the way in which the question period dominates the news. As TV cameras and tape recorders are not allowed in the Commons chamber, a room—Room 130S—has been set aside in the basement where the politicians can face the cameras and microphones and repeat—or occasionally amend—what they said in the House. The TV and radio reporters usually follow up with questions, while print reporters are more inclined to listen and take notes, as if they were following an exchange in the Commons itself. It is here in Room 130S, rather than in the Commons, that the news of the day is defined. This is what the public sees on TV and hears on radio, this is what print editors see and hear and demand from their reporters, rather than a report of the actual question period.

The question period and the sessions in Room 130S are in a sense management of the news by the opposition parties. They seek to arrange a confrontation on the floor of the House which will be reported in such a way as to convey a critical message about the government through the media to the public. The government can defend itself by defusing the confrontation or by changing the message—and of course it tries to manage its own news in the form of ministerial statements.

The Prime Minister and departmental ministers also manage news by making speeches, issuing statements, holding press conferences, permitting leaks of inside information and other devices intended to attract the attention of the news media and convey a message to the public.

All this is fine by Gallery reporters, and indeed by almost all reporters. While journalists may complain for the record about managed news and manipulation, they could hardly exist without it. Their basic task is to provide so many hundred words, so many stories, every day, and much the easiest way to get them is by way of handout, written or oral. The press gets really angry only when there is not enough managed news—as for example when the Prime Minister declines to hold a news conference.

Without a supply of ready-made news organized by press officers of one kind or another, reporters would have to go out and find their own stories. That would be hard, often unrewarding labor, and the danger of being scooped would be great. It is much better to go in a group to a briefing or a press conference and be fed the story of the day.

Incidentally, the idea that journalists at a press conference can make politicians squirm and extract all sorts of hitherto hidden information is largely romantic fiction. Any reasonably competent politician can turn questions to his own advantage, answering those which suit him and twisting others. Reporters are usually too disorganized or too jealous of each other to follow a persistent line of cross examination. It is only when a politician is on the defensive because damaging information is already public and the reporters already know or suspect the answers to their questions that a conference is likely to be an important source of new information.

The Task Force on Information estimated that there were about 400 information officers in the federal service and at least as many more men and women performing information duties but not classified as information officers. The federal information budget was said to be between $60 million and $148 million.[11] According to some sources the cost could now be about $200 million.[12]

Only a fraction of this effort goes in servicing the Press Gallery, in manipulating and managing news. The bulk of the resources goes into programs designed to make known information which sections of the public need but the mass media won't carry because it is not regarded as news. The Task Force report, written by that sparkling journalist Harry Bruce, put it this way:

> The Press Gallery at Ottawa would rather report the rivalry of Cabinet Ministers, or the gay times in the Commons question period, than the technicalities of some new social legislation to aid immigrants. The mass media, as a whole, would rather report the daily score of

prime ministerial kisses than government subsidies for adult education, and that's all perfectly understandable because that's what most
readers want. We're not knocking it. Those fellows have all got a job
to do. But the immigrant housewife is not hearing many of the things
she needs to know, and her many children are Canadians, and what
we're suggesting is that the government has a job to do, too, and that
part of it involves reaching them.[13]

That's an interesting comment on the news values of the mass media.
And if there is a tendency to doubt whether it is fair, Larry Zolf said much
the same in a different way in *Dance of the Dialectic.*

He said Trudeau was a hero to the paparazzi of the Press Gallery as long
as he was kissing pretty girls and making colorful copy, but then the reporters discovered to their dismay that he really hoped to be a serious Prime
Minister running a careful administration in a stable political climate. As
Zolf put it:

Now the hapless paparazzi had to wrestle with strange phenomena
like capital gains, depreciation and depletion allowances, standing
orders, closure and the Phillips curve. Hardly the proper bread nour-
ishment for even a third-rate flea circus, let alone the Great Forum
on the Rideau.[14]

The answer of part of the Gallery was to go into opposition against Trudeau
and, with a good deal of help from the man himself, they set the scene for
his near defeat in 1972.

This raises the question of the proper relationship of the press to government and how changing attitudes affect political reporting. Leo Rosten
described the cycle in the United States in terms which are equally applicable in Canada:

Newspapermen greet (a newly elected leader) with the hope that here
at last is the great man incarnate. The great man's talents are sung,
oversung, in the struggle for journalistic existence. Then "incidents"
occur, a political compromise of not admirable hue, a political set-
back, attacks come from the Opposition, the newspapermen begin
to see the feet of clay. They have been taken in, their faith has been
outraged. How did they ever "fall for that stuff"? . . . Other newsmen,
columnists, publishers cry that the press corps has been hamstrung
by phrases. The correspondents are hurt. They are irritated. And they
feel guilty. The breaking of the myth begins by the very men who
erected it.[15]

Remember how the press, led by the Gallery, fell in love with Diefenbaker in 1958 and out of love in 1962 and 1963; with Trudeau in 1968 and 1972; to a lesser extent with Lester Pearson and Robert Stanfield.

It is a pity we have to repeat the cycle of unbalanced reporting about political leaders. Perhaps it is the nature of journalists to be idealistic cynics, and therefore the cycle is unavoidable. But what we should be able to avoid in Ottawa is the importation of the U.S. idea that the press is a natural adversary of government.

In the U.S. system of government, this may be so. Instead of an adversary politics, there is a distribution of power among several branches of government. The President may oppose Congress on some issues, the Congress may legislate its way around the Supreme Court, the Court may discipline the President. But all are branches of the same government and there is no opposition offering an instant alternative. In this situation, the press may be justified in regarding itself as the watchdog, critic and adversary of government, and indeed its role in the political system is recognized and protected in the constitution.

In Canada, the situation is utterly different. The watchdogs, critics and adversaries are the opposition parties on the floor of Parliament, daily confronting and challenging the government and ready at a moment's notice to assume executive power and responsibility. The public therefore does not need another opposition in the form of the press. It needs a full and fair account of the actions of government and the criticisms of the opposition so that it can form a judgment about which to entrust with power.

This is not to say that reporters will never find themselves in an adversary relationship with some branch of government. Politicians and civil servants sometimes want to keep secret information which should be public and it is the reporter's job to beat them if he can.

Nor should there be confusion between the roles of adversary and investigator. The whole thrust of this article has been to argue that the press should be doing a great deal more to investigate and analyse the activities of government. In so doing, it would turn up some material favorable to the government and other material which would strengthen the opposition parties by providing ammunition for debate and criticism in the House of Commons. The point is that the primary role of the media should be that of the fair reporter and not that of the adversary with a duty to balance the power of government or even to bring down the government, as many political journalists now seem to imagine. It is simply easier and very much more flattering to regard oneself as a crusading journalist—confronting the Prime Minister and the bureaucracy, shaping public opinion, exercising political influence—than it is to be a conscientious reporter.

This entire criticism of political reporting rests, of course, upon the assumption that the public does in fact want information about federal affairs and that the media have a duty to supply it. A colleague to whom I showed a draft of this article provided a careful criticism, agreed in general with the thesis and then wrote:

> The question which haunts and taunts me constantly in any discussion of the Gallery and the reporting of politics and government in Ottawa is this: Who cares? If the ideal Press Gallery bureau were created—ideal by the standards of those of us who take ourselves and our jobs very seriously and perhaps even solemnly—what would it accomplish? Its members would know more and be able to write more, with more understanding and sensitivity and information. Would anyone really care? Would anyone except a few academics, probably misanthropic, read it at all? Would any paper print it? The answer is clearly No.

My despairing friend may be right. If so, those reporters and editors who see political reporting primarily in terms of chasing the daily fire engine to entertain a public basically not interested are right, and all my criticism falls to the ground. But so, I think, does the belief in popular democracy.

In closing this criticism of the reporting of federal affairs, I should make my own position clear. I write not as a superior outsider, but as one who has worked in the Press Gallery for almost 10 years and shared fully in the shortcomings and vanities which I have described.

NOTES TO CHAPTER FOUR

1/In a letter dated 1787, quoted in *Thomas Jefferson on Democracy,* ed. Saul K. Padover (New York: Mentor Books, 1946), p. 93. It is less often recalled that experience seemed to modify Jefferson's faith in a free press because, according to the same source, he wrote in a letter dated 1807, ". . . the man who never looks into a newspaper is better informed than he who reads them; inasmuch as he who knows nothing is nearer the truth than he whose mind is filled with falsehoods and errors".

2/A phrase enshrined in the folk memory of the Gallery.

3/*Report of the Task Force on Government Information,* Vol. II (Ottawa: Queen's Printer, 1969), p. 116.

4/It is necessary to distinguish between the importance of the press in the political system and the power of the press. Power implies an organized effort by some or all media to achieve a political end. Politicians sometimes allege that there is such a conspiracy by political journalists, or by editors or publishers. But all that is intended here is to say that by communicating or failing to communicate information, with no plan, intention or conspiracy, the media have an important influence on the political process.

5/LARRY ZOLF, *Dance of the Dialectic* (Toronto: James Lewis and Samuel, 1973).

6/For a detailed analysis of the issue, see my articles in the *Toronto Star,* December 5, 1970, and March 14, 1972. See also the records and reports of the Public Accounts Committee of the House of Commons.

7/WILFRED H. KESTERTON, *A History of Journalism in Canada* (Toronto: McClelland and Stewart Ltd., 1967), p. 163.

8/*Report of the Task Force, op. cit.* p. 115.

9/*Canada, Report of the Special Senate Committee on Mass Media,* Vol. II (Ottawa: Queen's Printer, 1970).

10/For another view of these events, see the Canadian edition of *Time,* September 23, 1974.

11/*Report of the Task Force,* Vol. I, pp. 5 and 17.

12/*Report of the Standing Senate Committee on National Finance on Information Canada* (Ottawa: Information Canada, 1974), p. 17.

13/*Report of the Task Force,* Vol. I, p. 11.

14/ZOLF, *op.cit.* p. 13.

15/*The Washington Correspondents* (New York: Harcourt, Brace and Company, 1937), p. 254.

chapter five

How Government Uses the Media*

T. JOSEPH SCANLON

In 1969, a special task force appointed by Prime Minister Trudeau chided the federal government's information programs for being unco-ordinated, archaic, aimless, even illiterate.[1] It was so critical that its authors admitted to a touch of nastiness and "unbecoming zeal" in their criticism. However, they admitted in the same breath that if the federal information apparatus was strengthened "the possibility of a government's manipulating public opinion" was raised. The implication was that such manipulation would be both new and undesirable.

In their desire to record glib criticisms with catchy phrases, the authors of the *Report of the Task Force on Government Information* took insufficient time to examine the record. The information services of the federal government have, at times, been extremely efficient. On a number of occasions, they have successfully manipulated public opinion by effectively exploiting the communication systems of Canadian society, including the news media system.

In the cases discussed below, the news media have been willing and sometimes unknowing partners in their own seduction as journalists responded enthusiastically and, on the whole, uncritically to government manoeuvres.

Four case studies of information campaigns by the federal government of Canada are used to show the range and effectiveness of federal propaganda and the extent to which the news media amongst other media collaborated in these publicity campaigns. They are: a campaign by the Department of Labour to change Canadian attitudes about winter work; a campaign by the Department of Public Works to improve its image; a campaign by the Department of Agriculture to get Canadians to eat more pork; and a campaign by the federal government to convince Canadians to convert wartime saving bonds to a new bond issue.

---

*The material in this chapter is drawn mainly from T. Joseph Scanlon, *Promoting the Government of Canada,* unpublished M.A. thesis, Queen's University, 1964.

I

The first is the best-known of all government campaigns. "Why Wait For Spring? Do It Now" was instituted in the mid-fifties after a government study concluded that the problem of declining activity in the Canadian labor force in winter was not simply a result of the cold weather preventing outdoor work. It was a reflection of a set of attitudes about the timing of work regardless of the temperature. The study concluded, therefore, that seasonal unemployment could be attacked by a campaign to change public attitudes.[2]

The job of creating such a campaign was given to the director of information for the Department of Labour, George Blackburn. He was given the small sum of $25,000 to launch the campaign, apparently because the government of the day did not have enough faith in its own study to risk more. A report of the department's information branch recorded what happened.

> ... the information branch prepared and placed advertisements in all daily and weekly newspapers and spot announcements on all radio stations during January. At the same time, a film trailer was circulated to all first-run motion picture theatres and to television stations.

Additionally, the director undertook two personal initiatives to get "Do It Now" off the ground.

First he approached a personal friend in Ottawa and convinced him to start a "Do It Now" campaign in his own lumber business. Prodded, the friend decided to:

> ... offer a home improvement "package deal"—free estimates, guaranteed workmanship, materials and financing. And to get sales leads, he took newspaper ads showing two men who would go to customers' houses and make free estimates.
> He started this campaign in the first week of January ... some of his staff had already been laid off, including six tradesmen in the woodworking shop attached to the store ....
> Within one week he had rehired all his staff and the six tradesmen in the woodworking shop, had hired ten additional tradesmen including carpenters to handle the initial rush of home improvement work. When customers complained they could not get through on the telephone, he increased his telephone lines from five to eight and hired an additional girl just to handle the office work involved in the rush of home improvement orders.
> During the next three months, he completed more than one hundred

home improvement jobs each month running between $250 and $2,-
500 each.

Although he offered to finance the jobs, seventy-five per cent of the
business was cash. He kept forty-six tradesmen who normally would
have been unemployed, working all winter.[3]

This success story was publicized by the department to encourage other
firms to try the same approach. Trade magazines were encouraged to run
articles about such ventures. One of them, *Building Supply Dealer,* chose
an annual dealer-of-the-year based on "Do It Now".

However, it was the director's second personal approach that brought
"Do It Now" to national prominence. Realizing that the advertising budget
was not enough "to brainwash the Canadian people", he interviewed officers of firms with large advertising budgets or facilities and convinced them
to support "Do It Now". Imperial Oil, *Reader's Digest,* General Electric,
General Foods and General Motors were among the companies that co-
operated. Imperial Oil gave him one-minute spots on three Saturday night
hockey broadcasts—a total audience at that time of 27,000,000 persons.
Reader's Digest gave him the inside front cover position for an advertisement.

As the annual "Do It Now" budget climbed to $285,000 the outside
support did too. On January 31, 1962, Labour Minister Michael Starr said:

> More than 90 per cent of all we see and hear promoting the "Do It
> Now" principle is either contributed as a public service or paid for
> by business and industry . . . . We estimate that we receive at least
> $10 public service support for every dollar spent on behalf of the "Do
> It Now" campaign and public support will again exceed $3,000,000
> this winter.[4]

The department estimated outside support for "Do It Now" eventually
passed the $3,500,000 mark.

The "Do It Now" campaign, of course, involved far more than free-time
advertising. As many as 2,350,000 envelopes containing single advertising
sheets were distributed by the department and co-operating firms. These
sheets carried a message from Mr. Starr suggesting that putting things off
until spring was "simply a matter of habit born of custom and tradition
of the past."[5] The department purchased metal dies which were supplied
to the post office department and used for stamping government mail. In
addition, the department supplied dies, advertising layouts, posters, pamphlets, film strips, etc., through its advertising agency to firms which would
make use of them. Newspapers carried 1,050 photos and 4,234 stories in

a single year, 1960-61. The Poster Advertising Association of Canada donated 2,000 billboards and paid the men who put up the posters. As one final gesture, the director himself wrote a singing commercial which has been played and replayed ever since.

The "Do It Now" campaign was a clear-cut case of a federal government attempt to change public attitudes. It was in no way insidious for its purpose was clearly stated and clearly understood. But it illustrates just how readily the federal government can get a response from the public using advertising and public relations techniques.

II

The second campaign—the publicizing of the blowing up of Ripple Rock—was accompanied by just as much publicity as "Do It Now". Again the media were overwhelmingly co-operative. But, unknown to the public or to the media, this campaign had a hidden agenda. The *public* purpose of the campaign was to publicize the removal of a shipping hazard; the *private* purpose was to change the image of a federal government department.[6]

Ripple Rock was a two-headed underwater peak in the Seymour Narrows—the shipping channel between mainland British Columbia and Vancouver Island—110 miles north of Vancouver. It was a shipping hazard which, in the time for which there were records, had claimed 200 large ships, 100 smaller ones and 114 lives. Its destruction had been tried before with limited success. But on April 5, 1958, it was blown up with 2,750,000 pounds of explosives—and the explosion was reported live on North American television.

This publicity bonanza was a matter of great satisfaction, for its authors were the information staff of the Department of Public Works. For many years, DPW had been regarded by many as patronage-ridden and incompetent. Its deputy-minister, Major-General H.A. Young, had accepted the post in 1954 only after personal assurances from Prime Minister Louis St. Laurent that the department and its image could be overhauled.

It was the view of those in the information division that the one thing which would alter the image would be a highly successful and highly publicized event associated with the department. The Ripple Rock explosion was to be that event. It was especially appropriate because the department had been responsible for the two earlier unsuccessful attempts. In 1943 cables on the drilling barge broke. In 1945 the same thing happened and nine persons died. This time, determined to be successful, DPW took a new approach—drilling from underwater up into the base of the rock.

In 1955, a $3,100,000 drilling contract was awarded to a group comprised of Northern Construction Company, J.W. Stewart Limited, and Boyles Brothers Drilling Company Limited. The work was to take 30 months. At the same time, engineers studied possible effects of the blast on nearby communities, shipping, and the fisheries. The Department of Mines and Technical Surveys advised that 9:31 a.m., April 5, 1958, would be the best time for an explosion because of tide conditions. The Department of Fisheries agreed with an April blast time because fish destruction could be kept to a minimum and the Department of Transport agreed to warn ships to keep clear of the blast area.

As the time for the blast approached, the information director launched a publicity drive. He wrote personal letters to all the Canadian daily newspapers, to The Canadian Press, to British United Press, to U.S. magazines such as *Life, Time* and *Look* and Canadian publications such as *The Star Weekly* and *Weekend.* Assessing the replies, he advised all publications that a maximum of two persons—normally one photographer and one reporter—would be allowed into a bunker 6,700 yards from the blast site.

The night before the explosion the press was briefed and each representative was given a British Columbia centennial silver dollar in "return for a signature on a release form in case of injury". Special planes were hired to fly film to Vancouver and pool arrangements were made for the circulation of wirephotos.

The next morning the blast went off like clockwork. No one was hurt. A count revealed that roughly one hundred fish of commercial value were killed. Ripple Rock was removed so well that within five hours after the explosion Public Works Minister Howard Green was able to announce that the channel had a minimum 40-foot clearance, the target depth. The Public Works Department had achieved the first aim of a public relations effort. The project had gone off smoothly. More important, however, international press coverage was phenomenal and the press was enthusiastic about cooperation from the department. The Public Works Department achieved its objective of publicizing a good effort. No one in government could be unaware that Public Works was capable of a professional performance under the glare of intense publicity. Of course, at the time, no one was told that one of the reasons for all the fuss was to improve the department's image.

III

The Ripple Rock campaign was an open campaign with a hidden agenda. The "Great Pork" project of 1959 was a completely hidden campaign. It involved the deliberate use of the established channels of communication between government and media without any notification to the media. It accomplished its purpose without a formal announcement of its existence.

In order to understand the background and reasons for this campaign aimed at increasing pork consumption, it is necessary to review conditions in the hog market at that time. From May 1956 to October 1958, the hog market had been light and prices favorable. With ample grain, as a Department of Agriculture internal bulletin reported at the time, the result was: "(a) a gradual build-up in hog numbers with a 'surplus' of pork beginning in October 1958; and (b) an explosion in hog numbers in the United States and Canada on the heels of high prices".

This explosion in production, under free market conditions, should have led to an immediate price drop followed by both a decline in production and an increase in consumption. But this would not happen because the Agricultural Stabilization Board had guaranteed producers a minimum of twenty-five cents a pound. To hold this price, the board purchased pork from the producers. By May 14, 1959, the board had seventy million pounds of pork cuts in cold storage compared with normal storage of eighteen million pounds. Desperately trying to stem the hog tide, the board announced the supported price would be dropped to 23.65 cents effective October 1, 1959. However, in the meantime the board had to contend with a huge pork surplus.

On January 28, 1959, the Director of the Livestock Division of the Department of Agriculture met in Toronto with officials from Canada Packers, Swift Canadian Company, the Retail Merchants Association, and the Meat Packers Council. Those at the meeting agreed that it would be helpful to increase consumer awareness of pork. The group decided to exploit "all the regular channels of communication rather than [launch] a special advertising campaign. Publicity instead of advertising should be used."[7] The meat packers met February 18 on their own. The meeting concluded:

> ... that the council as such should not appropriate funds for promotional activities to support pork sales since packers in general are already contributing toward this activity .... It was felt that such releases would receive more attention if issued through a government channel rather than by the council.[8]

The government agreed. The head of the special projects of the information division of the Department of Agriculture took charge of the campaign. He was allotted a budget of $41,800 and he used this money to produce booklets entitled "Pork; How to Buy: How to Cook". Two million were printed in English and 145,685 in French. The head of the department's consumer section was called in and told to stress pork rather than other meat products in its regular publicity services. In addition, the section was given $7,600 to produce three television films on pork. A special pork promotion luncheon was held in May at Toronto's Park Plaza Hotel.

Daily and weekly newspapers and radio stations were reached through the news and feature service of the Department of Agriculture. Since these media depend on the service for their regular food columns and broadcasts, at no extra cost, the department was able to supply them with material such as this:

> More and more people are enjoying pork in summer meals and fortunately this year there's no shortage. You can buy so many cuts prepared in so many different ways . . . fresh, or cured, pickled, canned or cooked . . . that you can serve pork as often as you wish with innovations.
> The primitive ham was a far cry from the scientifically prepared masterpiece of today . . . exacting skill is used to produce the tested, fine-flavoured, firm Canadian ham that will be the centre of Easter tables . . . [9]

With such copy coming to them free, it's hardly surprising that food writers felt prompted to produce articles like this one in the *Star Weekly:*

> Father's day is as good a time as any for father to don his apron and be boss of the barbecue. And, though steak is often the feature item for the outdoor chef, we suggest pork for a change.[10]

What is surprising is that the department never graced the campaign with an official announcement of either its start or its end. Douglas Harkness, Minister at the time, was deliberately not identified with the campaign, for, as a memorandum explains, "such action would focus too much attention on the pork surplus, and the consumer would be led to expect lower prices".

The campaign was successful. Pork consumption rose to 76,000,000 pounds in July 1959, higher than in 35 of the 49 surrounding months even though July is the month which normally marks a seasonal decline in pork consumption. In all but three months of 1959 higher figures were recorded than in comparable months in 1958, 1960 and 1961. The total pork consumption (in millions of pounds) for the years in question was: 1958, 763; 1959, 901; 1960, 839; 1961, 820.[11] While these figures are not conclusive, it would appear that the Department of Agriculture was successful in using its promotional resources to convince the public to eat more pork and thus eliminate an embarrassing pork surplus created in part by the policies of the Agricultural Stabilization Board.

IV

The eat-more-pork campaign may have never been dignified by a government announcement; the great conversion campaign, in which Canadians were urged to convert wartime Victory Bonds into new Conversion Bonds, was exactly the opposite. It was announced and accompanied by the greatest fanfare of all. It involved the unleashing of a massive government publicity campaign which, in retrospect, appears to have gotten sadly out-of-hand. It turned out to be quite possibly the most expensive campaign ever undertaken by the federal government—its total cost estimated at $10,000,-000.

The campaign began on July 14, 1958, when Prime Minister John Diefenbaker told the largest television audience in Canadian history up to that time:

> We often hear it said that nations and governments seem to be able to achieve things under the stress of wartime emergency that they can not do in time of peace. Surely it need not be so. Let us prove that it is not so by entering upon this undertaking [i.e. converting Victory Bonds to Conversion Bonds] in the same spirit and with the same determination that brought such distinction to Canada during the two great wars.

The publicity that surrounded the opening announcement was not confined to television. It received front-page treatment in such papers as the *Halifax Chronicle-Herald, The Montreal Star,* the *Toronto Daily Star, The Globe and Mail,* the *Winnipeg Free Press* and the *Vancouver Sun.*

The origin of the conversion campaign has never been established. One authority states "most informed, if unofficial speculation attributes it to a Toronto investment dealer who brought the proposal to the authorities in May or June". According to official government documents the

> conversion loan was issued in order to lengthen out the term of the debt, by selling to the public longer term bonds in exchange for the shorter victory loan bonds. It [the government] offered to convert all 3 per cent Victory Loan bonds into new 4½ per cent ones due September 1, 1983; 4½ per cent bonds due September 1, 1972; and 3¾ per cent bonds due September 1, 1965 or 3 per cent bonds due December, 1961, providing that the term of the new bonds was not less than that of the victory loan bonds converted . . . .

At the time the loan was offered most of the remaining five series of Victory Loan bonds were selling below par on the market.

The Ninth Victory Bond, for example, was selling at a discount of about $5 per $100 of par value. By the terms of the Canada Conversion Loan the holders of Victory Bonds were advised that they could exchange Victory Bonds for Conversion Bonds at par and, in addition, cash bonuses were offered to those who were willing to take the longer-term Conversion Bonds.

As Professor H. Scott Gordon has pointed out, from the standpoint of the holder of Victory Bonds, "the offering appeared very attractive indeed".[12] He received an immediate capital gain plus a cash bonus, for exchanging a government bond that paid him $3 a year for one that paid him $4.50 a year.

The government not only produced an offer that appeared extremely attractive to the small bond holder, it also went to great pains to win the support of the investment community. C.S. Mallory relates what happened:

It is appropriate that the new securities being issued in exchange for the Victory Loans are designated "Conversion Bonds" because there are heavy theological overtones to the operation, both in purpose and in execution.

In the first place, the manner of its announcement was in the nature of Moses receiving the tablets. A selected list of dealers and bankers was mysteriously summoned to Ottawa, where the new truth was revealed in solemn conclave by the Minister of Finance and the Governor of the Bank of Canada, after the brief appearance of a Commissioner of Oaths. The fourteen senior apostles from Bay Street and St. James Street who first received the word on Thursday were held incommunicado from the next platoon of twenty-four arrivals on Friday, and the latter were in turn sealed off from the world until the tablets were delivered to the Presidents of Canada's major financial institutions on Saturday, July 11th.

. . . the secrecy rituals . . . had certain advantageous side effects. The most important of these was to convey to the selected group of initiates a feeling of participation . . . and at the same time to prevent the initiates from talking to cynical outsiders, who might conceivably introduce seeds of doubt.

It is an interesting reflection on human nature that some of the men who were called to Ottawa to participate in . . . the conversion were prominent among those who wanted the Governor's head only two short weeks before . . . .

By Saturday afternoon, when a fleet of Viscounts had lifted the indoctrinated financial fraternity back to Toronto and Montreal, there was universal praise for the Minister's courage and vision and for the Governor's boldness, and cooperativeness and, indeed, charm. What had produced this conversion? The elements of mystery and secrecy have been mentioned.

There was, besides, the effect of the moral force which the combined weight of [Finance Minister Donald] Fleming and [Governor James] Coyne produced: let there be no mistake, the power and majesty of Government can awe most men, especially men of goodwill who wish to do the right thing by their country, and especially men who see a substantial profit in the deal.[13]

Mallory's final reference is, of course, to the substantial commissions paid investment dealers.

In any case, the government went all out to sell the Canadian people on conversion, using the theme "new bonds for old", although it was never quite explained just why a new bond should be better than an old one. The publicity that surrounded the great Canadian conversion was, itself, introduced by a ministerial statement:

> To make sure that each and every holder, in so far as humanly possible, is made aware of the opportunity, we are arranging for a widespread publicity campaign using all appropriate media.

A press release dated July 17, 1958, revealed that advertising and public relations personnel from outside the government had been called in to form an "advertising and publicity group" to aid in putting the campaign across. The government accounts show that the total advertising bill was just short of $1.5 million for the government alone. It must have been almost equal that for outsiders.

> The selling campaign for the Conversion Loan was mounted with a fervour that had not been experienced in Canada even in the most difficult days of the war. The selling techniques were not quite the same as those used by soap manufacturers, and the people who recommended the bonds on television bore very little resemblance to the ladies who regularly demonstrate there how soap is used, but, nevertheless, it was unmistakably, the 'hard sell.' The sales campaign carried through this patriotic wartime theme. It was well organized and highly effective, and was backed by an extensive advertising campaign . . . .[14]
>
> . . . it must rank as one of the great Canadian selling jobs of all time.

> It could only have been accomplished as a national effort, and then only if those engaged in persuading the holders of Victory loans to convert them into bonds had been fully convinced of the merits of their story . . . [A]s several of the dealers have since remarked, it was difficult for people to argue with a package wrapped up in a flag, particularly when most observers regarded the package as attractive in its own right.[15]

These statements were fully supported by an examination of the material used during the campaign.

One full-page advertisement, in particular, stood out. It was cited in the Commons on September 4, 1958, by Dr. W.H. McMillan (Lib., Welland), the only strong critic of the loan in Parliament.

> . . . I have also a full page advertisement inserted by the government of Canada in a leading publication . . . . It shows a picture of a lady. . . . [B]eneath the picture we find these words:
> "Look who's wearing her 'immediate cash adjustment'." Gracious! What next?
> A body can hardly keep up with things these days. What with dogs spinning around in the sky and all. And all the excitement changing over your victory bonds. I was sorry to see mine go. Had it so long you know . . . .
> But when the young man at the bank explained that these new bonds paid more interest. Well! I know a good thing when I see it. Besides, he gave me a nice cash adjustment which I straightaway spent on a new bonnet. Like it?[16]

The tone of this advertisement was designed to appeal to the small, unsophisticated investor; Mr. Fleming said that was the purpose of the advertising campaign.

> An effort . . . has been geared . . . to reach anybody we can possibly reach . . . . [M]any of these bonds are held in small accounts . . . . They are scattered in safety deposit boxes and other places of safe keeping. We must bring the message to the small bond holders.
> My message tonight is directed to the individual Canadian whatever his personal circumstances and whatever he may be in this broad land—the industrial worker, the farmer, the fisherman, the small merchant, the housewife, the school teacher, the office worker, the retired worker . . . .[17]

Unfortunately, it is necessary to point out that, according to Fullerton and others, $4.3 billion of the $6.4 billion outstanding was held by the Bank of Canada, government accounts, chartered banks and other large institutions. This sort of campaign seemed somewhat out-of-place for such experienced investors.

The government used another technique to convince the public and the large bond holders that conversion was the thing to do. It churned out a series of press releases timed and worded to indicate a trend. The releases, quoted below in part, are examples of government news releases designed to create a bandwagon effect.

> At last count, just before the Canada Conversion Loan was announced, about 1,898,000 $100 pieces and 857,000 fifties were outstanding . . . .(August 12) To see every one of these converted is the Bank's aim. Large scale conversions of Victory Bonds by corporations and institutions in both east and west continue to add to the impressive sales totals . . . . (August 15) The Department of Finance again stressed the importance of small conversions pointing out that from the standpoint of the success of the refinancing program every individual conversion, however small, is important. (August 19)
> In addition to conversions, a volume of business is developing with people who were not original holders . . . who are acquiring them in order to participate. (August 26)
> Weekend totals from all parts of Canada also revealed a growing tide of individual conversions as small unit Victory Bond holders invaded banks and investment dealers. (September 9)[18]

The releases usually included lists of names of large converters: Northern Electric, $5.2 million; Prudential Insurance, $42 million; Canada Permanent Mortgage, $7 million ; Aetna Casualty, $11 million and $3.6 million; the Milwaukee Insurance Co., $1,281,000.

The press releases did not tell the entire story—especially as it affected the unsophisticated bond holder. Bonds, except for parity bonds such as Canada Savings Bonds, can fluctuate in price. The Canada Conversion Bonds fell sharply in price when the interest rate rose soon after the cutoff date. One year later, one issue fell as low as $83—a level entailing a serious loss for an investor forced to sell. Yet the government never indicated this danger to the small investor.

In the initial Canadian Press story about the issue, the writer, Alan Donelly, mentioned this possibility. He suggested that "some bond holders might switch to the new bond issues to get the cash and later dump the bonds on the market". He was obviously dissuaded by government officials for he added, "While the experts conceded this was possible, they also suggested the bonds might sell at a premium higher than their face value".[19]

Any doubt that Donelly's latter statement reflected the official view is discounted by a press release dated July 25:

> Bond dealers report that already premium quotations above par exist on the 3¼-year 3 per cent and 7-year 3¾ per cent issues while the 14-year 4½ per cent and 25-year 4½ per cent maturities are trading *around par level.* (Italics added.)

This last release, issued in July, was the only one that gave an indication that the bonds could fall in price. Yet there is no reason to believe that government officials were not aware of this possibility. One dealer, whose firm dissociated itself from the loan, said, "We felt the selling and publicity would intimidate the sophisticated and seduce the innocent with both facing sharp losses".

Professor Gordon summed up:

> The conversion had developed into a campaign to induce all and sundry to take long-term bonds, whether such securities were suited to the investment needs of the person or institution or not. Many long-term bonds were sold to buyers who had cash for a short time only, and who were ignorant of the dangers inherent in such bonds or else were counting on a rise in bond prices.[20]

Small investors would likely be ignorant of the dangers of fluctuations in bond prices; yet Mr. Fleming told the bond holders that Canada Conversion Bonds were "new bonds . . . which are backed by the nation itself". He managed to convince 90.4 per cent of bond holders to convert.

The evidence suggests the media handled the news of the campaign uncritically. Stories such as the following, based on government releases, normally appeared on the financial pages of the newspapers:

HARD WORK AHEAD
PRIZES, BANNERS USED
IN CONVERSION DRIVE
It's often easier to complete a $1,000,000 conversion for a company than to discover an individual holding a $1,000 bond and persuading him to convert," one investment dealer said. (*The Globe and Mail,* August 11, 1958, p.22)
CONVERSION BOND DRIVE IS STUDIED
A bond "blitz" reminiscent of the Second World War may soon be

staged in at least 80 Canadian communities. (*London Free Press,* August 22, 1958, p.22)

A critical story arose when CCF Members of Parliament alleged that the whole campaign was an attempt by the Conservatives to pay off party supporters. The story got page one coverage in the August edition of *Le Devoir* but relatively minor treatment elsewhere.

The Canada Conversion Loan must be one of the greatest mass merchandising campaigns ever undertaken in peacetime. From the time the government used mystery and secrecy to impress the investment community until the time carefully scheduled press releases attempted to create a bandwagon effect, no effort was spared to sell persons on conversion. From the material presented, however, it would appear that sometime during the course of the campaign, motivation became confused. The government forgot possible needs of individual bond holders and the public interest was made secondary to a government interest—total conversion. There is some evidence, in fact, that Mr. Diefenbaker himself later felt that the conversion loan had been mishandled.

V

Whatever one thinks of the purpose and approach of the four campaigns described, it seems clear they are a far cry from the kind of bumbling, stumbling attempts at government information portrayed by the task force. "Do It Now" was a brilliant selling job done on a shoe string. Ripple Rock would be the envy of any corporate public relations department. The pork campaign cleverly exploited existing communication channels. The conversion campaign shows just how powerful government propaganda can be.

The four campaigns suggest in different degrees that the news media stand ready to assist government in its attempts to manipulate public opinion. In the first three cases, there was virtually no critical comment; in the last, criticism was made but was largely passed over. Taken together, the campaigns point to the existence of publicity networks extending from government through advertising and public relations agencies into the mass media and the campaigns demonstrate that there is a ready clientele of government information services comprised of reporters who specialize in areas such as food and agriculture or financial news.

Even though the campaigns described took place some years ago, the networks still exist. The agriculture information division, for example, still distributes weekly radio tapes to 105 English and 62 French radio stations and television tapes to 17 English and nine French TV stations. The department's feature service circulates 445 English and 315 French items each week and it has a specialized mailing list of 231 groups to which it sends as often as four times a week such things as ministers' speeches. It has the capacity at any time to divert this network to special purposes such as the ones described above.

NOTES TO CHAPTER FIVE

1/Report of the Task Force on Government Information, Vol. I, *To Know and Be Known* (Ottawa: Queen's Printer, 1969), p. 47 and p. 49.

2/Canada, Department of Labour, *Seasonal Unemployment in Canada,* undated, circa 1952.

3/Canada, Department of Labour, Information Branch, "Plan Now to Increase Your Winter Sales", undated, p. 3.

4/Canada, Parliament, *Official Report of Debates,* January 31, 1962, p. 404.

5/Canada, Department of Labour, "Why Wait For Spring?" undated pamphlet.

6/The material in this section is drawn entirely from interviews with departmental officials.

7/Memorandum from H.J. Maybee to L.W. Pearsall, January 29, 1959.

8/Meat Packers Council, "Memorandum re Pork Promotion Campaign", Toronto, February 18, 1959, p. 1.

9/Most of the material in this section is drawn from interviews and from C.H. Kenney, "Pork Promotion Committee: A Summary Report on Activities to Date", September 24, 1959.

10/MARJORIE ELWOOD, "Sparerib Barbecue", *Star Weekly Magazine* (June 20, 1959), p. 47.

11/Figures supplied by the Economics section, Canada Department of Agriculture.

12/H. SCOTT GORDON, *The Economists versus the Bank of Canada* (Toronto: Ryerson Press, 1961), p. 18.

13/C.S. MALLORY, "The Great Conversion of 1958", July 16, 1958. Quoted in Douglas H. Fullerton, *The Bond Market in Canada* (Toronto: Carswell Co., 1962), p. 346. C.S. Mallory is a nom de plume for Robert MacIntosh, who is currently executive vice-president of the Bank of Nova Scotia. Chapter 15 in Fullerton's book, pp. 235-64, contains the author's review of the loan. Appendix C, pp. 346-52, contains the full text of MacIntosh's comments.

14/GORDON, *op. cit.* p. 20.

15/FULLERTON, *op. cit.* p. 244.

16/Canada, Parliament, *Official Report of Debates,* July 14, 1958, p. 4592.

17/DONALD FLEMING, Minister of Finance, text of radio and TV address, September 2, 1958, p. 6.

18/The quotations are taken from a file of press releases maintained by the Bank of Canada.

19/The story is taken from the Canadian Press wire. It was printed in *The Ottawa Journal,* July 15, 1958, p. 17.

20/GORDON, *op. cit.* p. 20.

chapter six

The Canadian Press: A Force For Consensus?

CARMAN CUMMING

The consensus which is necessary for the maintenance of social structures does not come about through some metaphysical entity of a group or social mind, or a general will. Rather, the unifying of value themes is achieved through the control of media of communication. . . .

John Porter[1]

The Canadian Press may be one of the most overlooked institutions in Canadian life. Like the purloined letter, it is so much in view that it is not seen. Those who direct and operate it make no attempt to alter that situation, because Canadian Press is one of the few news organs that thrives on anonymity. The reason is that those who use CP news—daily newspapers, radio and television stations—have a vested interest in underplaying their reliance on it while accentuating their own individuality. This is true especially of radio and television. If CP is little known, its broadcast subsidiary, Broadcast News, is almost totally anonymous. Newspaper readers, especially those in smaller cities, are at least familiar with the (CP) logo, although they may not realize that news items designated (Reuter), (AP) and (AFP) have also passed through CP selection and editing. Radio and television news coming from CP/BN is almost never identified by source, even in the case of a voice report.

Yet the CP service constitutes the basic infrastructure of the news communication system in Canada. Its print and broadcast operations serve some 700 outlets—TV and radio stations and daily newspapers. In most cases the CP/BN wires provide either the main supply or the only supply of non-local news. Anyone in Canada who reads newspapers or listens to radio or television exposes himself probably dozens of times each day to messages that either originated in CP or were processed by it.

While it is easy enough to show that the CP system is both pervasive[2] and anonymous, it is much more difficult to define its significance for the country or demonstrate that its overall makeup, or particular aspects of its operation, affects the nature of the news it circulates and, thereby, the formation of public opinion. Conventional wisdom dictates that it has little such effect. Within the media, the view is that CP is essentially a pipeline for the transportation of neutral, objective fact. CP executives speak of it as a mechanism through which society works out new attitudes and values, rather than one which has an effect of its own. In this view, CP is like a municipal water system, noticeable only when the water supply becomes polluted.

The analogy may be seriously misleading if, as in Walter Lippmann's[3] view, the study of public opinion should be approached through examination of the *pictures of reality that people see.* While The Canadian Press as an institution never seeks to shape public opinion, anonymous CP editors make literally millions of decisions each year on what images of reality Canadians will receive—on whether, for example, they will "see" a demonstration of strikers in Trois-Rivières or the opening of a new art gallery in Winnipeg. The fact that such decisions are made by many individuals and shaped by the demands of hundreds of editors, whose decisions are in turn shaped by their publishers or their publics, may be a sign that the medium is the message, that the pressure on CP to respond to so many demands turns it into an agency actively promoting consensus without being aware that it is doing so. This may be the case even if it applies only to selection of the issues that will be discussed publicly, rather than to the manner in which they are discussed.

The question can be approached on two levels: whether the overall system has a definable effect, and whether specific features of the structure or operation tend to affect the news. Detailed consideration of either question demands at least a summary description of how CP works.

I

Basically, CP is a news exchange, formed in 1917[4] and, in 1974, owned by 110 daily newspapers. It services, through its Broadcast News subsidiary, 380 private radio and television stations while another subsidiary, Press News Ltd., supplies news to the Canadian Broadcasting Corporation's 192[5] stations. The system is also the main route by which news comes into the country and leaves it.

In effect it is a sophisticated barter system operating on the principle that a news story gathered by one newspaper or station may have value else-where—a spinoff return that doesn't detract from the value to the original collecting agency. On any given day, for example, a score of events may take place in Halifax which are of interest to one, ten or a thousand newspapers and broadcasting stations elsewhere. It makes sense to have a means of identifying and processing these stories and delivering them (quickly, because news is highly perishable) to the points where they have value. CP member papers achieve this by agreeing to supply all their local news to the agency in exchange for the news gleaned from other papers.

The CP bureau in Halifax thus makes the primary decision on whether a given news story will leave the city. From that point, the story passes through a number of checkpoints (or "gates" in the terminology of some social scientists)[6] where other filing editors ("gatekeepers") make decisions on how far it is to go and in what form. One editor will decide whether the story is to be distributed only to papers in the Maritimes or whether it will go to English-language papers in Ontario or the West. Another will decide whether it goes to French-language papers; another whether it will go to radio-TV stations; another whether it will go out of the country to New York, where crucial gatekeepers in the Reuter and Associated Press agencies will decide whether it will get international circulation.[7]

In return, through arrangements based partly on cash and partly on barter, CP obtains the news reports of AP, Reuter and Agence France-Press, including material obtained from other agencies associated with them. The English-language wires of the three services go into the CP head office in Toronto and the French-language wires go into Montreal. CP editors in the two cities select and distribute this foreign news to papers and stations in the two language groupings.

Together with this basic news exchange, a number of other services are provided by CP. Pictures are exchanged by wirephoto networks in a manner similar to the news exchange. Stock market lists are transmitted. CP reporters cover major news stories abroad and in Canada, particularly in Ottawa and at the provincial legislatures. In fact, one of the major trends in the agency is the increasing proportion of news that is staff-written rather than simply being reworked from material supplied by the local newspapers. In a 1974 interview, the CP general manager, John Dauphinee, estimated that the proportion of staff-written copy, most of it from the Ottawa bureau, was approaching 50 per cent.

The members include all but a handful of Canada's daily newspapers, and they share the cost through assessments based on circulation, with a reduction factor built in as circulation goes higher. In 1974 the smallest member, with a circulation just under 3,000, paid $7,000 for the basic service while the largest, with a circulation of nearly a half-million, paid almost $200,000. The company operated in 1974 on a budget of $9,100,000, more than double the figure for a decade earlier.[8]

The Broadcast News subsidiary,[9] so closely interlocked with CP that the two can almost be regarded as one system, receives all of the news put out by CP and rewrites it in broadcast style for its own wires. This arrangement has not been without tension. CP began selling news to radio stations before the Second World War, but it did so only after years of controversy about whether newspapers should allow their product to go to a competing medium. The system that developed contains a tenuous balance of advantages: The broadcasters, drawing on news gathered primarily by the papers, obtain a service more cheaply than they would if they had to organize their own. The newspapers in return obtain revenue from the broadcasting operation and hence have a less costly service. The formation of Broadcast News Ltd., in 1953 gave the broadcasters a voice in the overall BN operation; the company is controlled by a board of ten directors of whom five are chosen by the private broadcasters and five are named by CP.

Unlike the CP situation, BN clients are not required to make their local news available to BN, but in practice some voluntary exchange has been developed. Since 1956 BN has offered an expanding Voice Service in which reports of CP and BN staff and those supplied by participating stations are transmitted on a national network and on regional networks. Because there are several competing voice services, this is one of the most competitive areas of the CP/BN operation.

II

With this background in mind, the question may be raised again: What aspects of the operation or structure affect content or presentation of the news? Since CP's major role lies in choosing what news will be disseminated, the first attention should probably be given to the selection process—the "gatekeeper" function of filing editors.

Their decisions, of course, are made at high speed. On a major story, such as the crash of an airliner, a 25-word bulletin may pass through all the "gates" in seconds, to be reproduced in thousands of newsrooms in Canada and abroad. The very speed of dissemination raises one of the basic hazards: When the news is diffused so quickly, error is difficult to overtake. It is not surprising that CP makes accuracy a virtue above all others and places a premium on hard, provable fact.

While a major story goes quickly through the checkpoints, many others are never put on the wire, or are delayed or discarded at various points along the line. The significance of CP therefore lies just as much in the news that goes into its wastebaskets as in the news that goes on its wires. During an international crisis involving Britain or the United States, for example, the CP filing editor may have to choose almost hourly between the view of events presented by the British Reuters agency or the American AP. If there is a national bias, (and both agencies work to eliminate it) the CP editor may select on the basis of whether or not he shares the same bias. Even excluding the national bias, there is a danger that the CP editor may choose the version consonant with his image of the situation. The Vietnam War was a case in point: Editors who opposed U.S. involvement could easily be tempted to select stories that put the Americans in a bad light.

The importance of the CP selection is qualified by the fact that the agency in most cases depends on primary decisions made in the newspapers or agencies which supply the raw news. The whole complex chain, in fact, is as strong or as weak as the first link—the reporter on the local paper who covers the story. If this reporter considers that the event, or one aspect of it, is not worthy of note, CP itself will probably not overcome the deficiency. It is true that CP staff, if they know a local reporter has dealt inadequately with the story, are expected to develop it independently. But the step requires both knowledge of the gap and a fairly strong motivation. It is self-evident (and a rarely considered aspect of the media monopoly situation) that the CP news will have fewer gaps if versions of the event are received from reporters on two or three newspapers rather than one.

Another aspect of the structure that affects content, although recent technological changes make this less important, is the location of the most important checkpoints, or "gates", in Toronto. Aside from a small amount of news circulated regionally, and the French-language services centered in Montreal, all news is funnelled into the Toronto head office. It comes in via collector wires from east and west and from the major cities of Ontario and Quebec, by telephone and telegraph from smaller Ontario cities, by wire from the international agencies. In Toronto the news is rewritten or edited—usually only the latter—and computer stored for transmission to newspapers. Thus a decision on whether a story on language problems in Quebec schools should go to Cornwall, which has also had a language problem in its schools, will be made in Toronto where the editor may lack familiarity with the issue in either the sending or receiving city. It is axiomatic that a CP filing editor must try to understand the needs of his clients and make judgments accordingly, sending a story on potato prices to New Brunswick or a fish marketing story to British Columbia even if he personally finds the content uninteresting. The danger here is one of over-reaction. The CP editor in Toronto quickly finds that he can protect himself by sending all stories on potatoes to New Brunswick or all stories on wheat to Saskatchewan. At the least, the concentration of editorial decisions in Toronto is worth noting in connection with frequent charges from west or east that media decisions generally reflect the tastes and priorities of Toronto.

Similarly, it is significant that until 1972, decisions on what international news would come into Canada were made by editors living and working in New York. It would not be surprising if these editors selected a higher proportion of American news to other international news than would be the case with a similar group in Canada. A useful "gatekeeper" study could be done on this point, simply to determine whether a smaller proportion of American items, as opposed to other international items, has been carried on CP's wires since the international desk was moved to Toronto from New York. It might also be asked whether editors living and working in Toronto tend to take decisions reflecting a more parochial view of Canada's significance in the world—a view that might come through, for example, in a decision on whether to give more prominence to a minor Canadian speech at the United Nations than to a major British speech.[10]

III

Yet another structural problem has to do with the control of the agency. As a non-profit co-operative it is run on a one-paper, one-vote basis. In theory, the voice of the *Penticton Herald* equals the voice of the *Toronto Star*. In practice this is hardly the case, but major decisions of the agency are nevertheless made at annual meetings where smaller papers vastly outnumber the larger. The Thomson group alone makes up almost one third of the CP membership and thus carries at least potential influence out of proportion to its total circulation. These smaller papers generally are the most reluctant to put money into CP for expansion of foreign service or for such "frills" as specialized reporting on the arts or sciences. At the other end of the spectrum, the very largest dailies, working in competitive situations, are inclined to put their money into their own reporting rather than bolstering a service that will benefit their competitors equally. These natural tendencies do not always hold true. Some editors and publishers on the largest and smallest dailies have been the most consistent in supporting improvement of CP. In a general way, though, it would appear that the nature of CP lends itself best to the medium-sized daily in a one-newspaper town. These are the papers that have the largest interest in improving CP, but they are heavily outweighed in CP voting by the largest and smallest. CP executives insist that they detect no pressure of a group kind from smaller or larger papers. The effect, of course, might be a negative one, showing up in the absence of pressure to expand rather than in pressure to reduce services.

CP must not only shape its news to the needs of small and large papers—and to broadcasters as well as papers—but it must also address two language and cultural groups. The agency is the main "gate " through which English-language news goes to the French-speaking community and French-language news to English Canada. This function is carried out by the Montreal bureau, which operates French services for both print and broadcast and also translates and selects French-language news for transmission to the English side. The French service with 40 staff members in Montreal, Ottawa and Quebec City is inevitably slimmer than the English editorial staff of some 200 because there are fewer French media (14 newspapers and 48 private broadcast outlets aside from Radio-Canada). Translation problems are also inevitable and are made more acute because competent bilingual staff members are regularly tempted by higher paying jobs in government, business or other parts of the media. The complaint is often made that CP, while providing an accurate account of main developments in each culture to the other, has difficulty interpreting the nuances of change. Christopher Young, editor of *The Ottawa Citizen,* commented to an interviewer in 1972,[11] for example, that CP is very deficient in providing interpretation on Quebec news. In a 1974 interview, Young said the situation had improved somewhat with the assigning of Joe MacSween, a senior CP reporter, to interpret Quebec affairs, but that more was needed. "We find the CP report out of Quebec in general and Montreal in particular to be very slow and not adequate to our needs, particularly in terms of bridging the gap between the two cultures. It's amazing how much material appears in the French-language papers that doesn't show up on the CP wires."

The CP Ottawa bureau also provides a service that deserves separate attention. Unlike other bureaus, where there may be only one reporter to ten or fifteen editors and rewrite men, CP Ottawa has some twenty-five reporters working on political news. The significance is that only CP provides comprehensive coverage of official Ottawa. Individual newspapers may have one or more staff members of their own assigned to the Parliamentary Press Gallery, but none has sufficient manpower to cover all parliamentary committees, to provide hour-by-hour coverage of the Commons and Senate or to allocate specialists to departments. Typically, Press Gallery members of the individual papers concentrate on the big story, or on digging out a special, while CP provides bread-and-butter coverage of the plethora of committees, press briefings, speeches and departmental announcements.

In addition, other Press Gallery members have access to CP's stories and may rewrite them for their own use. The result at times is that if a major story breaks in an obscure committee, all news services in the country will see it through the eyes of the only CP reporter who was there—even though that image may be transmitted through a dozen other gallery reporters. The effect may be accentuated if a CP reporter, covering a series of committee hearings, develops a bias in one direction or another and shapes his fact selection accordingly. It is conventional wisdom among CP Ottawa staff that a reporter can easily select material to create a desired effect, while remaining within the CP tradition of factual objectivity. The difference could be subtle, as narrow perhaps as the choice between opening a story with an opposition member's charge or a cabinet minister's denial. The point is not just that the reporter allows his conscious or unconscious leanings to affect his selection and arrangement of facts; in the case of a CP political reporter, the effect may be amplified in a way that is not generally perceived because other reporters use his raw material.

Technological changes may be alleviating the problems of CP's monopoly. In 1974 the agency was completing technological changeover costing some $1½ million and designed to improve the speed and flexibility of copy-handling while reducing operational costs. The changes will have an effect not only on delivery but also on news selection:

1. Installation of storage and routing computers in the Toronto head office.
2. Use of Video Displays Terminals (VDTs) for writing and editing stories in part of the system.
3. Introduction of multiplex circuitry for delivery of news.

The first two changes allow CP to deliver more news faster, and to a more clearly defined area, while sharply reducing operating costs. In effect the editor no longer tears the story off a teleprinter and edits it by pencil; he "calls up" the story from the computer on to a Video Display Terminal, a device resembling a television set with a keyboard below it. The editor then rearranges the story as he wishes and decides where he wants to send it—without the necessity of having it set again by a teletype operator.

The third change—introduction of multiplex circuitry—may be the most important in terms of news decision-making. The system takes the wide frequency of a voice channel and divides it into 24 narrow-range channels sufficient for news wire transmission, and thus adds considerably to available "wire space". In practical terms, this means that the full range of CP news that was before available only to a handful of major papers in central Canada can now be offered at small cost to all major papers across the country. Whereas the larger papers in Winnipeg or Vancouver or Halifax have in the past been forced to delegate a large part of the news selection responsibility to editors in CP Toronto, they now can receive the full report and do their own selection.

Broadly speaking, the last generation of technology inhibited choice and editing freedom at the newspapers (and placed correspondingly more power in the hands of CP editors). The new generation will reverse the trend. The last generation was dominated by the teletypesetter, a device by which the papers received not only printed stories but also perforated tape which could be fed into a linotype machine for automatic typesetting. It meant that the editors outside the main cities of central Canada received a much cut-down version of the CP report and received it in a form that made changes within the newspaper difficult. The editor had the choice of having the copy set in type automatically without change or of editing it at the cost and nuisance of re-setting.

In the new technological generation, many more newspapers will be able to receive the full CP report and make their own selection rather than trusting the judgment of a Toronto editor. New technology also makes it possible for the newspapers to regain editing freedom while retaining the advantages of automatic typesetting. John Dauphinee has predicted that the future pattern will involve transmission of news from the CP computer directly to the newspaper's computer. The local editor will then be able to call up a story on a VDT and edit it as extensively as he wishes before approving it for automatic typesetting. The newspaper will either receive the full CP report at data speed or will view extracts of available stories and decide which ones it wants transmitted.

IV

Discussions of CP's structure may leave the impression that the company is a coldly efficient machine for packaging and transporting news, with none of the distinctive character that marks, for example, the CBC or the *Toronto Star*. In fact, the CP corporate character has probably been unique; a curious blend of military efficiency and family warmth.

The combination derives largely from the personality of one man—Gillis Purcell, general manager of CP for 24 years until his retirement in 1969. Under Purcell, CP acquired a reputation as an authoritarian, efficient, highly centralized news service—but also as a closely knit, paternalistic company. Within the news fraternity it was spoken of as a good place to break in and a good place to leave. Yet there was also agreement that the company commanded a surprising degree of respect and loyalty.

Staff relations were damaged by a union dispute in the early 1950s, when the company became the battleground in a fight between the American Newspaper Guild and the publishers over unionization of newsrooms. CP management fought the union with tactics that included dismissals (the company insisted they were purely for budgetary reasons) and barring of

✓ union members from the Parliamentary Press Gallery. Management won and staff resentment dissipated very slowly.

While salaries of CP staff have generally been competitive with newspapers, including unionized newspapers, there has been a consistent flow of talent from CP to the papers. The papers have not been reluctant to raid CP for its best people, while CP has been inhibited about retaliating. In recent years salaries have increased significantly. In 1974 the minimum pay for a five-year man was $265 per week, up from $210 in 1972 and $240 in 1973. The figures are somewhat misleading since virtually all staff members are above the minimum, particularly in larger cities.

Under Dauphinee there has also been a move to decentralize the agency, placing more decision-making in the hands of bureau chiefs and individual staff members. Staff turnover remains high, however. The company suffers particularly from loss of trained staff members in their 30s, as the graph below indicates.

The number of staff members in the 35-45 brackets points to a special problem for CP. Senior executives are selected from that group, and the small number available limits the selection scope. The choice is narrowed still further because some of those available prefer to remain on the more creative reporting or editing side rather than becoming executives.

V

In the light of this structure, then, how well does CP fulfil its function as the country's news infrastructure?

The Senate Committee on Mass Media, better known as the Davey Committee after its chairman, Senator Keith Davey, provided in 1970 one of the few outside looks at CP.[13] For the most part it eulogized the agency, at times in language that became almost lyrical ("Think of news agencies and you think of CP . . . . [T]he familiar (CP) logotype speckles the pages of Canada's newspapers like raindrops on a pond . . .").

The Davey report said CP is a strong force for national unity, that it does its job as a news exchange "supremely well" and that it provides news that is fast, comprehensive, reliable, tough, and more colorful than it is often considered to be. It brushed aside criticisms that CP's rate structure was unfair to smaller newspapers ("the remedy is in their own hands") and that CP has acted as an exclusive club, keeping out prospective competitors ("We could find no evidence that this was the case, though it may have been close to the truth in former years . . . "). The Committee was also not much disturbed by suggestions that CP's very universality made for drabness among Canadian papers (". . . it is a criticism that should be directed

EDITORIAL STAFF AGE GROUPINGS, JULY, 1974 [12]

Number of Employees —
▼

Ages ▶	Under 25	26-30	31-35	36-40	41-45	46-50	51-55	56-60	61-65
Number	64	61	42	16	19	24	15	11	5

to the newspapers themselves . . .").
In other areas, the Davey report was mildly critical.

> We are somewhat more sympathetic to the argument that CP is weak
> in its attention to the arts and cultural matters, and to the currents
> of social change. We think it is somewhat too slavishly attached to
> the hard-news, who-what-where-why-when tradition of journalism
> and too little concerned with interpretation, imagination, and the
> stirring of the spirit.
> But we're sympathetic to CP in this too. Its assignment is to run the
> record and to run it complete. It is surely up to the newspapers
> themselves to build on that bedrock job.

The Davey Committee in the end offered only one strong recommendation: that CP should post more staffers abroad, to report the world scene
"as Canadians speaking to Canadians". Even in making the recommendation, though, it acknowledged that it could find little support for it either
among publishers or the public. Other critics have been harsher, particularly concerning CP's foreign coverage, but the criticism has tended to fall
more on publishers than on CP staff. Peter Worthington, executive editor
of *The Toronto Sun,* has written:

> . . . based on its potential for doing a competent and necessary job
> for the Canadian newspaper public, CP makes a blatantly lousy effort.
> [This refers only to its overseas coverage, not its domestic reporting.]
> The blame does not lie so much with reporters, or CP's individual
> talents. More, it is the fault of the organization, its policies and lack
> of financial resources made available from member newspapers.[14]

Worthington found CP too concerned with the Canadian angle and too
concerned with pinching pennies.

> The concern with doing things on the cheap is not entirely CP's fault,
> since Canadian newspaper contributions keep CP functioning. But
> the obsession with cheapness aptly reflects the parochial, narrow out-
> look of most Canadian dailies, which aren't basically interested in
> foreign news.

John Dauphinee argues that the Davey criticism of CP's foreign coverage
was a matter of difference of viewpoint between members of the Senate
committee and of CP members on how foreign news should be covered.
He said a special news study committee of the CP membership agreed with

management that in a time of fast communications, it was more efficient to build up a team of reporters with background in foreign affairs within Canada rather than stationing men abroad permanently. The idea would not be to send teams of "firemen" to compete with AP and Reuter on major stories, but to make sure the Canadian aspect is well handled. Dauphinee pointed out that it costs $40,000 to $50,000 to station a man abroad—and for this price the agency could afford fifteen or twenty assignments abroad by Canadian-based reporters. In line with that philosophy, CP in 1974 had only nine staff members stationed abroad: four in London, one in Paris, two in Washington and one in New York.

A more serious weakness of CP, one almost overlooked by the Davey Committee, may be that its news decisions are too often defensive, designed to forestall criticism rather than fully report a situation. Within the objective tradition of news-gathering, brought to its finest pitch in news agencies, it has usually been sufficient for a reporter to cover a controversy by relating what each side says publicly, without explaining how the conflicting positions relate on whether the reality is different from what the spokesmen say it is. Reporters who go beyond this simple reporting of public positions make themselves vulnerable because they begin to take personal responsibility for what the story says rather than leaving it all on the shoulders of the conflicting spokesmen.

After the 1974 election, CP executives noted with satisfaction that the agency had not received a single complaint on the fairness of its campaign coverage. This is an achievement, but it raises deeper questions about whether CP escapes criticism because it deliberately shapes its product so that it will escape criticism. Hugh Winsor, in a *Globe and Mail* article, observed:

> The conventional wisdom about news agencies decrees they must write to the lowest common denominator—bland and harmless. There is a growing body of opinion, certainly among the metropolitan papers, that this is not necessarily so . . . .
> But CP has been reluctant to move toward more digestion of the facts it transports . . . .[15]

This is by no means a new complaint and would appear to be more related to the nature of news agencies than to the competence or motivation of their staff. In 1940 Carlton McNaught wrote:

> The news agency . . . because it serves many newspapers with varying policies, must at least pretend that its accounts are strictly factual and devoid of bias . . . . The result is apt to be a kind of specious

objectivity, in which "facts" are presented in an isolated and unrelated manner, often confusing the reader, yet unavoidably giving him a partial or one-sided view of affairs.[16]

The weakness can sometimes be best seen in the perspective gained by time. The following story, for example, was carried by CP in 1971, when the public had little sympathy for American draft dodgers, communes or the federal government's Opportunities for Youth program.

4 FROM COMMUNE ORDERED DEPORTED

OTTAWA (CP) - Four Americans on British Columbia rural youth communes supported by federal youth funds have been ordered deported and further investigations are under way by immigration officers.

The immigration department here confirmed Wednesday that a field investigation has turned up numerous Americans on 20 communes in southern B.C. The communes received grants in the one-thousand to two-thousand range from State Secretary Gerard Pelletier's 25-million-dollar Opportunities for Youth program.

Officials here were unable to confirm a report that there were no native Canadians in eleven of the twenty communes . . . .[17]

On first glance the story appears to be a routine, factual, objective report. After a closer look the reader may wonder: Why are the four Americans being deported? Because they were on communes receiving federal youth funds? In fact, why are the four linked with the grants at all? The question may be defined by asking how CP might have handled the story if the four had been working for a B.C. company assisted by federal grants. It is unthinkable that the story would have read:

OTTAWA (CP) - Four Americans working at one of the 83 B.C. corporations assisted by the Industry department's $100 million grants-to-industry program have been deported . . . .

Furthermore the wording of the second paragraph ("*confirmed* . . . that a field investigation has *turned up* numerous Americans . . .") lends an aura of guilt. Is it illegal or immoral for Americans to live on communes in southern B.C.?

The story illustrates the kind of "specious objectivity" noted by McNaught. The selection and arrangement of facts, especially the questionable linking of the deportation to the commune grants, creates a message at least as potent as a polemic, since unlike a polemic it presumably circumvents the readers' psychic guards. It may be argued, of course, that neither the slanted message nor the polemic can be proven to have a predictable effect on public opinion. The story will also presumably escape censure only if the slant reflects general values, and this raises a chicken-and-egg question of whether the medium is reflecting audience opinion or shaping it.

Leaving aside those difficult questions, one may still ask: Is there anything about CP that makes its messages distinctive? One partial answer is that CP is a national medium in a country that has few such media. It must address all significant sectors of the society, or at least avoid alienating them. There is a school of thought that national media by their nature act as a centripetal force in society. James W. Carey, for example, has written:

> Such [national] media attempt to create a consensus or at least a centre of value, attitude, emotion and expressive style. Their success in doing this is highly problematic but national media strive for this consensus. They also tend to block out of communication those values, attitudes and groups which threaten the tenuous basis of social order.[18]

CP officials often speak of the organization as a force for national unity but they reject the notion that the agency deliberately seeks to create a consensus or to block out unpopular messages on a given issue. They tend instead to attribute the unifying effect to the fact that, through CP, various groups and areas receive information about each other. The commune story cited earlier makes clear, however, that the agency has little difficulty reporting on an unpopular phenomenon in a manner conforming with majority values. It also is clear that in a situation where the country is sharply divided—as, for instance, the bilingualism issue—the agency has an interest in presenting both sides in a dispassionate manner. This at least ensures that all parts of the country learn that there *is* another side to the story. It could also be argued that CP editors are more comfortable handling aspects of such an issue that are likely to gain sympathy from both sides. That is, it would be highly unlikely that CP would do anything in a national election campaign to suggest that one party leader should be favored over another. But it would be entirely consistent with CP's nature to stress views that tended to envelop both sides in consensus (for example: "This is a dull campaign", or "The public is concerned about inflation").

If there is such an effect, it is questionable to what degree it cuts across the country's main language barrier. The Canadian Press staff in Ottawa, for instance, has a French-language staff which operates with almost complete independence from the English-language group, and it presumably feels no pressure to address a national consensus. Similarly, foreign news enters the country in two distinct language channels and there is minimal Toronto control over the selection of French-language news at Montreal.

A more striking pattern associated with consensus formation is CP's tendency, mentioned earlier, to make news decisions in a defensive manner, transmitting easily those stories that meet a known demand and therefore, automatically, delaying or excluding items that are off the known pattern. That tendency applies all along the line, starting with the individual bureau where editors faced with a decision on whether to staff a "known" event such as a parliamentary committee or an unknown one such as a demonstration, are more likely to choose the first because they are more vulnerable to criticism if they miss the known event. Along the line, editors are more likely to give priority to those stories where there is a known demand rather than the ones that appear to be out of pattern. The implication is that CP has an important role in what has come to be known as agenda-setting: the defining of what issues are to receive public attention.[19]

This is not just a question of whether it sets a given agenda through a blending of the pressures from various directions—the news source, the editor, the reader—but of whether the agency itself adds something to the pattern. Proof that CP's reactions differ from those of any other news organ would have to rest on evidence that its feedback differs in kind from that of the others, and this is not easy to show. It could be argued, in fact, that it is in the CP editor's interest to identify himself precisely with the news values of the newspaper editors he supplies, including the search for what is off-pattern and therefore news. The contrary argument is that the cumulative effect of the known demands from newspaper editors creates a pattern different from the individual demand; that the act of meeting many demands tends to eliminate from the mix the news stories that don't fit the known pattern. If that is the case, it would indicate that CP's role in agenda-setting is to keep the national perspective focussed on the known and accepted issues at the expense of the new and different. At the least, this would seem to be a danger inherent in the CP system.

NOTES TO CHAPTER SIX

1/ *The Vertical Mosaic* (Toronto: University of Toronto Press, 1956), p. 460.

2/A study prepared in 1969 for the Senate Committee on Mass Media by T. JOSEPH SCANLON, Associate Professor at Carleton University's School of Journalism, showed that of 6,758 items selected randomly from 30 Canadian dailies, 40.8 per cent were staff-written and 34.8 per cent came from CP and associated agencies. In some cases the percentage of wire service copy was much higher. Of the items randomly selected from *The London Free Press,* 52. 7 per cent came from CP and its associated agencies and 24.2 per cent were staff-written. For *The Sudbury Star* the figures were 55.4 per cent from CP and associated wire services and 27.9 per cent staff-written. T. JOSEPH SCANLON, *A Study of the Contents of 30 Canadian Daily Newspapers* (Ottawa, 1969).

3/WALTER LIPPMANN, *Public Opinion* (New York: The Macmillan Company, 1960).

4/For a full discussion of CP's early history, see M.E. NICHOLS, *(CP) The Story of The Canadian Press* (Toronto: Ryerson Press, 1948).

5/The figure includes 59 CBC radio stations and 72 affiliates, and 25 TV stations plus 36 affiliates. It does not include rebroadcasting stations.

6/DAVID MANNING WHITE, "The 'Gatekeeper': A Case Study in the Selection of News", *People, Society and Mass Communications,* eds. Lewis Anthony Dexter and David Manning White (New York: The Free Press, 1964).

7/The Soviet news agency Tass and the French Agence France-Presse also make selections of CP news, but both do it within Canada—Tass at Ottawa and AFP at Montreal.

8/Figures supplied by The Canadian Press.

9/In 1974 BN served 247 AM radio stations, 72 FM radio stations, 61 TV stations and 14 cable TV stations. One television station, 16 AM stations and 4 FM stations did not subscribe.

10/The Scanlon study of newspaper content showed that in 1969, when CP's international selection was being made in New York, more of the items randomly selected (9.8 per cent) concerned the U.S. role in world affairs than the Canadian role in world affairs (4.4 per cent).

11/HUGH WINSOR, "Is the Canadian Press Doing its Job? *The Globe and Mail* (Toronto), July 4, 1972, p. 7.

12/Data supplied by The Canadian Press.

13/Canada, *Report of the Special Senate Committee on Mass Media,* Vol. I (Ottawa: Queen's Printer, 1970), pp. 229-235.

14/"Foreign Affairs: The Irrelevant Beat", *A Media Mosaic,* ed. Walt McDayter (Toronto: Holt, Rinehart and Winston of Canada Limited, 1971), pp. 75-77.

15/*Loc. cit.*

16/*Canada Gets the News* (Toronto: Ryerson Press, 1940), p. 81.

17/*The Vancouver Sun,* July 2, 1971, p. 1.

18/"The Communications Revolution and the Professional Communicator", *The Sociological Review Monograph,* No. 13 (1967).

19/For a review of agenda-setting work, see MAXWELL MCCOMBS AND DONALD L. SHAW, *A Progress Report on Agenda-Setting Research* (Paper presented to Association for Education in Journalism, 1974).

chapter seven

The Not So Mass Media: The Role of Individuals In Mass Communication

T. JOSEPH SCANLON

It is not hard to provide evidence of the "mass" nature of mass media. According to the Special Senate Committee on Mass Media (the Davey Committee) adult Canadians spend 30 to 40 minutes a day reading a newspaper.[1] Television audiences are sometimes as large as the one attracted by the second game of the Canada-Russia hockey series in 1972 when there were more than 12 million Canadian viewers.[2] The Liberal leadership convention at which Pierre Elliott Trudeau was elected party leader was watched by 13.6 million on CBC and CTV[3] and, to confirm what most of us already know, the Davey Committee reported that "eight in ten (Canadians) use all of television, newspapers and radio . . . " on a daily basis.[4]

The studies that have sought to determine how people first learn about news events strengthen this impression of the "mass" nature of mass media. For example:

- three quarters of those interviewed in a survey in Calgary learned of the death of Governor General Vanier directly from the media;[5]
- the returns of an Ottawa-Hull survey showed that four fifths of the population learned about the murder of former Quebec labor minister Pierre Laporte directly from the media;[6]
- more than four fifths of those interviewed in another Calgary survey learned about the surprise marriage of Prime Minister Trudeau directly from radio and TV;[7]
- two thirds of a similar sample in Kingston, Ontario learned directly from the media that kidnapped British diplomat James Cross had been found.[8]

Major news stories—whether startling, happy or sad—reach most people directly through the mass media, usually radio or TV.[9]

Yet this evidence of the "mass" nature of mass media can be deceiving for two reasons. First, although the audience may be vast it is not homogeneous. The audience is comprised of individuals of various backgrounds, intellects and habits whose reactions to media events are equally varied.

Second, the media are not the only means of communication. Parallel to and intertwined with the media are "people" networks (that is, networks of communication based on face-to-face conversations or telephone conversations). The news communication system of a modern society consists of both the media and people networks.

These two propositions, the first dealing with the heterogeneity of the audience and the second with the informal people networks, are central to an understanding of the problems with which we will be concerned.

I

Evidence of the "mass" character of the media should not obscure the fact that the media do not reach everyone.[10] While the Davey Committee found that there are 2.33 radios for every Canadian and, further, that 88 per cent of Canadians receive a daily newspaper, it also found that these figures varied according to regional and socio-economic factors. At the time, 2 per cent of Canadians did not have a radio, and the figure for those whose incomes were below $4,000 a year was 5 per cent. The Committee discovered that 12 per cent did not receive a daily newspaper; the figure was 24 per cent for those living in the isolation of the large rural areas of Saskatchewan. These findings bear out earlier research showing that the availability of media was far below normal in an isolated and depressed area such as the region of Quebec which includes the Lower St. Lawrence, Gaspé and Iles-de-la-Madeleine:

> 16% of the persons interviewed had no television set, 19% did not listen to radio, 31% did not read magazines, 37% did not read newspapers, 71% did not see motion pictures, and 74% did not read books.[11]

There is other evidence, perhaps more important, about the nature of media contact. Not surprisingly, it shows that regardless of availability, people are highly selective in their listening, watching and reading behavior, especially when very basic values, such as political ones, are at stake. A study of the 1940 presidential election in the United States between Wendell Willkie and Franklin Roosevelt showed that people tended to pay attention to the material they knew they would agree with. "More Republicans than Democrats listened to Willkie and more Democrats than Republicans listened to Roosevelt . . . [E]xposure was consistently partisan and the partisan exposure resulted in reinforcement".[12] The same kind of thing was found seven years later when a research unit operating in Cincinnati examined a campaign to promote the United Nations. This group found the campaign reached mainly the younger, better educated persons who were already supporting the U.N. The study concluded, "The people reached by the campaign were those least in need of it . . . . [T]he people missed by it were the new audience the plan hoped to gain".[13] This phenomenon, referring to media choices tied to already-held values, is usually called selective exposure.

The selective nature of media exposure has been examined further in a Canadian study of people who watch relatively little television.[14] Supervised by Maclaren Advertising, the study found that such people were more likely to be younger, better educated and from larger families than those who watched a great deal of television. The light viewers were more likely to choose Canadian over U.S. programs and choose FM in preference to AM radio. And they were very selective about those TV programs they did watch. The same study also revealed the "staggering" fact that 20 per cent of the population accounts for 40 per cent of the total television viewing. At the other end of the scale 20 per cent of the population accounts for only 4 per cent of the total viewing. In other words, that some persons watch a truly staggering 53.9 hours of television a week should not obscure the fact that others average only 4.8 hours. Mass audience figures conceal individual differences in media uses.

Whether people come in contact with a medium is one thing. What they do once they are contacted is another. In addition to the phenomenon of selective exposure, social scientists have identified two other phenomena to which the labels selective perception and selective retention have been given. Regardless of the nature of exposure, there is a clear tendency for individuals to see and retain only what conforms to deeply-held convictions or desires. The phenomena are discussed by such scholars as Joseph T. Klapper in his book *The Effects of Mass Communication*[15] and by Raymond Bauer in his excellent article "The Obstinate Audience".[16] One illustration here will be enough to elucidate the terms these scholars used.

A group of people that included smokers and non-smokers was asked how well-proven were statements about the relationship between smoking and ill health. As the figures below show, the conclusions of the individuals were very much related to their smoking behavior. Non-smokers were far more ready than smokers to accept data about the relationship of smoking and ill health:[17]

	Smokers	Non-Smokers
Accepted the relationship	28%	54%
Did not accept it	70%	38%
Didn't know	2%	6%

Data dealing with the manner in which people accept information—and which media they accept it from—also come from two other areas of research: the study of diffusion of innovation (how people learn about new things) and the study of crises or disasters. Studies in both these areas suggest, as will be shown later, that individuals may accept information from the media for one purpose, but reject it for another. They also show that acceptance or rejection may depend on the individual's previous experience, or sometimes, on the reaction of others concerning the information supplied. The fact that a message reaches someone does not tell us a great deal about what will be done with it.

In the area of diffusion of innovations, the leading researcher is the University of Michigan's Everett Rogers.[18] He has concluded that while media are important as sources of information on new products or ideas, the persuasive influence of friends or neighbors is a more important factor leading to the adoption of such products or ideas. It appears that information from the media is received and noted; information from peers is acted upon. In a study of how Canadian farmers heard of and adopted a new grain variety, Carleton University student Bryan Lyster found evidence to support Rogers's ideas.[19] Lyster discovered that farmers in Saskatchewan heard about a new grain variety mainly through the farm press but their decision to adopt that variety depended largely on consultation with registered seed growers and with neighbors.

Research into the problems of communication in crises exposes even more variations. In one study it was found that over half of those who received a hurricane warning by radio evacuated their community. Only 38 per cent of those warned by TV did the same.[20] In another study, it was found that people in two communities, one on each side of the Mexico-United States border, reacted differently to warnings of a flood threat. Mexicans placed more faith in radio warnings than warnings from official sources. Those in the United States discounted the media warning but paid attention to official requests to evacuate.[21] In both communities the official warnings were conveyed directly in face-to-face contacts. The same message, "evacuate", was evaluated in terms of carrier rather than content.

The discussion of the impact of messages on individuals does not stop here. There is also evidence that people do not act entirely on their own. They act the way they see others acting or the way they think others would expect them to act. They do not respond to media messages—or to other messages—as individuals but as members of a group or a society.

A study of reactions to air raid sirens going off on three different occasions in three different cities concluded that behavior of the individual related to behavior of others:

> When an individual observes persons in his immediate environment
> acting in such a way as to indicate that they [the others] believe the
> signal to be valid, then [he] the observing individual is likely to treat
> the signal as valid . . . . People tend to look around them to see how
> others are responding to a situation.[22]

The study conducted after the famous Hallowe'en broadcast by Orson
Welles of an alleged invasion from Mars, reached similar conclusions. Persons responded differently to the broadcast if their attention was called to
it by an excited friend.[23]

None of these ideas is new. The political study of the 1940 U.S. election
mentioned earlier concluded that people's political views are influenced by
those of the people around them. "Personal influence is more pervasive and
less self-selective than the formal media".[24] A study of how people formed
opinions about such things as fashions, movies and public affairs explored
this idea and found that it is possible to locate leaders of opinion in such
areas—persons who pass on their views and have them accepted by others.[25]

It has gradually become clear that relationships involving the transfer
of information or opinions from one person to another are very structured.
In his book *The Human Group,* George Homans described such relationships as part of a human communications network. He described, for example, the role of a foreman.

> He deals with certain men in the plant and not with others. He goes
> to certain men and talks to them; others come to his desk and talk
> to him. He gets his orders from a boss and passes on the orders to
> members of his own department. That is, he communicates or . . . in-
> teracts with certain persons and not with others, and this communi-
> cation from person to person often takes place in a certain order—for
> instance from boss to the foreman and then from the foreman to the
> workers—so that we can say . . . the foreman occupies a position in
> a chain of communications.[26]

William Whyte did the same thing when he outlined the nature of a gang
in his book, *Street Corner Society.* Homans analyzed the communication
patterns in the gang Whyte described; Homans wrote:

> If Doc felt the group ought to take a particular line of action, he was
> apt to talk the matter over first with Mike and Danny, and, perhaps,
> Long John. If the decision reached Long John it went no further; he
> influenced no one. But if it reached Mike, he was apt to pass it on
> to Nutsy and through Nutsy it reached Frank, Joe, Alec, Carl and
> Tommy. Or Doc could influence Nutsy directly.[27]

Human relationships assume a regular pattern, a pattern that involves communications. "People" networks obviously exist.

II

What we are interested in here is not just the question of whether such human networks exist but whether they exist as part of a news communication system. Do the kind of networks illustrated above carry news? The answer, as the steadily growing evidence shows, is clearly Yes.

The first collection of data on the nature of human communication chains was presented in two of the studies quoted earlier—one dealing with the 1940 U.S. presidential election[28] and one dealing with the problem of how people make decisions about such things as public affairs, movies and fashions.[29] The first study suggested there was a clearly defined two-step flow of communication which took ideas from the media to some people and from them to others. The second study explored this concept and attempted to analyze this relationship further. The problem with both studies was that neither offered very much in the way of the description of person-to-person communication. The authors of the second study, Elihu Katz and Paul Lazarsfeld, reported that the reason for this gap in description was that it was extremely difficult to track down the links in the chain of communication. In one case, for example, three out of five interpersonal contacts could not be identified, located or interviewed.[30]

Other researchers had little more success in tracing the flow of interpersonal communication. One after another they reported failure or partial failure. One research group, for example, that tried recruiting observers in the system reported ruefully that the recruits may have been key links.[31] Because the research group had asked their recruits not to pass on rumors, the normal lines and the contents of communication were upset. Another group reported planting a rumor in a community then finding that even one of the persons with whom it had been planted could not remember it.[32] The conclusion was: interpersonal chains might extend many links but it would be difficult to follow or trace these links.[33]

Recently, however, a research group at Carleton University in Ottawa— now formally established as the Carleton "Crisis Research Team"—has had more success in establishing the nature of interpersonal communication networks. The team has completed four studies, three of which have provided data about the "people" side of the news communication system.[34] All these studies are based on research into the diffusion of news, the study of how people get news.

These news diffusion studies have suggested that interpersonal channels of communication are most active when the news is most important.[35] At the time of the Kennedy assassination, for example, 49 per cent of the population of the United States first heard the news about Kennedy from someone else. In Dallas, where the shooting occurred, 57 per cent learned first from another person. These contacts sometimes took place on a face-to-face basis, sometimes as the result of a telephone conversation. In the nationwide survey, it was also discovered that two thirds of the sample started conversations with someone else as soon as they heard the news.[36] Other research supports this evidence that major news events stimulate human communications activity and are, therefore, an excellent time to study this phenomenon.

The first Carleton study was a pilot study. The community selected was Kingston, Ontario, and the event was the discovery of kidnapped British diplomat James Cross.[37] Cross had been kidnapped and held prisoner in Montreal by the terrorist Front De Libération du Québec (FLQ), a group committed to the separation of Francophone Quebec from Canada. The day Cross was found in a house near Montreal, a research team from Carleton moved into Kingston, drew a sample according to statistical procedures, asked respondents if they had heard the news that Cross had been found, and if so, where they had heard it. If the respondent had heard from someone else, the team then began the process of locating that person and others in the chain so that the flow of information could be established. The researchers were able to follow 39 chains across the community as far as seven stages. In most cases they were able to trace the story back to the point of origin in the broadcast media.[38]

The Kingston/Cross study showed that interpersonal communication chains which began in the home usually originated with television. Those outside the home originated mainly with radio, often car radio. It also showed that the bulk of interpersonal contacts took place outside the home and that long communication chains inevitably spread beyond a single family group. In Kingston, in every case, the chains originated with the media.[39]

The Kingston/Cross study established that human networks are not only a reflection of the group structure of society but they also efficiently transmit news which originates with the media systems.

The second Carleton study followed up on this success: it involved the study of how the people in North Bay, Ontario, learned about a shooting incident that took place in a downtown parking lot on a Saturday night. The incident involved two policemen. The first, Alex McCourt, was shot and seriously injured when he investigated a report that there was a "man with a gun" in a downtown parking lot. The second, Len Slater, was shot and killed when he answered a radio call for help from Constable McCourt. The North Bay/Slater study revealed, as had been the case in the Kennedy death, that roughly half the population, 48.5 per cent of those interviewed, had heard first from someone else.[40] More important, the research group successfully traced 73 of the sources of this first information along communication chains—in each case following the data from the person in the sample to the original source (either media or, in all the longer chains, to a participant or eyewitness).

In almost half of the cases the chains were of two stages; that is, one person heard from another. But there were some involving three stages—one person heard from a second who had heard in turn from a third.[41] In one case the chain involved ten stages. This is how the 73 interpersonal chains broke down:

- two stages   – 35
- three stages   – 15
- four stages   – 9
- five stages   – 2
- six stages   – 4
- seven stages   – 4
- eight stages   – 3
- ten stages   – 1

In North Bay, interpersonal chains were more active than in Kingston because the event was a local one involving the direct contact of many persons and because it took place in a public area (a parking lot by the main station) at a time when many persons were in the vicinity (while the bars were still open).

The 73 chains represent enough data to begin a detailed examination of the nature of human communication chains. The analysis of these chains is still going on, but the work that has been done suggests that most people associate and communicate with those like themselves—with persons of the same religion, the same educational attainments and same incomes—and that, further, this pattern prevails even when vital information is involved. Even in a crisis it seems people pass on information to those with whom they normally come in contact through family, work or leisure. But the North Bay/Slater study also reveals just where information channels cross these normal lines to persons other than relatives, friends or co-workers. Such breaks are most common where official transactions are involved—a policeman explaining a roadblock, a bus driver explaining a delay—or where overhearing is involved such as a waitress overhearing a customer or a nurse overhearing patients and their friends.

The North Bay/Slater study provided a detailed picture of an interpersonal communication network. The accompanying chart shows how eight persons in the sample of 200 first heard the news about the shooting of Constable Slater. It showed how that information flowed from person to person from the original source, a source who for each of these eight was the informant who first told the police that there was a man with a gun in a downtown parking lot.

The numbers in the chart (191, 120, 35, etc.) represent different persons in the original sample. An X beside the number means that the person told someone else who did not know. Unbroken lines connecting persons mean that there was communication between them. Unbroken lines surrounding individuals indicate that communication was by telephone rather than face-to-face. A box composed of broken lines indicates that the person so enclosed overheard a communication not intended for him. The line marked "A" that goes across the chart represents the normal break that takes place in communications during the night. All persons above the line received information after this break. Note: there was no communication in any of these chains between 2:30 A.M. and 6:30 A.M.

The nature of these interpersonal communication chains can be seen by looking at one of them in isolation (#191):

1. A lady heard the news at home in bed on Sunday morning about 12 hours after the shooting. She overheard her daughter talking to a friend.
2. The friend heard from her father the night before when she got home from baby sitting.
3. The father heard first from a policeman he had gone to school with. The policeman had been on duty at the scene of the shooting and had been forced to stop the father from getting his car. (The car was in the parking lot where the shooting occurred.)
4. The policeman heard first when he was on the phone to his station. He had been talking to the station duty officer when the first call came in.
5. The duty officer had overheard the original call from Constable Alex McCourt, the policeman who was shot first. McCourt had called in for help.
6. Slater got the first information from informants. They told him they had seen a man with a gun in the Oak Street parking lot.

It should be noted that the message passed along each interpersonal communication chain is not constant. What Slater heard first was not what he told the duty officer. Slater heard first only of a man with a gun; by the time he called for help he had been shot. What the other policeman heard originally was not what he told the father; by the time he talked to the father, he knew that not just one but two policemen had been shot, one fatally. What the father heard first was not what he told his daughter. The

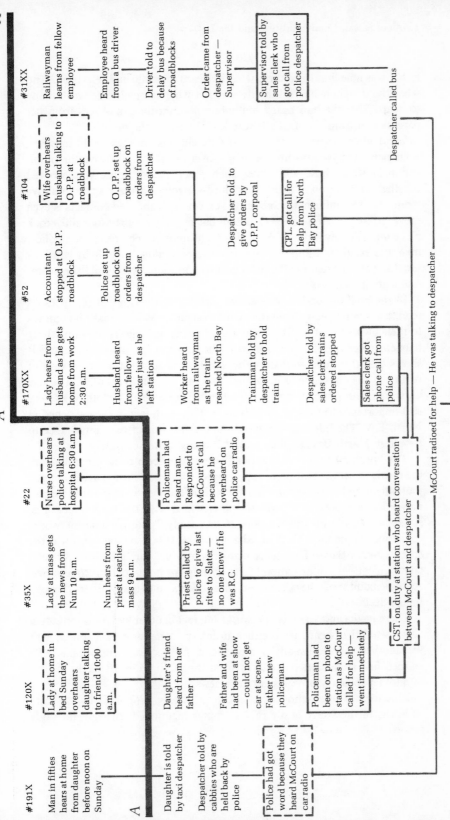

father was able first to confirm what he heard on radio and television. And what the daughter heard initially was not what the child she was talking to heard first; she had heard a number of confirming messages from her parents and from the media before she passed on the news.

Incidentally, there are thirty-four different links in these eight interpersonal networks: twenty-three of them—over two thirds—involve communication between those who knew each other and/or those who worked together; only eleven of them—one third—involved contact among relative strangers. This information about the extent of established contacts is even more striking when it is noted that all but five of the thirty-four links took place immediately after the Saturday night murder. The death of a policeman was exciting, dramatic news. It was passed along quickly by word-of-mouth. Yet it tended for the most part to flow along well-established communication channels.

In the brief discussion of selective perception it was noted that persons tend to assimilate news from the media in such a way as to make it conform to their own view of reality. Some recent research suggests the same thing happens when people are involved in the transmission of information.[42] It shows that they tend to distort the information to suit their own view of reality as they pass messages along from one person to another. The one variation from this pattern occurs when the message is something of very real importance to those transmitting it. This is, in fact, what happened in North Bay. The information about the murder was of real importance to people in North Bay, so they passed it along quite accurately.

The "people" networks described above may seem to be separate from the media networks that preoccupy most of the authors who have examined journalism and mass communications. But the fact is that these human networks exist both alongside and intertwined with the media networks. As shown earlier by the Kingston/Cross study,[43] interpersonal networks sometimes originate with the media networks. It is also true—this was the case in North Bay—that media networks may be *started* by interpersonal communications. Information starts flowing from one person to another. At some point it reaches the media, then it flows on to many others through the media.

These media and "people" networks interact in other ways; persons often check what they heard from either an interpersonal or media source with yet another source, usually a media one; furthermore, individuals who learned first from someone else or from the radio are most likely to turn to another media source, usually the newspaper.

This idea of interaction or checking is clearly supported by the data collected in the study of air raid warnings mentioned earlier. The study reported:

... the most conclusive general finding is ... that hearing the warning siren is totally inadequate to stimulate people to immediate protective action. What people do, in fact, on hearing the siren, is to seek additional information either to validate or refute their own initial interpretation of the meaning of the signal ... .[44]

In a study of warning systems, Benjamin McLuckie reports how common this checking procedure is.

In most situations people aware of a warning usually seek to validate their own initial interpretation of its meaning (which is usually that "it doesn't mean anything") by observing the reaction of those around them, by watching the sky, by telephoning significant persons, by listening to the radio ... .[45]

In his study of *Invasion from Mars,* Hadley Cantril shows the same behavior may alert others.

People who were frightened or disturbed by the news often hastened to telephone friends or relatives. In the survey made by the American Institute of Public Opinion, all the people who tuned in late were asked, "Did someone suggest you tune in late after the program had begun?" Twenty-one per cent said, "Yes". In a special telephone study made for CBS by Hooper Inc., it was found that 15 per cent of the 103 persons interviewed had tuned in late to the program because they were telephoned to do so; in the CBS survey 19 per cent were found to have listened after the beginning because others told them to hear the news.[46]

Finally, this conclusion of interaction is also supported by data obtained when researchers looked at how people reacted to rumors of a flood threat in a community that had already experienced severe flooding. About half the people who heard the rumor that a dam had burst fled immediately. But even under such conditions 42.8 per cent tried to get official confirmation before fleeing, a feat that was somewhat difficult because the local radio station had not resumed broadcasting after the original flood.[47]

What emerges from all these findings, therefore, is a whole system of interpersonal networks which interact with each other and with the media in various ways. These networks carry various kinds of information (including news) sometimes on their own, sometimes touching the media at some point, then moving along independently once again. These two kinds of networks both exist to service people who, as individuals and as members of a group, are capable of interpreting all messages regardless of source as they see fit. In other words, the whole system assumes a distinctly individual human flavor which somewhat modifies the "mass" notion of mass media. As W. Phillips Davison once commented, "an audience can not be regarded as a lump of clay".[48]

NOTES TO CHAPTER SEVEN

1/ *Report of the Special Senate Committee on Mass Media,* Vol. III (Ottawa: Information Canada, 1971). This report is hereinafter cited as the Davey Report.

2/The CBC English and French Audience Panels, 1972-73. This information was provided at the author's request.

3/"Audience Research & Audiences to CBC Television and Radio Network Programs". Extract from CBC Annual Report, 1968-69. Information provided by CBC.

4/Davey Report, p. 5.

5/ASGHAR FATHI, "Problems in Developing Indices of News Value", *Journalism Quarterly,* (Autumn 1973), p. 498.

6/DENNIS P. FORCESE, HUGH MCROBERTS, STEVEN RICHER AND JOHN DE VIRES, Paper presented to annual meeting of the Canadian Anthropology-Sociology Association, St. John's, Newfoundland, June 1971, p. 4.

7/ASGHAR FATHI, "Diffusion of a 'happy' News Event", *Journalism Quarterly* (Summer 1973), p. 272.

8/T. JOSEPH SCANLON, "News Flow about Release of Kidnapped Diplomat researched by J-students", *Journalism Educator,* Vol. XXVI, No. 1 (Spring 1971), pp. 35-38.

9/There is a whole series of articles done in the United States in the area of diffusion of news. The best two summaries are: BRADLEY S. GREENBERG, "Person-to-Person Communication in the Diffusion of News Events", *Journalism Quarterly* (Autumn 1964), pp. 471-94; RICHARD J. HILL AND CHARLES M. BONJEAN, "News Diffusion: A Test of the Regularity Hypothesis", *Journalism Quarterly* (Summer 1964), pp. 336-42.

10/All of the figures cited in this paragraph are taken from the Davey Report, Vol. III.

11/JACQUES DE GUISE, "Information Media in the Pilot Region: Lower St.

Lawrence, Gaspé, & Iles-de-la-Madeleine", Agricultural and Rural Development Agency condensed report CR-#7, Ottawa (1967), p. 3.

12/PAUL LAZARSFELD, BERNARD BERELSON AND HAZEL GAUDET, *The People's Choice* (New York: Columbia University Press, 1968), p. 89.

13/SHIRLEY A. STAR AND HELEN MACGILL HUGHES, "Report on Educational Campaign: The Cincinnati Plan for the United Nations", *The American Journal of Sociology* (January 1950), p. 397.

14/HUGH F. DOW, "We Seek Them Here, We Seek Them There", a study of MacLaren Advertising, March 1973. All of the data in this paragraph are quoted from this study.

15/ *The Effects of Mass Communication* (Glencoe, Illinois: Free Press, 1960). The material on selective perception is found on pp. 21-23, 25, 64-65; on selective retention, 23-24, 64-65.

16/"The Obstinate Audience: The Influence Process from the Social View of Communication", *The Process and Effects of Mass Communication,* eds. Wilbur Schramn and Donald F. Roberts (Urbana: University of Illinois Press, 1971), pp. 326-46.

17/CHARLES F. CANNELL AND JAMES C. MACDONALD, "The Impact of Health News on Attitude Behavior", *Journalism Quarterly,* Vol. 33, No. 3 (1959), pp. 315-23. Evidently 2 per cent of the non-smokers were not accounted for.

18/The work in this area is summarized and reviewed in EVERETT N. ROGERS WITH F. FLOYD SHOEMAKER, *Communication of Innovations* (New York: Free Press, 1971).

19/BRYAN LYSTER, "Information and the Farmer in Southern Saskatchewan", *Canadian Journal of Agricultural Economics,* Vol. XVIII, No. 2, p. 18.

20/HARRY ESTILL MOORE, FREDERICK L. BATES, MARVIN V. LAYMAN, VERNON J. PARENTON, "Before the Wind: A Study of the Response to Hurricane Coreen", Publication 1095, National Academy of Sciences, National Research Council, Washington (1963), p. 36.

21/ROY A. CLIFFORD, "The Rio Grande Flood: A Comparative Study of Border Communities in Disaster", Publication 458, National Academy of Sciences, National Research Council, Washington (1956), pp. 77-82. The study shows, for example, that 41 per cent of the Mexicans but only 14 per cent of the U.S. residents, took the first warning by radio very seriously.

22/RAYMOND W. MACK AND GEORGE W. BAKER, "The Occasion Instant: The Structure of Social Responses to Unanticipated Air Raid Warnings", Publication 945, National Academy of Sciences, National Research Council, Washington (1961), p. 45.

23/HADLEY CANTRIL, *The Invasion from Mars* (Princeton, N.J.: Princeton University Press, 1966), p. 140.

24/LAZARSFELD, *et al., op. cit.* p. 152.

25/ELIHU KATZ AND PAUL LAZARSFELD, *Personal Influence* (New York: The Macmillan Company, 1964).

26/*The Human Group* (New York: Harcourt, Brace and Company, 1950), pp. 11-12.

27/*Ibid.* pp. 160-61.

28/LAZARSFELD *et al.* See especially Chapter 16, pp. 150-58.

29/KATZ AND LAZARSFELD, *op. cit.* pp. 150-58.

30/*Ibid.* p. 363.

31/KURT BACH *et al.,* "The Methodology of Studying Rumour Transmission", *Human Relations,* Vol. III, p. 32.

32/LEON FESTINGER, STANLEY SCHACHTER AND KURT BACH, *Social Pressures in Informal Groups* (New York: Harper, 1950), pp. 120-21.

33/ELIHU KATZ, "Interpersonal Relations in Mass Communications: Studies in the Flow of Influence", Ph.D. Thesis, Columbia University, 1956, p. 244. Katz reported the difficulty of tracing in an article a year later, "The Two-Step Flow of Communication: An Up-to-Date Report on an Hypothesis", *Public Opinion Quarterly* (Spring 1957), p. 27.

34/The three studies relevant to the discussion below are: T. JOSEPH SCANLON, "Not Two Steps but One and One Half" (Ottawa, 1968), unpublished; T. JOSEPH SCANLON, "The North Bay/Slater Study", working paper, National Emergency Planning Establishment (Ottawa, 1974); T. JOSEPH SCANLON AND JAMES JEFFERSON, "The Sidney/Big Storm Study", working paper, Emergency Planning Canada (Ottawa, 1974). These studies are described hereinafter as the Kingston/Cross Study, the North Bay/Slater Study and the Sidney/Big Storm Study.

35/The material in this paragraph is quoted entirely in a series of references in BRADLEY S. GREENBERG AND EDWIN B. PARKER, eds., *The Kennedy Assassination and the American Public* (Stanford: Stanford University Press, 1965), p. 181.

36/GREENBERG AND PARKER, *op.cit.* p. 108.

37/SCANLON, The Kingston/Cross Study.

38/*Ibid.*

39/*Ibid.*

40/SCANLON, The North Bay/Slater Study.

41/*Ibid.*

42/The research in this area is summarized in T.M. HIGHAM, "The Experimental Study of the Transmission of Rumour", *Interpersonal Communication: Survey and Studies,* ed. Dean C. Barlund (Boston: Houghton Mifflin, 1968), pp. 273-91.

43/SCANLON, The Kingston/Cross Study.

44/MACK AND BAKER, *op. cit.* p. 39.

45/BENJAMIN MCLUCKIE, "The Warning System in Disaster Situations: A Selective Analysis", Disaster Research Centre Report Series, No. 9 (July 1970), p. 43.

46/CANTRIL, *op. cit.* pp. 83-84.

47/ELLIOTT R. DANZIG, PAUL W. THAYER AND LILA R. GALANTER, "The Effects of a Threatening Rumour on a Disaster-Stricken Community", Publication 517, National Academy of Sciences, National Research Council, Washington (1958), p. 36.

48/"On the Effects of Communication", *Public Opinion Quarterly* (1959), p. 360.

PART
THREE

Journalism
and the Law

EDITOR'S NOTE: The law of the press in Canada including the status of the constitutional right of freedom of the press are the subjects with which this section is mainly concerned.

In Chapter Eight, Ronald G. Atkey surveys the legal environment which circumscribes journalism practice. Central to this environment are the powers in the possession of a judge to cite a journalist for contempt of court; statutory restrictions on the coverage of certain kinds of judicial proceedings such as preliminary hearings or trials of juveniles; and the various libel and slander acts which are intended to protect private individuals from unwarranted damage to their reputations through writing or broadcasting by journalists. Atkey analyzes a series of cases in which the rights and obligations of journalists were at issue. At the same time he describes the defence strategies likely to occur when journalists run afoul of the law.

Although there are several classes of events or situations such as the ones Atkey describes in which the journalist is restrained from publishing or broadcasting freely, a fundamental axiom of our political culture is that the freedom of the press will be preserved. The force of that axiom was tested in the Supreme Court of Canada in 1938 when the Alberta Press Act was referred to it. The act had provided the provincial government with such extraordinary powers as the right to prevent specific journalists from writing in provincial papers and the right to insert stories in newspapers of Alberta when it felt its views had been misrepresented. Predictably the Supreme Court found that the act was unconstitutional.

In Chapter Nine, the events leading to the passing of the bill by the Alberta legislature are presented with a view to explaining why the Alberta premier sought to control the press. The conclusion is reached that the attempt to control was partly a retributive action against the press by a premier who had been thoroughly attacked by it, but it was additionally part and parcel of an ideological and practical scheme, inspired by C.H. Douglas, the father of social credit theory, for implementing social credit principles in Alberta.

In Chapter Ten, the decision reached by the justices of the Supreme Court in the Press Act hearing is reviewed critically by E.A. Tollefson. Of central importance to his critique are the uncertain grounds on which the justices based their decision. First among these is the fact that the justices considered the constitutionality of a statute which was not referred to the Court and then used their finding on that statute to justify their decision on the Press Act. Of equal significance are the arguments supporting freedom of the press inspired by the preamble to the British North America Act in which it is written that Canada's constitution is to be "similar in principle to that of the United Kingdom". Tollefson argues that freedom of the press was, in 1867 as now, a condition subject to the supremacy of

Parliament and, further, that the supremacy of Parliament in Canada is complicated by the division of powers, enumerated in the B.N.A. Act, between the federal government and the provinces. It is noteworthy that despite the enactment in 1960 by the federal Parliament of a Bill of Rights in which the freedom of the press is specified as a basic right, the split jurisdiction and the principle of the supremacy of Parliament still complicate the status in Canada of the constitutional principle of freedom of the press.

In the concluding chapter of this section, Peter J. Goldsworthy examines the privilege, secured by statute in some U.S. jurisdictions and claimed by some newsmen, to keep secret in the face of judicial interest the sources on which news stories are based. In Canada, a judge may permit a journalist to refrain from disclosing his sources under examination, but such a decision rests with the Court and is applied by discretion under special circumstances. After surveying the customs and practices in Britain, the United States and Canada, Goldsworthy concludes with the recommendation that it would be desirable to create a statute defining and limiting the extent to which a journalist may exercise this privilege in courts of law.

The articles in this section contain legal terms which may not be familiar to students of journalism. A glossary of legal terms is provided in the order in which they appear in the text.

GLOSSARY

CORAM CURIA:	in the presence of a court of justice.
SUB JUDICE:	under a judge or before a court; under judicial consideration.
PRIMA FACIE:	at first appearance; at first sight.
INTER ALIA:	among other things. A term used in pleading, especially in reciting statutes, where the whole statute is not set forth at length.
INDICTMENT:	a written accusation of one or more persons of a crime or misdemeanor presented to a grand jury. If the grand jury decides the accused ought to be tried before a court the return is made a "true bill" and thenceforward it is called the Indictment.
INTRA VIRES:	an act is said to be "intra vires" of a person or corporation when it is within the scope of his or its power or authority.

ULTRA VIRES: an act is said to be "ultra vires" of a person or corporation when it is beyond the scope of his or its power or authority.

CIVIL PROCEEDINGS: a legal action against a person or corporation initiated by a private citizen as distinct from a criminal proceeding in which it is the responsibility of the entire community, represented by Government agencies, to initiate.

INTERLOCUTORY PROCEEDINGS: a temporary or intermediate action with special reference to a suit not final; something provisional intervening between the commencement and the end of a suit which decides some point or matter but is not a final decision of the whole controversy.

RATIO DECIDENDI: the grounds of a decision; the point in a case which determines the judgment.

RES JUDICATA: a matter which has been adjudicated.

DICTA: sayings, remarks or opinions of a judge during the hearing of a case, which do not embody the resolution or determination of a case.

PERSONA DESIGNATA: a person pointed out or described as an individual as distinguished from a member of a class.

APPELLANT: the party who takes an appeal to another, usually a higher, court in order to have the case in which he is involved reviewed or reconsidered.

COMMON LAW: the body of law and juristic theory which was originally developed and formulated in England as distinct from Foreign, Civil or Canon Law; written and unwritten rules and authoritative principles embodied in judicial decisions as opposed to statutory law enacted by legislatures.

CIVIL LAW: it means two things: a) a system of law derived from Roman as distinct from English law; b) in the English system of law (and in the article) it refers to that division of municipal law concerned with the regulation of ordinary private matters, i.e. civil rights, as distinct from laws regulating public matters, i.e. criminal, political or military.

chapter eight

The Law of the Press in Canada*

RONALD G. ATKEY

PART B: CONTROL OF THE PRESS IN
THE ADMINISTRATION OF JUSTICE

1. The Criminal Offence of Contempt of Court

All criminal offences in Canada are specifically included under the Criminal Code or other federal statutes, with the sole exception of the common law offence of contempt of court.[16] This offence has its historical antecedents in the common law of England. It has been applied as a common law offence in Canada up to the present time much in the same way as it was in eighteenth century England by Lord Hardwicke in the famous *St. James Evening Post* case, where he gave the rationale for the offence:

> Nothing is more incumbent upon courts of justice to preserve their proceedings from being misrepresented; nor is there anything of more pernicious consequence, than to prejudice the minds of the public against persons concerned as parties in causes, before the cause is finally heard.[17]

The offence of criminal contempt can be committed either in the court itself (*coram curia*) or outside the court through publication or comment (constructive contempt). It is the latter situation which is most likely to confront the members of the press.

There are essentially three types of constructive contempt which can arise: 1. publications tending to pervert the impartiality of the judicial proc-

---

*A two-part study which appeared first in *Gazette,* International Journal for Mass Communications, Vol. XV, No. 2, pp. 105-124 and No. 3, pp. 185-200, 1969. It appears here with the permission of the publisher and the author. Part A, "Freedom of the Press in Canada", has been omitted. The sections of the Criminal Code cited in this article bear the numbers that were used prior to 1970. The Code was revised and re-numbered in that year.—Editor.

ess in criminal cases; 2. publications scandalizing the Court or members of the judiciary through undue criticism; and 3. publications unnecessarily abusing the parties involved in civil causes before the courts so as to cause them to compromise or refrain from using the courts.

Of the three types of constructive contempt, the third is the rarest. In only one reported Canadian case has the offence been committed, that being a situation in 1934 in which the publisher and a writer of the Edmonton *Bulletin* were found guilty of contempt and fined $300 and $100 respectively after publishing two articles which prejudiced the interests of one of the litigants in a civil action then in progress.[18] Although other attempts have been made to procure a conviction for publication of this sort, they have been largely unsuccessful.[19] In the most recent English case of this type, the Court was quite prepared to allow newspaper discussion or opinion concerning the law in a pending civil case, as long as it didn't deter the parties from continuing or defending the action or attempt to influence the judge.[20]

The second type of constructive contempt (scandalizing the Court) occurs somewhat more frequently. For example, an Ontario Court in 1963 convicted a monthly magazine publisher for contempt for repeatedly publishing abusive, nasty and vulgar references to certain County Court judges accusing them of bias, perverting justice and breach of their oaths of office.[21] In a Newfoundland case in 1954, newspaper accusations, couched in contemptuous and insulting language, that the Court had assumed dictatorial powers to assist in a campaign for the suppression of the free press, brought contempt convictions for both the owners of the newspaper and the columnists involved.[22] Perhaps the most spectacular case involved an article by Eric Nicol in the *Vancouver Province* following the murder conviction and imposition of the death sentence on a nineteen-year-old boy. Intending an allegory on capital punishment, Nicol wrote:

> Although I did not myself spring the trap that caused my victim to be strangled in cold blood, I admit that the man who did was in my employ. Also serving me were twelve people who planned the murder, and the judge who chose the time and place and caused the victim to suffer the exquisite torture of anticipation.

Nicol was convicted for contempt in that he imputed improper motives on the part of the judge who imposed the sentence.[23]

Contempt convictions for scandalizing the Court have generally been reluctantly imposed on the Canadian mass media however. For the most part contempt has been regarded more as a "hovering judicial right",[24] allowing reasonable criticism of the administration of justice where the public good has demanded it, but standing in readiness where acute circumstances require it. The press has been allowed a certain degree of freedom in criticizing both individual judges and the judicial system, and the courts have tended to be tolerant of journalistic impertinence. For example, in 1965, a cartoon was published of a certain judge in Quebec, implying criticism of certain of his judicial actions. Yet the Court dismissed the motion for contempt.[25] A more recent case in Quebec involved a book entitled *J'accuse les assassins de Coffin* written by Louis Hébert some seven years after the famous murder trial and execution of Wilfred Coffin. Although Hébert in the book had strongly criticized several persons involved in the conduct of the Coffin case including the judge, the Court refused to convict for contempt because on balance it preferred to protect the right of free discussion and comment notwithstanding the effect on the process of justice.[26]

Judicial tolerance was clearly illustrated in another Quebec case where a newspaper had been ordered by a court to publish a judgment condemning it for a defamatory libel, and the newspaper published the judgment in very small print on the back page. The Court refused on appeal to convict for contempt in spite of the obvious disrespect for the original order.[27]

The general reluctance of the Canadian courts to find contempt of this sort would appear to be in accord with the English position illustrated in a leading case before the Judicial Committee of the Privy Council in which a newspaper article on the inequality of sentences in criminal cases by different judges was held to be not in contempt.[28] The standard of proof in most cases seems to be subjective and arbitrary,[29] but the courts would seem to rule in favor of the accused where there is any doubt present.

The first type of contempt (perverting the impartiality of the judicial process in criminal cases) provides the most significant restriction and constitutes the greatest danger in court reporting by the mass media. Its arbitrary application by the courts represents the balance that is often struck in the classical conflict between free press and fair trial. Not only can the contempt power be exercised by the courts during a trial, but, perhaps more frequently, before a trial as a result of press reporting of spectacular crimes, witnesses' statements, arrests, preliminary inquiries and coroner's inquests.

The position of the mass media has been perhaps best expressed in a recent case involving two Vancouver newspapers which had published, under such headlines as "I'll Kill Anyone! Four Held Prisoners by Crazed Gunman", articles based on interviews with eyewitnesses. In one of the articles, the accused's name was mentioned in the concluding paragraph. The Court declined to cite the newspapers for contempt, stating:

It is the business of newspapers to gather and publish information

to their readers of matters of public importance and that right will
not be interfered with unless the higher right of the courts to determine the guilt or innocence of an accused is thereby prejudiced or
interfered with.[30]

However, the very task of determining the "higher right of the courts"
involves an exercise of judicial discretion not always consistent in its application, and depending in each case upon the particular facts and circumstances, the time of publication, the causes leading to publication and the
tenor of what is published. In short, there are no clear and easily defined
guidelines for the press to follow.

On the one hand, the courts have convicted a Toronto newspaper for
reporting a police officer's statement that an accused had admitted guilt,[31]
a foreign publisher and local distributor of an article containing inadmissi-
ble hearsay evidence about a pending murder trial,[32] and a broadcasting
company for a radio report on a case that was *sub judice* of information
tending to prejudice potential jurors.[33] The absence of knowledge or lack
of wrongful intent has been held to be no excuse, though it has mitigated
the penalty.[34] On the other hand, the courts have refused to convict a Saint
John, New Brunswick, newspaper for reporting the verdict of a coroner's
inquest that the accused (not then charged) fired the gun in question and
killed the deceased,[35] and, more recently, Toronto Controller Allan Lamport and *The Telegram* for a newspaper and television report that Lamport
"urged" and "hoped" that the Court would impose a certain penalty on
a number of hippies charged with creating a disturbance.[36]

Perhaps one of the clearest cases of contempt for prejudicing a fair trial
was the feature article by Robert Fulford entitled "Tragedy of a Sex Criminal" published in the September 21st, 1963, edition of *Maclean's Magazine.*
The article discussed the case of Leopold Dion, alleged sex killer of four
boys, who was being held in custody awaiting trial. Although Fulford
primarily directed his attack at the parole system and authorities who granted parole to Dion even though he had a history of sex deviations, the article
dealt with Dion's criminal record, the evidence he gave at the coroner's
inquest, and statements and confessions alleged to have been made by him.
The article was published three weeks before Dion's trial. The Court found
no difficulty in convicting the author and publisher for contempt, particularly since those who would be constituting the jury could have been easily
affected by such comments.[37] However, Dion was subsequently convicted
and sentenced to death.[38]

It is generally accepted that the press can print a factual account of
preliminary inquiries (with the exception of a confession tendered in evidence—see *infra*), notwithstanding that only the Crown's evidence is usual-

ly entered to establish a *prima facie* case. The same rule applies for coroner's inquests as well.[39]

Photographs are subject to the same restrictions as written reports, particularly where publication would tend to affect the identification of an accused if it were in issue. However, it is often the practice that newspapers will co-operate with the police in publishing the photograph of a wanted man. As commendable as this practice would appear to be, it would not exculpate a newspaper from a possible contempt charge should identification later be a key issue in the trial.

Photographs, televison cameras and tape recorders are forbidden in the courtroom by custom and practice of the judiciary. Their deliberate use would undoubtedly constitute criminal contempt in the court itself (*coram curia*) and would likely result in a conviction meted out on-the-spot by the presiding justice.

Even after a criminal trial is over, newspapers are not completely free to comment on the facts or the decision or the sentence until the time for appeal has passed or until the appeal has been heard and judgment pronounced.[40] However, the risk of potential unfairness to the accused here is not particularly great,[41] and newspapers have been inclined to ignore this restriction, generally in the public interest.

The only definite guideline for newspapers in avoiding contempt would seem to be the factor of time. "When in doubt, delay publication" was the advice of the late Honourable Ivan C. Rand to a symposium of journalists and lawyers at Osgoode Hall Law School in 1966. He considered this necessary to afford sufficient benefit to the accused individual. At the same time he was critical of the investigation of crimes by the press which often led to undue pre-trial publicity. Yet the time element is probably the most important factor in the competitive world of newspaper reporting and publishing and therefore to suggest it as a guideline merely begs the question to the editor concerned with publishing the hottest news within the limits of the law.

The vagueness and uncertainty of the contempt sanction in Canada has given rise to recommendations for specific legislation to define the powers of the press in crime reporting. Some would suggest that the press be confined to the publication of only the facts of arrest and charge, as in England, and of any apparent procedural abuses. Accurate reports of the trial would still be allowed, but comments on the merits of the cases would be prohibited until the verdict was known.[42] Coroner's inquests and preliminary inquiries would not be publicized except where the court considered it in the public interest to allow it. Indeed, at the time of writing of this paper, an amendment to the Criminal Code is before the Canadian Parliament which would allow an accused to apply for an order directing that evidence taken at a preliminary inquiry not be published or broadcast until the subsequent trial is over or the accused discharged.[43]**

The enactment of restrictive legislation is not the only remedy suggested however. The Honourable J.C. McRuer in his 1968 Royal Commission Inquiry Into Civil Rights (Ontario) devoted an entire chapter to the problem of publication of proceedings before trial, and recommended, *inter alia:*

1. A self-governing council should be established in Ontario to control and discipline the press and other news media with respect to the publication of news and comment that may tend to prejudice the fair trial of an accused should a charge later be laid, unless it is shown that the publication is in the public interest.

2. The Attorney-General should act promptly to prosecute for breaches of the law respecting contempt of court, and not leave the initiation of prosecutions to the individuals affected or to the court.[44]

The concept of a self-governing Press Council as a restricting force, rather than specific legislation, is a novel one in Canada. The British Press Council, made up of an independent chairman, representatives of press associations and members of the general public, has had only a limited degree of success in controlling and disciplining the press. Whether a Canadian Press Council will ever be created, and, once created, whether newspapers would pay any attention to it, are matters which only the members of the press in Canada themselves can determine.

In any event, McRuer also considered the problem of preliminary inquiries and concluded that "there should be no further restriction provided by law on the reporting of proceedings at preliminary inquiries". Thus, he placed himself in opposition to the proposal now before Parliament as outlined above, stating that such a restriction "would in large measure remove from this branch of the administration of justice an essential safeguard of civil rights—the right of the public to know, to criticize and to debate".

One further proposal to remedy the problem of the vague and uncertain contempt power was made by E. U. Schrader of the Ryerson Polytechnical Institute. He recommended the establishment of "written professional guidelines, jointly arrived at by lawyers and editors, which would serve as a chart on prejudicial reporting".[45] As an exercise in self-discipline, this proposal is not significantly different than the Press Council proposal.

Finally, mention should be made of the existing rights of appeal from

**The amendment was passed in the same year.—Editor

a contempt conviction. By a new section added to the Criminal Code in 1953-54, constructive contempt convictions can be appealed to the court of appeal of the province in which the proceedings take place both as the conviction itself and also the punishment imposed.[46] Where contempt is committed in the face of the court (*coram curia*), the appeal can be taken only with respect to the punishment imposed, and not the conviction.[47] The latter situation is one of the few instances in our law where a man can be summarily convicted on the spot and then denied a right of appeal.[48] The potential danger of abuse is substantial, and it is hoped that the sanction will be used sparingly.

2. Other Restrictions on the Press

Apart from the common law offence of contempt, there are other specific statutory restrictions in the Criminal Code and elsewhere which operate in varying degrees to control the press in the administration of justice. Since criminal law and procedure in Canada are by the constitution a matter of federal and not provincial jurisdiction, these restrictions apply to all newspapers in Canada, and to the other forms of mass media.

a. Restriction of Reports of Confessions At Preliminary Inquiry

Section 455(2) of the Criminal Code creates an offence for the publication in any newspaper or broadcast of a "report that any admission or confession was tendered in evidence at a preliminary inquiry or a report of the nature of such admission or confession so tendered in evidence" until the accused's trial has ended or he is discharged.

This provision of course would be partially subsumed by the present amendment before Parliament allowing an accused to make an application for a preliminary without publicity should the amendment be adopted by the law-makers.

The offence was first created in 1959, following a New Brunswick case earlier referred to.[49] There are few reported convictions under the section, although it is quite clear that in the *Dion*[50] case, Fulford and *Maclean's Magazine* would have been convicted had they not been successfully convicted for contempt.

b. Trial of Juveniles To Be Without Publicity

Section 427 of the Criminal Code provides that "where an accused is or appears to be under the age of sixteen years, his trial shall take place without publicity . . .".

While the restriction on the press appears to be of general application in criminal cases, it applies only to the trial and not the preliminary inquiry. Most juvenile (under age sixteen) prosecutions proceed under the *Juvenile Delinquent Act,*[51] in which there is no preliminary inquiry. However, section 9 of that Act provides that a juvenile court judge may order a juvenile over age 14, charged with an indictable (serious) offence, to be "proceeded against by indictment in the ordinary courts in accordance with the Criminal Code". In this latter instance, there is a preliminary inquiry. Therefore, there is occasionally created the anomalous situation in which the press is perfectly within its rights in publishing the factual account of a preliminary inquiry of an accused juvenile over fourteen for whom an order under section 9 has been made, but is absolutely prohibited from publishing a factual account of the subsequent trial by section 427 of the Criminal Code. In view of the fact that only Crown evidence is usually adduced at a preliminary inquiry in order to establish a *prima facie case,* it would appear that the potential prejudice to the accused would be increased, not decreased, by the Code restriction on the press at trial prohibiting balanced reports of both Crown and defence evidence there adduced.

This actual situation arose in the famous Truscott murder case in 1959 in which a fourteen year old juvenile was convicted for murder in the ordinary courts following a section 9 order.[52] The newspaper publicity of the preliminary inquiry was substantial and might well have helped to convince the readers and potential jurors of Truscott's guilt. Yet when the actual trial started, newspaper coverage was completely stopped (although reporters were allowed to sit in until the end of the trial). Truscott's conviction and life imprisonment sentence later became the subject of a public furore largely as a result of a book written by one Isabel Lebourdais. The federal Cabinet eventually became involved, and re-submitted the case on a reference (advisory opinion) to the Supreme Court of Canada. The Court reaffirmed the conviction[53] with only one of the nine judges dissenting from the majority decision.

c. *Exclusion of the Public and the Press in Certain Cases*
Section 428 of the Criminal Code provides for the trial of an adult accused

> in open court, but where the court, judge, justice or magistrate . . . is of opinion that it is in the interest of public morals, the maintenance of order or the proper administration of justice to exclude all or any members of the public from the court room, he may so order.

This section has seldom been invoked, the concept of "open court" being a much cherished tradition in the administration of justice in Canada.[54]

In a case in Manitoba in 1961, a magistrate under this section excluded members of the public from a preliminary inquiry on a charge of gross indecency, but did not exclude representatives of the press and members of the police force. Upon the objection of the accused's counsel who argued that his client's right to a fair trial was prejudiced, the Court held that the magistrate properly used his discretion under the section and that, in consideration of the generally broad power given to him in the conduct of an inquiry by other Code provisions, the objection was not well founded.[55]

In a preliminary inquiry to capital murder charges against five men in Hamilton, Ontario, taking place at the very time of writing of this paper, the judge invoked a related section 451 (i) to exclude both the public and the press from the courtroom. The counsel of one of the accused had made the request for such a move because there had been a great deal of publicity about the shooting incident and because a particular radio station had been constantly reviewing the case in subsquent weeks. The particular section of the Code gives a judge at a preliminary the power to order everyone out of the courtroom except the prosecutor, the accused and their counsel where it appears that the ends of justice will be best served by so doing. The section has seldom if ever been used. Shortly after this sequence of events, a lawyer appeared on behalf of the radio station and requested the readmittance of the press on the grounds that the public had a right to know what was going on. The court refused the request, pointing out the proposed Criminal Code amendment concerning preliminaries before Parliament, and indicating defence lawyers had full opportunity to say what was going on.[56]

d. *Restriction on Publication of Indecent Matters in Judicial Proceedings or of Certain Matters in Divorce Proceedings*
Canada has adopted from the criminal law of England the following restrictions now found in section 151(1) of the Criminal Code:

A proprietor, editor, master printer or publisher commits an offence who prints or publishes

(a) in relation to any judicial proceedings any indecent matter or indecent medical, surgical or physiological details, being matter or details that, if published, are calculated to injure public morals;

(b) in relation to any judicial proceedings for dissolution of marriage, nullity of marriage, judicial separation or restitution of conjugal rights, any particulars other than:

I.   the names, addresses and occupations of the parties and witnesses,

II.   a concise statement of the charges, defences and counter-charges in support of which evidence has been given,

III. submissions on a point of law arising in the course of proceedings, and the decision of the court in connection therewith, and

IV. the summing up of the judge, the findings of the jury and the judgment of the court and the observations that are made by the judge in giving judgment.

There have been no cases of any great consequence under this section, implying the general adherence of the press to the stated restrictions.

e. *Restrictions on the Press in Civil Proceedings*

The rules as to whether the press can be excluded from civil or administrative proceedings are generally determined by the statute law of the particular province in which the proceedings are being conducted. The statutes and the various types of proceedings are too numerous to set forth in the context of this paper. Generally, there is an express power of exclusion in proceedings relating to mental incompetents, deserted wives' and children's maintenance, and other family court matters.[57]

PART C: THE LAW OF LIBEL AND THE PRESS IN CANADA

1. General Nature of Libel

The clearest and most accurate definition of libel that there is comes from England in 1882 in the words of Mr. Justice Cave: "A libel is a false statement about a man to his discredit."[58] This definition would appear to apply to libels of practically all the forms of mass media in Canada: newspapers, magazines, reviews, books, broadcasts and telecasts. And with respect to newspapers in particular, virtually all parts of them are capable at some point of being libellous: cartoons, editorials, news reports, letters to the editor, photographs and even advertisements.

Intention to libel is largely irrelevant in determining liability, with the exception where malice is an issue when the defence of qualified privilege (*infra*) is pleaded. However, lack of intention will help to mitigate any damages to be awarded to the successful plaintiff.

It must be pointed out at the outset that all libel actions in Canada are tried by both a judge and a jury (comprised of six persons). The judge's task, in addition to conducting the trial, is to determine whether the alleged libel is capable of having a libellous meaning. Once he is able to answer this in the affirmative, the judge then, and only then, will put the words to the jury to determine whether the plaintiff was actually libelled and the extent of his damages.

Two recent examples are illustrative of judicial attempts to apply the general definition. In a 1963 newspaper editorial in the *Vancouver Province,* a candidate for re-election to the school board was discussed and indeed praised, but his age was stated as over 80 when in fact it was 73, and the editorial commented that his age made the wisdom of electing him questionable. The Court dismissed the candidate's libel action since the false statement of age by itself was not libellous as no senile incapacity verging on insane condition was suggested. In short, there was no real possibility that readers would shun the candidate or that he would be exposed to ridicule as a result of the editorial.[59] The words were therefore incapable of libellous meaning.

The other case arose out of an article appearing in *Maclean's Magazine* on September 5th, 1964, entitled "These Were the Years that Made Our World". Igor Gouzenko was a person who had become famous by assisting the Canadian government in the post-Second World War period in uncovering a spy ring, at great risk to his own personal safety. *Maclean's* in the article made seventeen references which might have been construed as being derogatory about Gouzenko, for which he instituted a libel action, claiming that the remarks were meant to mean that he, Gouzenko, was a spend-thrift, a person whose contribution to the security of Canada was incidental and of no great value, a troublemaker, a ward of the R.C.M.P., a dishonest man seeking to have the government do his family chores, a lazy man and a work shirker, a man deluded by delusions of great wealth, a washed-out author, an ungrateful person, and a person not worthy of the goodwill of his fellow Canadian citizens.

Maclean's pleaded justification and fair comment. The trial judge allowed only three of the quotations to be put to the jury, and they returned with a general verdict of libel and assessed damages of $1.00.[60] Gouzenko appealed the assessment of damages, and a new trial on that issue was ordered by the Supreme Court of Canada[61] (at the time of writing the new trial had not been reported). The jury's general verdict of libel stands however.

Where words taken by themselves would not be considered libellous, the plaintiff may allege that the words in the particular context in which they appeared contain an imputation not expressly stated. This is what is called pleading *innuendo.* It is the latent or secondary meaning which the public would attach to the phrase complained of. The danger in a plaintiff alleging *innuendo* is that it enables the defendant newspaper to plead the truth of the *innuendo* and thus drag into the trial any bit of damaging fact about the plaintiff they may have been able to discover. The effect of this on the jury is obvious.[62]

2. The Various Libel and Slander Acts

Although libel was and still is a common law civil remedy, all the Canadian provinces have enacted legislation for the purpose of specifying certain statutory rights and obligations in connection with alleged defamatory words in a newspaper or broadcast. While these statutes represent a large part of the law of "newspaper and broadcast" libel in each provincial jurisdiction, they do not exclude the operation of the common law. Therefore, there are in effect two parallel sets of rules which apply to newspapers and broadcasts, sometimes tending to confuse the situation. This confusion is most readily apparent in the defence of qualified privilege which will be discussed at a later point.

For discussion's sake, the Ontario *Libel and Slander Act*[63] provides a useful model of a statute which is not dissimilar to that in most of the other provinces. Section 2 of the Act states that defamatory words in a newspaper or in a broadcast shall be deemed to be published and to constitute libel. The section thus dispenses with the necessity for proving publication. Subsequent sections set forth instances of qualified and absolute privilege, but these are conditional upon the defendant inserting an explanation or contradiction of the impugned statement. Sections 5 and 6 are statutory limitation periods requiring a person allegedly libelled in a newspaper or broadcast to give the defendant a written notice of the libel within six weeks of its coming to his knowledge, and requiring that any action be commenced within three months.

The remainder of the sections relate to detail administration and other matters such as damages and procedural defences which will be discussed at a later point. Slander is dealt with in a separate section of the Act, but it is not directly relevant to the mass media.

3. Defences

a. Justification

No libel action will lie for the publication of a defamatory statement if the defendant pleads and proves that it is true. The burden of proof rests upon the defendant. On occasion, the defence has proved to be a dangerous one because an unsuccessful attempt to establish truth through evidence has "aggravated" the original injury and increased damages to a greater extent than had the defence not been pleaded at all.

Section 23 of the Ontario *Libel and Slander Act* provides that in instances of two or more libels, the defence of justification shall not fail by reason only that the truth of every charge is not proved, if the words not proved to be true do not materially injure the plaintiff's reputation having regard to the truth of the remaining charges.

This defence is almost always pleaded by newspaper defendants together with the alternative defence of fair comment. Therefore, case examples of justification will be considered in the next section.

b. *Fair Comment*

Statements of opinion made upon matters of public interest fall under the protection of this defence, if they are made in good faith and without malice. Opinion, in order to be "fair", must be based upon facts, although the particular facts upon which the opinion is based need not be set out in the article in question. Comment based on facts which are ill-founded are not entitled to the protection.

This defence is most often used for newspaper comments on politicians, entertainers and other public figures, although it is used in private situations as well if it meets the conditions set out above. Since most newspaper reports in editorials alleged to be libellous contain both opinions and facts, the defences of fair comment and justification go hand in hand (in technical terms, a "rolled-up plea").

As an example, a case arose in 1962 in Oakville, Ontario, when the *Oakville Record Star* editorially attacked a builder who had constructed a building which had been completely destroyed by fire. Although the building had been constructed in accordance with the town building bylaws and the National Building Code, the editorial asserted that it was a "fire-trap", "easily-combustible", "in no sense fire-resistant", and was built "on the cheap". The editorial also attacked the builder personally. In an action for libel, the Court refused to accept the defence of truth because the newspaper could not prove the allegations, and declined to accept the defence of fair comment since the opinions were based on erroneous facts. The newspaper was found liable for damages of $5,000, which included punitive damages since it had failed to offer a retraction and exhibited indications of malice.[64]

After the Eric Nicol allegory in the *Vancouver Province* and the resulting contempt conviction[65], eight of the jurymen brought a libel action against the publisher. The defence of fair comment was raised, but rejected by the Court since the comment was certainly not fair. Damages for libel were awarded in the amount of $4,000.

The allowable latitude for fair comment in political situations was set forth in a case in Toronto in the mid-forties in which certain advertisements attacking an elected official (who later became the mayor of that city) during an election campaign had appeared in a local newspaper. Although the actual issue in the appeal case concerned the perversity of the jury's decision, the Court stated:

> It was plain upon the face of the pleadings that this whole matter was a by-product of a heated election campaign, in which party feeling was aroused . . . . A jury is not necessarily perverse if it refuses to regard as seriously as the party assailed may do, the seemingly venomous attacks made upon such an occasion. No monetary loss is involved, and a jury is not likely to regard as serious the damage, if any, done by rough words applied to a political opponent, even though they may amount to gross abuse.[66]

A significant case arose in 1968 in England involving *The Daily Telegraph* and the publishing of letters to the editor which imputed dishonesty to a solicitor who had formerly been Town Clerk and then later legal advisor to a private firm with property interests somewhat conflicting with those of the town. The writer of the letters implied publicly that the solicitor used "back-door influence" with the employees of Town Council in the interests of the company. A libel action was brought by the solicitor and his company against both the writer of the letters and the *Daily Telegraph*. Lord Denning, Master of the Rolls, held that the letters were fair comment on a matter of public interest and then proceeded to lay out the test which will likely be followed in Canada:

> If he was an honest man expressing his genuine opinion on a subject of public interest, then no matter that his words conveyed derogatory imputations: no matter that his opinion was wrong or exaggerated or prejudiced; and no matter that it was badly expressed so that other people read all sorts of innuendoes into it; nevertheless, he has a good defence of fair comment. His honesty is the cardinal test. He must honestly express his real view. So long as he does this, he has nothing to fear, even though other people may read more into it . . . I stress this because the right of fair comment is one of the essential elements which go to make up our freedom of speech. We must ever maintain this right intact. It must not be whittled down by legal refinements. When a citizen is troubled by things going wrong, he should be free to 'write to the newspaper': and the newspaper should be free to publish his letter. It is often the only way to get things put right. The matter must, of course, be one of public interest. The writer must

get his facts right: and he must honestly state his real opinion. But that being done, both he and the newspaper should be clear of any liability. They should not be deterred by fear of libel actions.[67]

Finally, it should be pointed out that there are a number of authorities for the proposition that a newspaper pleading fair comment and/or justification as a defence in a libel action is required on discovery (i.e., pre-trial examination) to disclose its factual sources notwithstanding normal journalistic reluctance to do so.[68]

c. *Absolute and Qualified Privilege*

There is only one type of newspaper or broadcast report which is "absolutely privileged", and thus completely immune from a libel action, no matter how false and defamatory the report may be and even though it is made maliciously. This is a fair and accurate report of judicial proceedings. Although the specific wording of the immunity varies from province to province, section 4(1) of Ontario's *Libel and Slander Act*[69] illustrates the common example:

> 4(1) A fair and accurate report without comment in a newspaper or in a broadcast of proceedings publicly heard before a court of justice, if published in the newspaper or broadcast contemporaneously with such proceedings is absolutely privileged unless the defendant has refused or neglected to insert in the newspaper in which the report complained of appeared or to broadcast, as the case may be, a reasonable statement of explanation or contradiction by or on behalf of the plaintiff.[70]

This immunity applies to fair and accurate reports of statements in court of judges, counsel, witnesses and parties, whether the proceedings are preliminary or final in nature. And the privilege extends to statements in documents used in the judicial proceedings such as affidavits and pleadings.[71]

The defence of "qualified privilege" provides a somewhat broader protection for newspapers. Statutory protection is given in most provinces for fair and accurate reports of a variety of situations (as long as there is no malice and the newspaper has not refused to insert a reasonable statement of explanation or contradiction):[72] proceedings of Parliament or any legislative or administrative body or public commission of inquiry;[73] public meetings;[74] reports, bulletins, notices or other documents publicly issued by government;[75] and findings or decisions of public associations in various fields concerning persons who are members of or contractually subject to such associations.[76]

The common law also provides a number of forms of qualified privilege which are useful to newspapers. For example, statements made by a newspaper in discharging some moral, social or legal duty are protected. An erroneous news story reporting someone as missing might qualify for this protection if it were not made maliciously. Again, statements made to a person who has a common interest in a subject with the person who makes them provide another instance of qualified privilege. If one newspaper in a chain unjustly criticized another newspaper in the same chain by way of an open letter to that other newspaper, the privilege might well be invoked. Statements made in self-defence can also claim qualified privilege as well. For example, if one man attacks another in the public press, the latter may make a reply, and the reply may contain countercharges against his assailant, if they form a reasonably necessary part of his defence.[77]

The difference between qualified and absolute privilege, i.e., the waiver of the immunity if the publication is made maliciously in the case of qualified privilege, is a difference more apparent than real. Most Canadian newspapermen in their day-to-day operations regard the rules of qualified privilege as their primary "rules of thumb" in potentially libellous situations, and there have been very few cases in which a newspaper has been alleged to have maliciously published otherwise privileged reports.

One notable case however deserves mention in this context. *The Toronto Globe and Mail* in November 1957 had published a lead editorial entitled "Mission Accomplished" in which Harold C. Banks, the well-known vice-president of the Seafarers International Union, was sarcastically and severely denigrated for his union activities and general operation of the S.I.U. The *Globe and Mail* pleaded both qualified privilege and fair comment. In respect of the former, it was claimed that the newspaper had a duty to publish, in the interests of the public, information with respect to a particular strike called by Banks and the resultant transfer of eight vessels from Canadian Registry; therefore the information and comment thereon was privileged. Banks claimed that it was not, and that, in any event, there was malice on the part of the *Globe and Mail,* thus disqualifying the privilege.

The trial judge found that there was qualified privilege, but there was also evidence of malice to go to the jury. The jury however later negatived express malice, thus in effect dismissing Bank's action on the grounds of qualified privilege. However, on appeal to the Supreme Court of Canada, it was held that there was no qualified privilege in the statement since the "right" of a newspaper to publish matters of a public interest does not necessarily constitute a "duty" to do so, such as would bring the statement within the immunity of the common law qualified privilege. Therefore, the question of malice became moot, and Banks recovered $3,500 against the *Globe and Mail.*[78]

d. *Procedural Defences*

The most obvious defence which any newspaper will raise to a potential libel action is the failure of the plaintiff to provide adequate notice. Under the statutory requirements in most of the provinces, a person who is allegedly libelled in a newspaper or broadcast must give the newspaper or broadcaster written notice of the exact libel within six weeks after the alleged libel has come to his knowledge.[79] A libel notice is served on the newspaper much in the same fashion as a court document, and is the first clear and accurate indicator to a newspaper that there is a libel case brewing, aside from the usual rumors which tend to arise after a controversial article or report is published.

A second procedural defence open to a newspaper in most of the provinces is that the plaintiff failed to launch his court action within three months after the libel came to his knowledge, contrary to the requirement in each of the provincial statutes. This defence has seldom been the matter of court disputes, probably since the more onerous requirement of the six-week libel notice, once having been satisfied, would mean that solicitors were then involved and able to meet the three-month limitation in commencing formal proceedings with little difficulty.

Another procedural defence that is open is a newspaper defendant's application for security for costs to be posted by the plaintiff where the plaintiff is not possessed of property sufficient to answer the costs of the action in case judgment is given in favor of the defendant newspaper;[80] or where the grounds of action are trivial or frivolous;[81] or where the plaintiff was from outside the jurisdiction in which the action was commenced.[82] However, the intricacies of these defences are the province of the trial lawyer, and no useful purpose would be served by going into them in any great detail here, except to mention them.

4. *Damages*

The subject of damages is theoretically relevant only after the fact of libel has been established. However, as a practical matter, the amount of damages which a potential plaintiff can hopefully recover will most often determine whether an action will be commenced in the first place. Libel is technically an everyday occurrence in most Canadian newspapers, yet few actions are ever commenced because of the limited likelihood of the person "libelled" being able to prove substantial damages and thus make the suit worth his while.

The easiest and most practical way for a newspaper to reduce the size of damage claims for libel is to apologize—as promptly, graciously and fully as is reasonably possible. An apology does not completely exculpate a newspaper from liability however; in some cases, it might even amount to an admission of the libel. However, it does reduce the amount of damages which a potential plaintiff can claim to have suffered by reason of the libel.

Whether an apology will have the intended effect of reducing the plaintiff's damages remains a matter to be decided in each case by the trial judge and/or the jury, and will depend on the nature and effects of the original libel, the plaintiff's reputation, the promptness and effectiveness of the apology, and other surrounding circumstances such as alleged malice or negligence of the defendant. For example, in *Leonhard* v. *Sun Publishing Company*,[83] the *Vancouver Sun* had libelled Jacob Leonhard by falsely implying that he was head of an illegal drug syndicate. The *Sun* apologized fully, but Leonhard pressed on with his libel action. In defence, the *Sun* produced other newspaper clippings as evidence of Leonhard's bad reputation. Also, his examination for discovery showed evidence of a bad reputation. Therefore, because of the apology and these collateral facts, the Court was able to hold that Leonhard had no reputation capable of being injured, and nominal damages of $1 were awarded.

Generally, an apology will be more effective in cases where a plaintiff is suing for the purpose of clearing his name and reputation, as opposed to obtaining money damages as compensation. The incidence of this situation is, by some reports, remarkably high. For instance, one of the lawyers acting for the *Toronto Star*[84] in this field estimates that at least 50 per cent of the libel actions commenced against the *Star* in recent years have been to vindicate reputation rather than to obtain money damages. Of course, there is always the chance that an action starting out this way will turn into a claim for money damages as well. But the point is that apologies are more effective in the reputation cases. And the chances that a prompt apology will "nip in the bud", through satisfaction or settlement, a potential libel action involving the vindication of reputation are correspondingly greater than if money is the primary objective of the plaintiff.

On rare occasions, an apology has tended to aggravate rather than mitigate the damages. In *Brannigan* v. *Seafarers International Union of Canada*[85], a member of a rival union was falsely alleged to be a Communist in the S.I.U.'s newspaper known as *"Canadian Sailor"*. The newspaper some three months later ran an apology in which it explained how it had confused Brannigan with another man, but that Brannigan was engaging in the same type of conduct (carrying a placard in support of the policies of the Communist Party) as was the mistaken man. The Court held that the apology was simply a reiteration that the plaintiff was a Communist, and indicated a complete lack of any intention to withdraw or express regret for the original statement. Therefore, the original damage was aggravated instead of mitigated, and the S.I.U. was assessed damages of $5,000. The lesson to be learned here is that the apology must be sincere, and should not be used by a newspaper or broadcaster to subtly take another swipe at the plaintiff through the use of clever sarcasm.

Some of the libel and slander statutes in the provinces contain specific provisions limiting libel awards against newspapers or broadcasters to "actual damages" suffered by the plaintiff in certain situations. For example, section 5(2) of the Ontario Act limits recovery to actual damages if the libel was published in good faith, didn't involve a criminal charge, took place in mistake or misapprehension of the facts, and if a full and fair retraction of erroneous matters was published in the next regular issue or within three days of receipt of the libel notice, in as conspicuous a place and type as was the alleged libel.

If a newspaper cannot bring itself within specific statutory provisions such as that above so as to limit damages, then it is subject to libel awards being made against it for general damages—which include not only "actual" loss suffered, but compensation for such things as injury to feelings and reputation and loss of social status in the community.

Libel awards in reported cases in Canada have not in general been as large as those in the United States. One can thus assume that libel settlements made out of court are also not as great, since they are generally premised on lawyers' assessments of what the damages would be worth should the case go to trial. There are probably two reasons for this fact, aside from the general reluctance of Canadian juries to be as generous as their more prosperous American counterparts. One reason is the method by which court costs and lawyers' fees are determined in litigious matters in Canada. Unlike many U.S. jurisdictions where each party pays his own court costs regardless of outcome and the plaintiff's lawyer takes a fixed percentage of the award as a contingent fee, court costs of all parties to a libel action in Canada are a separate item and must be borne by the losing party, and this includes a large portion of both lawyers' fees. Thus a plaintiff receiving a sizable damage award for libel in Canada will be able to retain a much greater portion of it for himself without having to pay any court costs or large lawyer's fee (usually the allowable fee paid by the losing party will be 60 per cent to 70 per cent of the actual fee of the winner's lawyer, depending on the extent of services rendered). Most of the award therefore will accrue to the plaintiff's own benefit. In the United States, on the other hand, it is not unusual for a goodly portion of a plaintiff's libel award to be paid in costs and lawyer's fees, thus reducing substantially the portion left to the plaintiff. American juries, knowing of this fact, have set libel awards accordingly.

The other reason accounting for the difference is the practice of Canadian judges and juries with respect to awarding punitive damages. Only in extreme cases have there been damages of this type awarded in Canada, the courts preferring to maintain the primary purpose of libel awards as compensation for the injured plaintiff, not punishment to the newspaper libelling. However, in occasional cases where a newspaper has unjustifiably refused to apologize, or acted recklessly, or where the newspaper's profit from libel would be larger than the normal compensation to the victim libelled, the courts have assessed punitive damages.

In *Platt* v. *Time International of Canada Ltd.*,[86] punitive damages of $35,000 were awarded in the Supreme Court of Ontario. *Time* magazine had published in 1962 an article falsely implying that Platt, a major in the Canadian army, was a member of a dope smuggling group and that he was going to be charged in connection with such smuggling. The article was written with full knowledge that there was no suggestion that the plaintiff was in any way involved in dope trafficking. Both before and throughout the trial, the defendant displayed an attitude of defiant arrogance and persistently refused to give a proper apology. Therefore the court regarded the conduct as constituting malice in law, and imposed the punitive damages.

Then in *Morgenstern* v. *Oakville Record Star* referred to earlier,[87] in which a builder of a building destroyed by fire was libelled with respect to professional competence, the court included in its $5,000 award an amount for punitive damages because of the persistent refusal of the defendant to offer any retraction, and other circumstances suggesting malice on the part of the defendant. Thus, on the basis of these two recent cases, it would appear that the courts will award punitive damages if there is evidence of malice and the defendant refuses to apologize. However, it must be remembered that these instances of punitive damages are more the exception than the rule, as a review of all the Canadian cases will indicate.

Libel insurance is one method by which newspapers in Canada have attempted to protect themselves against large damage awards. However, the premiums for this type of insurance coverage are substantial, and most insurers will insist on a large deductible amount on the insurance contract as a deterrent to the insured newspaper engaging in libellous publishing. Thus, to this extent, the protection is somewhat limited.

An interesting case[88] recently came before the Supreme Court of Ontario regarding the right of a broadcaster against whom a libel award had been made to claim over for a contribution to damages against the news service who had supplied the libellous news information. Television station CJOH-TV in Ottawa had broadcast on December 7, 1964, two defamatory news reports that Brigadier Allan, an ex-Canadian army officer, had been criminally charged with bribery. A libel award in the amount of $58,000 was made in favor of Allan.[89] The television station then claimed over against Broadcast News Limited, a wholly-owned subsidiary of the Canadian Press corporation with whom it had a contract to receive news by means of an automatic printer service for $85.00 per week, and from whom it had received the information concerning Brigadier Allan. Mr. Justice Lieff found that Broadcast News Ltd. was in breach of its implied condition in the contract that the news it supplied would be reasonably fit for transmission to the public, since the news reports supplied were defamatory. Therefore the news service was held to have contributed to the eventual libel of Brigadier Allen to the extent of one-third, CJOH-TV being responsible for the other two-thirds resulting from their aggravation of the original defamatory news reports through editing. Thus Broadcast News Ltd. was assessed one third of the $58,000 libel award. In rendering judgment, Mr. Justice Lieff laid down the general nature of the protection which the Canadian people could expect against broadcast libel (often called, colloquially, 'defamacasts'):

> ... [T]here must be a safeguard to ensure that the television media which simultaneously reach out to people in all regions throughout Canada, broadcast accurate facts. Surely, [Broadcast News Ltd.] knew the consequences of breaching its contract, and although it is not in the position of an insurer, it must bear responsibility for its inaccuracy.[90]

This case clearly illustrates a judicial willingness to spread libel responsibility around among all the agencies collectively engaged in the investigation, gathering and dissemination of news and information, according to the extent of each agency's "participation" in the libel. No longer will the final broadcaster or publisher have to bear the sole responsibility when the misinformation originates from a prior source in the chain. And no longer can independent news services safely rely on contractual provisions exempting them from liability for libel claims made against the broadcaster or publisher arising from use of their news service, since the courts (as in the Brigadier Allan case) are more likely to regard the supplying of defamatory news as a breach of a *fundamental* term of the contract, disentitling the news service from relying on any exemption clause by virtue of the common law.

5. Criminal Libel

This offence, created under the Criminal Code, is characterized as "defamatory libel" and defined as "matter published, without lawful justification or excuse, that is likely to injure the reputation of any person by exposing him to hatred, contempt or ridicule, or that is designed to insult the person of or concerning whom it is published".[91] Defamatory libel may be expressed directly or by insinuation or irony in words or by any object (such as a cartoon) signifying a defamatory libel otherwise than by words.[92] A person guilty of publishing a defamatory libel that he knows to be false is liable to imprisonment for a maximum of five years, otherwise for a maximum of two years.[93] The proprietor of a newspaper is the one presumed responsible for a defamatory libel unless he proves that the defamatory matter was inserted in the newspaper without his knowledge and without negligence on his part. However, where he gives authority to another person to manage or conduct the newspaper as editor or otherwise, that other person generally will be presumed to be responsible.[94]

There are a number of saving provisions from defamatory libel in the Criminal Code which are tantamount to the usual defences in a civil action for libel: publishing proceedings of courts of justice;[95] publishing parliamentary papers;[96] publishing fair reports of parliamentary or judicial proceedings for public meetings;[97] publishing matters of public interest for the public benefit;[98] fair comment;[99] truth;[100] publications invited or necessary in self-defence;[101] answers to inquiries;[102] giving information to persons having a common interest,[103] and publications in good faith for the redress of wrong.[104]

In view of the fact that criminal libel tends to be duplicative of the civil remedy, thus putting newspapers in potential situations of double jeopardy of a sort, and also could be applied by the Crown in such a way as to smack of *ex post facto* censorship by the state, it is not surprising that there have been very few reported cases.

The cases in the area generally indicated that the Crown had to have very strong evidence to secure a conviction.[105] Indeed, the last reported case until recently was in 1938.[106]

However, a very recent case of criminal libel in the Supreme Court of British Columbia involving the Vancouver underground newspaper called the *Georgia Straight* has changed all this. In an article in the final edition of 1968, the editors had lampooned a number of local officials and administrators in Vancouver by satirically "presenting" them with various "dubious distinction" awards of the year. Among these awards was the "Pontius Pilate Award" which was "presented" to a Vancouver magistrate for convicting a resident hippie for loitering in or near a government building under a law which the magistrate himself had admitted was unfair but which he said he was bound to apply. The newspaper and its two editors were charged and convicted of defamatory libel and fined $1,000 and $250 each, respectively. It was not reported whether the magistrate commenced a civil action for libel, or whether there was an attempt to cite the newspaper and its editors for contempt for scandalizing the Court. However it is significant that the newspaper and its editors, about the same time as the charge and conviction of defamatory libel, were also charged and convicted of obscenity under the Criminal Code for other satirical pieces in which public figures such as the President of the United States had been depicted nude with their sexual organs in full view. This same newspaper had been deprived of its business license by the City's Chief License Inspector approximately one year earlier for "gross misconduct in or with respect to the licensed premises" in that the newspaper had been offered for sale and sold to children at the city schools.

Quite clearly, the charge of defamatory libel was just another in a series of legal devices being invoked by law enforcement officials in Vancouver to bring pressure to bear on the *Georgia Straight* in the ongoing "war" between the hippies and the city fathers. However, the Court was undoubtedly cognizant of this fact yet still chose to convict, not necessarily to vindicate the reputation of the particular magistrate involved (he had his civil remedy), but to punish conduct which tended to encourage disrespect for the law and legal institutions and officials. There was no suggestion here that the impugned article tended to provoke a breach of the peace (a requirement that had commonly been regarded as an essential condition of the offence during its lengthy period of disuse). One can only question then why the prosecution here chose to resurrect the dormant criminal offence of defamatory libel when a more usual contempt citation might have accomplished the same thing, unless of course it was a conscious attempt by the prosecution to publicly emphasize the seriousness of the matter so as to deter future publications of this sort by the *Georgia Straight* and other similar newspapers. In any event, the criminal offence of defamatory libel has been reactivated in a provincial Supreme Court decision, and Canadian newspapers are no longer in a position to ignore its possible invocation in serious cases. Whether the *Georgia Straight* conviction will result in demands to repeal the offence from the Criminal Code remains a matter of pure speculation at this point, although to the writer it does seem rather unnecessary to retain an offence which virtually duplicates the civil remedy and at the same time can supplement or substitute for the contempt sanction in certain situations.

CONCLUSION

In terms of governmental restrictions on the press, control of the press in the administration of justice and, to a lesser extent, the civil remedy of libel, the law of the press in Canada is now at a crossroads. In the past, the tendency has been to regard these areas as relatively uncertain, with most analyses being done on a case by case basis. In the courts, a heavy reliance has been placed on English cases and treatises as persuasive authorities, and U.S. precedents have largely been ignored, notwithstanding that the nature of the Canadian newspaper and broadcasting industry is probably much more similar to its American counterpart.

But now there are indicators that the government is not content to allow this area of the law to be determined by common law alone. Already most of the provinces have passed libel and slander legislation providing a much clearer delineation of the rules relating to newspapers and broadcasters. Legislative proposals for control of the press in the various aspects of the administration of justice are being made with increasing frequency in a number of quarters, and perhaps in the near future, there might be an attempt to codify the law of contempt as it applies to newspapers and broadcasters. And with the distinct possibility of a Bill of Rights being entrenched in the Canadian constitution within the next few years, the heretofore esoteric notion of "freedom of the press" as a legal right will become much more certain, at least in terms of its application by the courts.

But where does all this lead us? If members of the press are to come to rely solely on specific detailed statutory enactments for the source of the law of the press in Canada, aren't they losing something in terms of flexibility, autonomy and self-respect? Perhaps the growing interest of government in codifying the law and in controlling the press to a greater degree is based on the observation that not all facets of the press in Canada have exhibited a willingness to police their own interests to the fullest extent necessary.

E.L. Donegan, one of the counsel to the *Toronto Star,* reports that his newspaper attempts to police itself against libel and contempt by use of a rotating inspection system involving ten lawyers who take turns checking questionable news reports and articles in advance of printing and publication. This system is undoubtedly very expensive and probably could not be justified financially on this scale by a smaller newspaper. But the point is that the need for preventative inspection is clearly recognized and there is a conscious attempt to meet the uncertainties of contempt and libel through the use of legal experts in advance. Surely this is an approach which members of the press could adopt in varying degrees, not only to stem the tide of increasing government control through threats, investigations and codification, but to allow a certain amount of flexibility safely within the confines of the existing law. A more sophisticated manifestation of this approach might be inspection in advance carried out by legal officials or agents of a voluntary press council whose powers would be decided jointly by a broad representation of the press in each province or region, without any direct interference by government.

One thing is clear: the press in Canada by its own actions (or lack thereof) will determine where the law of the press goes from the crossroads. Regular inspection in advance is one of the practices that might hopefully become more widespread. And of course, the press itself will have to work out the problem of increasing concentration of ownership; otherwise the government will do it for them. The next decade will tell whether the press is equal to the challenge of deciding its own legal fate.

NOTES TO CHAPTER EIGHT

Since the first section of the original article has been omitted, the footnotes for this narrative begin at number 16.—Editor

16/*Criminal Code* Stats. Can. 1953-54, c. 51, s. 8.

17/*Roach* v. *Garvan,* [1742] 2 Atk. 469 (Chancery).

18/*In Re Campbell and Cowper,* [1934] 3 W.W.R. 593 (Alta.); see also *Hatfield* v. *Healy* (1911) 18 W.L.R. 512 (Alta.)

19/E.g., *Staples* v. *Isaacs and Harris,* [1939] 4 D.L.R. 556 (B.C.); *R.* v. *Bonnar,* (1903) 14 Man. R. 481; *In Re North Renfrew Election,* (1904) 9 O.L.R. 79 (C.A.); *Guest* v. *Knowles,* (1908) 17 O.L.R. 416; *Meriden Britannia Co.* v. *Walters,* (1915) 34 O.L.R. 518.

20/*Vine Products Ltd.* v. *Green* [1965] 2 W.L.R. 791.

21/*R.* v. *Glanzer,* [1963] 2 O.R. 30.

22/*R.* v. *Western Printing and Publishing Ltd.,* (1954) 34 M.P.R. 129.

23/*R.* v. *The Vancouver Province, sub nom. Re Nicol,* [1954] 3 D.L.R. 690.

24/See ZIEGEL, *Some Aspects of the Law of Contempt of Court in Canada, England and the United States,* 6 McGill L.J. 229 (1960).

25/*R.* v. *Larose,* [1965] Que. S.C. 318.

26/*Hébert* v. *A.-G. Quebec,* [1966] Que. Q.B. 197.

27/*Cie de Publication La Presse Ltée* v. *Simard,* [1962] Que. Q.B. 697.

28/*Ambard* v. *A.-G. Trinidad and Tobago,* [1963] A.C. 322.

29/See WATKINS, *The Enforcement of Conformity to Law Through Contempt Proceedings,* 5 Osgoode Hall L.J. 125, 145 (1967).

30/*Fortin* v. *Moscarella* (1957) 23 W.W.R. 91, 94.

31/*Steiner* v. *Toronto Star Ltd.,* [1956] O.R. 14.

32/*R.* v. *Bryan,* [1954] O.R. 255.

33/*R.* v. *Robinson & Co., R.* v. *Nfld. Broadcasting* (1954) 34 M.P.R. 257.

34/*R.* v. *Hamilton Spectator* [1966] 2 O.R. 503; *A.-G. Manitoba* v. *Winnipeg Free Press* (1965) 52 W.W.R. 129.

35/*R.* v. *Thibodeau; Re Saint John Telegraph-Journal* (1955) 23 C.R. 285.

36/*Re Depoe and Lamport* (1968) 66 D.L.R. (2d) 46.

37/*Re Editions Maclean and Fulford; R.* v. *Dion* [1965] 4 C.C.C. 318 (Que. C.A.).

38/See FREEDMAN, *Fair Trial-Freedom of the Press,* 3 Osgoode Hall L.J. 52, fn. 42 (1964).

39/See *supra,* note 35.

40/See MCRUER, *Criminal Contempt of Court Procedure* 30 Can. B. Rev. 225 (1952).

41/See *In Re O'Brien* (1899) 16 S.C.R. 197.

42/E.g., FREEDMAN, *supra* note 38 at 74, 75; Watkins, *supra* note 29 at 143; and Wright, *Newspapers and Criminal Trials,* 17 Can. B. Rev. 191 (1939).

43/*Bill C-150,* First Session 28th Parliament, 1968 (First Reading, December 19, 1968) Section 452A.

44/*Royal Commission Inquiry Into Civil Rights (Ontario),* Report No. 1, Volume 2, p. 769 (Honourable J.C. McRuer, Commissioner). (1968).

45/*Collision Course: Free Press and the Courts* 22-33 (Parker ed. 1966); A Symposium of lawyers and journalists at Osgoode Hall Law School.

46/*Criminal Code,* Stats. Can. 1953-54, c. 51, s. 9(2) (3).

47/*Id.,* s. 9(1).

48/See the recent case of *Regina* v. *Shumiatcher* (1967) 64 D.L.R. (2d) 24 (Sask.) for an example of summary contempt proceedings against a lawyer for tactics employed in defending an accused in a criminal case. The omnipotent power of a judge in exercising such a power is very apparent in this example.

49/See *supra,* note 35.

50/See *supra,* note 37.

51/R.S.C. 1952, c. 160.

52/*R.* v. *Truscott* [1959] O.W.N. 320.

53/*Reference Re Regina* v. *Truscott* (1967) 62 D.L.R. (2d) 545.

54/See Wright, *The Open Court: The Hallmark of Judicial Proceedings,* 25 Can. B. Rev. 721 (1947).

55/*Re Spence* (1962) 37 W.W.R. 481.

56/The Toronto *Globe and Mail,* February 25, 1969.

57/See generally *supra,* note 54.

58/*Scott* v. *Sampson* (1882), 8 Q.B.D. 503.

59/*Van Baggen* v. *Nichol* (1963), 38 D.L.R. (2d) 654.

60/Unreported judgment of Stark, J. on a jury verdict in favor of Gouzenko.

61/See *Lefolii* v. *Gouzenko,* (1968), 70 D.L.R. (2d) 337 (S.C.C.); affirming, in part (1967), 63 D.L.R. (2d) 217.

62/See Stark, *Newspaper and the Law of Libel,* 24 Can. B. Rev. 869 (1946).

63/R.S.O. 1960, c. 211.

64/*Morgenstern* v. *Oakville Record Star* [1962] O.R. 638.

65/See Part I, note 23.

66/*Dennison* v. *Sanderson* [1946] O.R. 601.

67/*Slim* v. *Daily Telegraph Ltd.* (1968) 1 All E.R. 497, at 503.

68/See *McConachy* v. *Times Publishers Ltd.* (1964) 49 D.L.R. (2d) 349 (B.C.C.A.); *Price* v. *Richmond Review* (1965) 54 W.W.R. 378 (B.C.); *Wismer* v. *Maclean-Hunter Publishing Co. and Fraser* (No. 2) (1954) 1 D.L.R. 481; *contra, Reid* v. *Telegram Publishing Co.* [1961] O.R. 418.

69/*Supra* note 6.

70/*Id.*

71/But see, for example the case of *Mack* v. *North Hill News Ltd.* (1964) 44 D.L.R. (2d) 147 (Alta.) in which it was held that the publication of pleadings *before* the trial (and not "*contemporaneously* with such proceedings") was libellous.

72/Again, the Ontario *Libel and Slander Act, supra,* note 63, is the most convenient model, and is perhaps the most important of all the provincial acts because of the greater number of sizable newspapers in that province as compared with any other single Canadian province.

73/*Id.,* s. 3(1).

74/*Id.,* s. 3(2).

75/*Id.,* s. 3(3).

76/*Id.,* s. 3(4).

77/See STARK, *Newspapers and the Law of Libel,* 24 Can. B. Rev. 861, 875 (1946).

78/*Banks* v. *The Globe and Mail Limited and Dalgleish* [1961] S.C.R. 474.

79/As an example of a case in which this procedural defence was applied, see *Leslie* v. *The Telegram Publishing Company Limited* [1955] O.W.N. 122; affirmed [1956] S.C.R. 871.

80/See, for example, *Oshanek* v. *Toronto Daily Star,* [1966] 1 O.R. 492.

81/See *New Era Home Appliances Ltd.* v. *Toronto Star Ltd.* [1963] 1 O.R. 339.

82/See *Sorokin Trail Times Ltd.* (1960) 33 W.W.R. 414.

83/(1956) 19 W.W.R. 415; 4 D.L.R. (2d) 514.

84/E.L. Donegan esq., of the firm of Blake, Cassels and Graydon, Toronto.

85/(1963) 42 D.L.R. (2d) 249.

86/(1964) 44 D.L.R. (2d) 17; affirmed, 48 D.L.R. (2d) 508n.

87/*Supra,* note 64.

88/*Allan* v. *Bushnell T.V. Co. Ltd; Broadcast News Ltd., Third Party.* (1969) 1 D.L.R. (3d) 534.

89/See (1968) 67 D.L.R. (2d) 499.

90/*Supra* note 46 at 548.

91/*Criminal Code.* Stats. Can. 1953-54, c. 51, s. 248(1).

92/*Id.,* s. 248(2).

93/*Id.,* ss. 250, 251.

94/*Id.,* s. 253.

95/*Id.,* s. 255.

96/*Id.,* s. 256.

97/*Id.,* ss. 257, 258.

98/*Id.,* s. 259.

99/*Id.,* s. 260.

100/*Id.,* s. 261.

101/*Id.,* s. 262.

102/*Id.,* s. 263.

103/*Id.,* s. 264.

104/*Id.,* s. 265.

105/See *R.* v. *Cameron,* 2 C.C.C. 173; and *Stone* v. *Newspaper World Co.,* (1918) 4 O.L.R. 33.

106/*R.* v. *Unwin* [1938] 1 D.L.R. 529; *R.* v. *Powell* [1938] 1 D.L.R. 535.

chapter nine

The Sovereignty of the Publicity System: A Case Study of the Alberta Press Act

G. STUART ADAM

Tension between journalist and politician arises naturally out of the absolute and reciprocal dependency of their relationship. To put it crudely, the politician needs the journalist, preferably a friendly one, to circulate his name and ruminations; the journalist needs the politician, as fodder for his enterprise. Political life breeds journalism; journalism breeds political life.

In a society such as Canada in which liberal theory is used to rationalize the social and political arrangements, the relationship between the journalist and the politician has special properties which nurture this tension. For one thing, the rights and privileges of the journalist (or his collaborators and managers) are defined in the common law and constitutional traditions in such a way that the journalist is unlikely to run into official sanctions for political writing that is embarrassing or objectionable to authorities.[1] The tension arises from a situation in which the journalist rather than the politician or emissary of the state decides what will be conveyed as political information. In such a society political life operates within an environment of uncertainty and indeterminacy created by a system of publicity[2] which is independent, or, one could even say, sovereign.

At the same time, the set of attitudes common to most journalists is such that adversary behavior is regarded as virtuous. Material that is perceived to be objectionable, however innocuous it is in fact, operates as an assurance that the sovereign rights of the system are operating. In the charters of his craft, the journalist sees himself as the agent of the sovereign people, as an exemplary democrat who scans the processes of government and politics as a member of the public accounts committee scans spending habits or the opposition surveys the claims of the government. He believes with some force in the legitimacy of his adversary role through which he acts as a custodian of civic virtue against the natural tendency of those in power to deceive or manipulate.[3]

C.V. Ferguson, in his biographical sketch of J.W. Dafoe, provided an insight into one way in which this adversary quality can express itself. He wrote of Dafoe's attitude to the Tories when the Liberals were in oppositon:

> He could hit out freely at the largest target any country has to offer:
> its government. The enemy was in possession of the fortress. Very
> well. It became, then, the carefree duty of an opposition editor to
> spend happy years in harassing action.[4]

In the conventional press, the harassment may not be obvious, at least
not as obvious as it is in the partisan writing of Dafoe or in the contemporary muckraking one finds in those journals the Davey Committee called
somewhat glibly the Volkswagen press.[5] Sometimes, as implied above, the
harassment is illusory—a simple function of the indeterminacy that arises
out of the division of political labor. In either case, the thrust of the common
law and constitutional traditions in Anglo-Saxon democracies is to institu-
tionalize rather than dissolve the tension that is endemic to the relationship,
and there has been an official willingness to live with the vagaries of the
free press.

But deviations from this tradition—cases in which governments attempt
to redefine the relationship—occur from time to time. One such deviation
occurred in Canada in 1937[6] when the Alberta government of William
Aberhart passed "An Act to Ensure the Publication of Accurate News and
Information".[7]

In the 1935 election, the Social Credit Party in Alberta, rising on the
ruins of the United Farmers of Alberta which had been in power since 1921,
swept into office by winning 56 of the 63 seats. Their victory has been
discussed elsewhere, as has their plan for political and economic reconstruction.[8] For now it will suffice to note that they brought with them an elaborate ideology which promised to restore sovereignty and material well-being
to a people who blamed their powerlessness and material privations in the
Depression on eastern "financial wizards" and their collaborators.

Their plans materialized in a series of bills which, when judged by conventional standards and the habits of the past, seemed bizarre. Most of this
legislation was aimed at repairing the economic system. The spectacle of
this bizarre legislation and the somewhat unorthodox rhetoric and behavior
of the Premier and his colleagues caused the provincial dailies to attack the
government with extraordinary zeal.

After two years of this harassing, the government acted retributively by
passing the Press Act, the object of which was to provide the government
with the power to silence the journalists and the people on whom they were
relying for information. It aimed further at providing the government with
the power to place in the newspapers "rewrites" of stories the government
felt had misrepresented their policies or goals. Thus, the terms of the press-
government (journalist-politician) relationship were redefined in the face

of an apparent Canadian tradition of freedom of the press to provide the provincial government with greater control over the publicity system.

As noted above, the act was a retributive action against the press by a man who had been thoroughly harassed. Had he been a thoroughgoing liberal on the subject of press freedom, Aberhart no doubt would have wished it, if not legislated it, into a more subservient role. But in addition, his theoretical view of society and politics, derived from Social Credit principles, justified an action against the press; and, further, he accepted the political strategy of his English adviser, Major C.H. Douglas, who was the founder of Social Credit. Major Douglas had argued as early as 1934 that political victory must be accompanied with the establishment of a news circulating system under the province's "unchallengeable control".[9]

The Press Act, then, was tied closely to the Social Credit ideology and a clearly-stated propaganda strategy.

For all the furor it caused, the Press Act was never enforced. It was reserved by the Lieutenant-Governor of Alberta and subsequently sent by the federal government to the Supreme Court on reference to determine whether the provincial government was acting *intra vires.* It wasn't. At least that was the opinion of the Supreme Court justices. The Bill was disallowed.

Accordingly, the effect of the Press Act was to test in Canada the principle of the publicity system's sovereignty. Needless to say, that principle was vindicated. The case in the Supreme Court led to an elaborate statement on the relationship between democratic life and a free press, giving us a touchstone, if not a first amendment, on the immunity of the press from government control.

What follows, then, is an attempt to trace the story of the Press Act from its source in the relationship between the political journalists of Alberta and William Aberhart to the Supreme Court's ruling.

As a methodological note, *The Edmonton Journal* for 1935–38, has served as the main source for the narrative.[10] It was the government's major critic and a special object of the government's vindictiveness. It led the fight against Aberhart in the courts of public opinion and the judiciary. For its editorial performance it was awarded a Pulitzer Prize. In the Supreme Court, it and its friends had their day and won.

I

A preview of the tension that was to develop between Aberhart and *The Edmonton Journal* was contained in the Conservative *Journal's* pre-election editorials. Mixing appeals to common sense with scare tactics, *The Journal* warned against any purchase of Aberhart's ideas.

Why . . . should any Alberta farmer think for a moment that Mr. Aberhart can assure him a "just price" in his wheat? The only hope of his obtaining a price that will give him a decent return for his efforts is through increased world demand or through support that the dominion is to continue to give the market . . . (July 8, 1935, p. 4).

Similarly, when the Calgary Board of Trade announced its opposition to Social Credit in a six-point statement which was published two weeks before the election, *The Journal* commented:

It is a straight appeal to the intelligence of the citizens that the chamber has made. . . . An organization that has given the public such good service over a long period of years and has at all times manifested so high a sense of its responsibility deserves to have the closest attention paid by every elector to the warning that it has issued. (Aug. 8, 1935, p. 4.)

Furthermore, playing on the same depression fears that Aberhart was exploiting, *The Journal* tried to ensure that the common sense it proclaimed would not be smothered by extravagant hopes. In a front-page editorial just seven days before the election, it wrote:

The Journal knows that one commercial house has already made preparations to move, bag and baggage, to a neighbouring province . . . . Think what will happen to the employees of this firm.
The Journal knows that one big firm is ready and anxious to open up for business in Alberta, is waiting until election day is over before going on with its plan . . . .
The Journal knows that men and women who have money lying idle in Alberta are waiting for election day to decide whether they will put that money to work here, or will take it away to some other province . . . .
The Journal knows that Alberta would have been enjoying a mild building boom right now if it had not been for the threat of Social Credit . . . . Things will indeed be worse. Much worse—if Social Credit carries next Thursday. And it is not the rich who will suffer most. Many of them will pack up and get out.

After Aberhart won the election, *The Journal,* resigned to a full term of Social Credit government, seemed willing to give the new Premier a reprieve:

> Even those who were most doubtful of their [the theories'] soundness should be prepared to give Mr. Aberhart every opportunity to justify the striking tribute of confidence that he has received at the hands of his fellow citizens. (Aug. 23, 1935, p. 4.)

But the reprieve was short-lived, as almost every move of Aberhart's and his government confirmed *The Journal's* pre-election suspicions. Almost immediately it launched its attacks on the government. For example, when a civil servant was fired in October, *The Journal* reprimanded the Premier for rejecting demands for an explanation on the grounds that it was "not a matter for public information". "The people of the province have always considered themselves entitled to information of this kind," said *The Journal,* "and to withhold it from them is wholly out of keeping with democratic practice." (Oct. 23, 1935, p. 4.)

In scalping material from other publications on Social Credit, the editors were careful to see that they discredited the Premier. One such article was introduced this way: "Roger Babson, noted U.S. economic expert, herewith presents first published opinion of Social Credit". (Nov. 1, 1935, p. 1.) In summary, Babson said that Social Credit was ridiculous. Another, by "an associate editor" of *Collier's* magazine, was entitled "Milk and Honey Ltd. or Another Paradise Lost". *The Journal* featured this article on page 1 of the January 17, 1936, edition:

> ... The Social Credit party was voted into power by a poverty-stricken electorate which is still wondering what Social Credit means. It is highly unlikely they are going to find out .... In these days of vaudeville economics and camp-meeting sociology, it has been given to Mr. Aberhart to demonstrate the something-for-nothing theory. He is the first prophet of any of the endless chain of non-Marxian share-the-wealth ballyhoos to have been taken at his word by a people and told to go to it ....

These and other criticisms of the government, whether of a general nature or directed at specific actions of the Premier and his government, continued for two years after the election. The catalogue of misdemeanors recorded by *The Journal* with elaborate comment included the suggested retail codes, the stamped script, the denials by Aberhart that he had made a promise during the election campaign to pay $25 monthly to Alberta citizens, the covenant with which the government tried to bind Albertans to the use of "funny money", and the default of Alberta bond payments.

In July 1936, almost a year after Aberhart had assumed office, *The Journal* summed up its view of the Social Credit government:

One thing that is claimed for the present Alberta government will not be disputed. It is, as its supporters have pointed out, making history. Never before under democratic institutions has so much been done that is so altogether out of keeping with those [institutions]. The aberrations during the past year in this province from what has hitherto been regarded as proper constitutional practice will doubtless receive plenty of attention from the historians. (July 30, 1936, p. 4.)

By the fall of 1937, when the Social Credit government was locked in its celebrated struggle with the federal government over the power of disallowance, Aberhart's policies and his approach to governance were compared by *The Journal* to "Hitlerism". It was a strong term but it symbolized the intense hostility that the adversary newspaper felt for its opponent in government. With such passion in the air, there was a certain inevitability that a counterattack would be launched. It came in the fall of 1937 in the form of the "Act to Ensure the Publication of Accurate News and Information". But before examining the bill, it is useful to trace the development of Aberhart's press policy.

II

At first, Aberhart equivocated in his references to the press. As a politician he no doubt accepted the fact that as long as the traditional arrangement of press control was maintained its special animosity would be damaging. Besides, his press policy would require time to take shape in the conditions of office. But from the start, he reflected a readiness to suspend the publicity system's sovereignty.

His first public statement on the press occurred only seven days after he was elected. In his statement Aberhart first denied any intention of entering the daily publishing field in Alberta as long as the "existing dailies" told the truth, gave people the facts and refrained from circulating "false and misleading propaganda". He continued:

If the newspapers co-operate with us, there will be no need of entering that field. All we ask is that the newspapers print the truth and the whole truth and not spread lies. I think you fellows are in the same position as the banks. We trust you will not try to hinder our attempts to give the people the facts and let them judge. I don't think you have any right to spread lies. (Aug. 29, 1935, p. 9.)

Aberhart could not have been completely sincere. Four and a half months later, *The Journal* reported the "sale of *The Calgary Albertan* in a deal by which the paper [was] merged with the Social Credit Chronicle to become the organ of the Social Credit Party". (Jan. 15, 1936, p. 1.) The deal included radio station CJCN. Aberhart said, "The sale of *The Albertan* doesn't involve the provincial government", but he qualified this by adding that it was his intention to work with it, and with other papers ". . . as long as other papers treat us fairly".

The testimony of a member of his cabinet, Solon Low, further suggests that Aberhart had not been sincere and that the policy of invading the communications field had been considered from the very outset. Low stated publicly in March that the Social Credit government had undertaken to follow a strategy suggested by Major Douglas. He said:

> Major Douglas asked that we have a paper and a radio. We have them and I submit that these are two very important things done by this government in its program of implementing pledges. (March 5, 1936.)

As the strategist and philosopher of the movement, Douglas had made his position on the media explicit at least once. He had been in Alberta during 1934 to testify on his economic theories before one of the provincial legislature's standing committees. Impressed by what he had heard, Premier Reid asked Douglas to accept a position with the Alberta government as "chief reconstruction adviser".[11] Douglas accepted, and in May 1935 he submitted his "First Interim Report on the Possibilities of the Application of Social Credit Principles to the Province of Alberta".[12]

In this report Douglas characterized the press as an agent of orthodox finance, and therefore as a natural enemy of the new order. But he also realized it was a powerful instrument for propaganda. Thus he wrote: "The practical importance of this in regard to Alberta is that vindictive action by the financial authorities could be pilloried through the agency of the press and broadcasting".[13]

He advised, therefore, that a preparatory step to be taken prior to the implementation of Social Credit should be the "systematic provision of a news circulating system under the unchallengeable control of the province, particlarly in regard to radio facilities, of sufficient power to cover a wide geographical area".[14]

As noted above, Aberhart on his part first denied that the government would enter the communications field as long as a condition was met, that is, as long as "the newspapers co-operate with us . . . print the truth . . . do not spread lies".

The fact is that, whatever Aberhart was hoping for when he made the statement, the newspapers were not likely to meet his condition. They had been stubbornly opposed to him from the day he entered politics. Accordingly, the necessity for implementing the Douglas press policy became increasingly apparent.

To gain support for the press policy he appealed directly to the people as he had done during the election campaign and subsequently as premier through his weekly religious broadcasts from his own Prophetic Bible Institute in Calgary. In January 1936 he told a radio audience that the "press was becoming a nuisance. The people of the world are beginning to realize they have to control and own their own press", and he warned that there was a possibility that he would have to do "something severe in the next few weeks. I am not sour or sore. I might have to do something severe". (Jan. 7, 1936, p. 1.) This was just prior to the purchase of *The Albertan.*

That was the beginning. The press fought back, writing editorial after editorial about the implications of press control. But Aberhart persisted, trying to rally the "people" behind him. In April 1936 he told them "it is of the utmost importance to keep free the channels of true information". Behind the press slurs, he argued, was the "iron hand behind the scene", the forces of orthodox finance. (April 28, 1936, p. 1.)

A page 1 news story in *The Edmonton Journal* on June 1, 1936, contained perhaps the most complete summary of the Premier's attitude toward the press. The lead read as follows:

> Licensing of newspapers as a governmental regulation in an effort to compel publishing of "uncoloured" and accurate news stories was advocated by Premier Aberhart when he addressed the Edmonton Prophetic Bible conference in the Strand Theatre Sunday.

In the story, Aberhart was reported to have attacked the handling of news by "the so-called free press". He said "they [the reporters and publishers] heed the dictates of the money barons", and licensing, therefore, was the only way "the people" would get accurate news accounts. Grocers, butchers and motorists are licensed, why not newspapers? he asked. He went on to complain that the daily press had pictured him as a man who didn't know what he wanted or what he was doing and that he was destined to wreck the country. He continued:

> One fact that I am always glad to remember is that people are beginning to recognize the voice of finance and therefore, these poor puppets and henchmen are unable to spread the confusion and alarm that they are trying to spread. Up to the present, the money barons have been able to hire numbers of poor benighted souls who deliberately undertake to confuse and double-cross their fellows in order that

economic slavery of mankind should continue. How despicable it all is. Thus it is that 100 money barons can control 10,000,000 people and crush them into the ground. Too many of the enslaved are willing to sell out. Thank God the common people are awakening to the racket and are refusing to accept money bribes to betray their fellows. (June 1, 1936, p. 1.)

Such was the rhetoric of Aberhart's campaign against the press. But the critical period in the conception and development of the press bill would not come until well into 1937 when a formal relationship between the government and Major Douglas had been established.

Although members of the cabinet, such as Solon Low, had maintained contact with Douglas in England after the election, Aberhart and Douglas had had a falling out over what Douglas considered to be Aberhart's whimsical interpretation and implementation of Social Credit theory. It was not until the spring of 1937 that the rift was healed and communication restored. With this restored communication and camaraderie came the appointment of the Social Credit Board which was composed of Douglas-trained experts whose special competence in Social Credit theory would enable them to "engineer" the new order. It was through this board that Douglas's influence over Aberhart and his government was secured and it was through its maneuverings that there emerged the bizarre legislation of 1937, including the Alberta Press Act.

On August 6, just as the legislature was prorogued, the Lieutenant-Governor, Hon. J.C. Bowen, assented to three bills passed during the four-day summer session. The bills—The Credit of Alberta Regulation Act, the Bank Employees Civil Rights Act, and an Act to Amend the Judicature Act—were aimed at controlling banking in the province according to Social Credit principles.[15] As the federal government studied the bills, Prime Minister Mackenzie King telegraphed Aberhart to tell him that they were being considered for disallowance. He suggested that in order to avoid the embarrassment of disallowance the bills could be referred to the Supreme Court if Aberhart would, in the meantime, suspend them. Aberhart refused. As events confirmed, the threat was in earnest, and on August 17, on the recommendation of Justice Minister Lapointe, the three acts were disallowed on the grounds that they interfered "with the operation of Dominion laws".[16]

Aberhart's reaction to this rebuff was to reject federal law as not having any meaning in Alberta, since, as he liked to say, "the people" were a higher court. But as a matter of strategy, he introduced a new set of bills aimed at meeting federal objections. Aberhart summoned the legislature to meet on September 24, in order to introduce Bills seven, eight and nine. Bills seven and eight amended the intent of the first three bills by devices such as the substitution of "credit institution" for the word "bank", and by proclaiming that they were not to be "so construed as to authorise the doing of any act or thing which is not within the legislative competence . . . of the Province".[17] Bill nine was the Press Act.

Emotions were running high in the days just prior to the official announcement. More than a year of threats had made the press attentive to its fate. But the event that signalled an impending frontal attack and demonstrated unequivocally that Douglas was engaged as a latter-day Rasputin, came in mid-August, a month and a half before its introduction to the legislature.

To recall, it was in the first week of August that the banking legislation was passed. Before Douglas knew that the federal government had disallowed the legislation—Lapointe's memorandum was issued on August 17—he cabled the Alberta government: "Great Work. Rush appointment Bank directors. Pass Press Act". The cable came on August 15. It was too late to act on Douglas's directive because the legislature had been prorogued. But the beans had been spilled and the "Mail Order Government" exposed.[18]

As noted earlier, Aberhart summoned the legislature to introduce his substitute bills on September 24. On October 1, the press was on the agenda as the provincial secretary, Solon Low, introduced Bill nine, "An Act to Ensure the Publication of Accurate News and Information" to the provincial legislature.

III

To the newspapermen of Alberta, the terms of the bill were drastic. As *The Edmonton Journal* pointed out, it made the chairman of the Social Credit Board a sort of "Super Editor" over the provincial newspapers by granting him the power to force any journal—daily, weekly or monthly—to publish any statement furnished by him relating to:

a) the objects of any policies of the Government of the province;
b) the means being taken or intended to be taken by the government for the purpose of attaining such objects; and
c) the circumstances, matters and things which hinder or make difficult the achievement of any such objects.[19]

With respect to the space the chairman would demand, the Act stated:

The length of any statement required to be published shall not exceed the length of the statement corrected thereby and such statements shall be given the same prominence as to position, type and space as the statement corrected thereby.

It furthermore provided the government with the power to "pillory" individuals and groups, as Douglas had counseled, without at the same time making the newspapers guilty of libel. It read:

No action for libel shall be maintainable on account of the publication of any statement pursuant to this act against any person who is the proprietor, editor, publisher, manager or printer of the newspaper publishing the same or against any employee or any such person or against any person on account of any subsequent publication or any such statement.

Section 4 of the act was aimed at eliminating "dishonest" writers and news sources. It required publishers to furnish the Social Credit Board chairman with the names of individuals who provided information on which news stories were based and with the names of editors, editorial writers and reporters who participated in the preparation of any objectionable story. These names and sources had to be provided within 24 hours of their being requested and the requests could occur at any time within sixty days of a cited edition. With this provision went the right to shut down newspapers which failed to toe the line:

In case the proprietor, editor, publisher or manager of a newspaper has been guilty of any contravention of any of the provisions of this Act the Lieutenant-Governor-In-Council upon the recommendation of the Chairman, may order prohibited:
a) the publication of such newspaper either for a definite time or until further order;
b) the publication in any newspaper of anything written by any person specified in the order;
c) the publication of any information emanating from any person or source specified in the order.

Finally, anyone who contravened any provision of the Act or defaulted in complying with its requirements would be liable to a $500 fine, except in instances where a newspaper or newspaperman:

a) contravened an order-in-council suspending publication;

b) permitted a barred writer to write; or

c) accepted information from a barred source.

The penalty for the last three contraventions was $1,000.

The third and final reading of the bill occurred on Monday, October 4. After a four-hour debate during which there were several bitter exchanges between members of the opposition and the government, a vote was taken on a formal division and the bill passed 44-10. One "semi-independent Social Credit-er" voted with the nine opposition members, which included four Liberals, two Conservatives and three Independents.

The debate is of limited interest here. Much of what was said by the opposition members merely echoed the sentiments of the newspapers as they had been reflected in a statement which appeared in *The Journal* on Friday, and in the editorials and news stories on the subject during the past two years. On the government side, there was simply a restatement of the position Aberhart had been maintaining in his speeches.

Aberhart did not participate directly in the debate. The bill was defended mainly by the provincial secretary, Low, whose cabinet post made him responsible for the legislation, and by Edith Gostick, an M.L.A. who had been close to Aberhart throughout his political career.

Low, the first speaker, told the legislature that the bill was in no way intended to muzzle the press and he was sure, furthermore, the provisions would cease to be offensive to publishers once they understood what they were all about. He denied that the Act was in any way undemocratic:

> It has been definitely known that the press were enjoying, not just a freedom, but a so-called freedom that is much in the nature of license, untramelled or unfettered, and I cannot see that this bill will in any way restrict them at all. (Oct. 5, 1937, p. 6.)

Low's *rationale* for his views was related to his Social Credit concept of truth which he believed the "so-called" free press had been irresponsibly ignoring. But the idea was better expressed by Mrs. Gostick who started her speech with the following statement:

> I am opposed to censorship of the press, I believe in free press and free speech and value very highly those qualities and am determined to guard them. Because I am in favour of a free press, I am going to support this bill. I think a free press should publish the truth. We hear that old cry of freedom of the press and we have no such thing today as a free press and there never has been. Our opponents are talking about our controlling the press. I want to tell you sir, it is

generally understood that the press is largely controlled by the financial interests. What do we mean by freedom of the press? Freedom for whom? Freedom for the class who profit through the press or freedom for the people? (Oct. 5, 1937, p. 6.)

Mrs. Gostick went on to elaborate on the now familiar theme of the relationship between the financial interests and the newspaper hacks who acted as flunkies for them. In sum, Mrs. Gostick and the government for whom she spoke believed that they were merely relieving the press from the sinister and manipulative grasp of the money barons. This meant investing that control in a more trustworthy group—the members of the government who expressed the will of the people and the Social Credit Board who "engineered" it. This, Mrs. Gostick sincerely believed, would emancipate the press, making it truly free.

IV

It is constitutional practice in Canada that legislative or parliamentary acts do not become law until they have received royal assent. In the provinces, this ritual completion of government business is carried out by the Lieutenant-Governor, whose status in the province is similar to that of the Governor General at the federal level. As a matter of custom, the royal assent is a rubber-stamp process. Yet in law, the Crown, acting through the Lieutenant-Governor, can exercise certain prerogatives. The Lieutenant-Governor can withhold his consent, or he can reserve the bills for the "signification of the Governor General's pleasure".[20] The latter alternative is a device of federalism relating to the question of disallowance or, as it will be shown, referral to the Supreme Court. It is aimed at preventing provinces from encroaching on jurisdictions and prerogatives of the federal or the Imperial government.

Bearing in mind the fate of the three Social Credit bills which were disallowed in August, it is understandable that the Lieutenant-Governor of Alberta, when confronted with the three new bills, had some reservations (so to speak). Still, it was inconceivable to Aberhart and a surprise to everyone else that on October 5, the day after the debate, Lieutenant-Governor Bowen reserved the bills for the "signification of the Governor-General's pleasure". As far as is known, Bowen had not been in touch with Dominion authorities on the matter and was, therefore, exercising a prerogative on his own authority that no Lieutenant-Governor had ever exercised in the history of the province.

Aberhart challenged his right to do this as he had earlier challenged the principle of disallowance. He maintained that disallowance was an obsolete power and had fallen into disuse, as Lapointe himself had said in the House of Commons only a few months before.[21] He asked the federal government to refer the issues of disallowance and reservation to the Supreme Court for a ruling. But he insisted that the Act to Amend and Consolidate the Credit Regulation Act and the Bank Taxation Act be allowed to stand and that their constitutionality be tested in the courts. For some unexplained reason he was willing to let the Press Bill be referred to the Supreme Court. On November 3, Prime Minister Mackenzie King announced the government's decision to refer everything—the three bills, and the question of the constitutionality of the Crown exercising the royal prerogatives of reservation and disallowance—to the Supreme Court.

Of course, much of the discussion in the Supreme Court focussed on the division of power between the federal and provincial governments rather than on the definition of press rights and privileges. And when the judgment was rendered on Friday, March 4, 1938—the hearings had begun January 10—the reasons for the decision were only partly related to the testament on the press which came, regrettably, as a postscript.

The unanimous opinion of the justices was that the powers of reservation and disallowance were still operative prerogatives of the crown; that the credit and banking legislation was *ultra vires* of the provincial government; and that the Act to Ensure the Publication of Accurate News and Information was similarly *ultra vires.*

Chief Justice Lyman Duff wrote the Court's majority decision on the Press Act. In it, he agreed with the Dominion and newspaper arguments that "this Bill is a part of the general scheme of Social Credit legislation, the basis of which is the Alberta Social Credit Act".[22] He said, "that Act is *ultra vires*.... This is sufficient for disposing of the question referred to us but, we think, there are some further observations upon the Bill which may properly be made".

Having said this, Chief Justice Duff proceeded to spell out in detail the *rationale* for freedom of the press in Canada. First, he described the traditions of representative government as they have been embodied in the British North America Act. He went on to say:

> The preamble of the statute . . . shows plainly enough that the constitution of the Dominion is to be similar in principle to that of the United Kingdom. The statute contemplates a Parliament working under the influence of public opinion and public discussion. There can be no controversy that such institutions derive their efficacy from the free public discussion of affairs, from criticism and answer and counter-criticism, from attack upon policy and administration and

defence and counter-attack; from the freest and fullest analysis and examination from every point of view of political proposals . . . .

The right of public discussion is, of course, subject to legal restrictions; those based upon considerations of decency and public order, and others conceived for the protection of various private and public interests with which, for example, the laws of defamation and sedition are concerned. In a word, freedom of discussion means . . . "freedom governed by law".

Even within its legal limits, it is liable to abuse and grave abuse and such abuse is constantly exemplified before our eyes; but it is axiomatic that the practice of this right of free public discussion of public affairs, notwithstanding its incidental mischiefs, is the breath of life for parliamentary institutions.

Chief Justice Duff agreed that some regulation of newspapers was conceded to the provinces. "Indeed, there is a very wide field in which the provinces undoubtedly are invested with legislative authority over newspapers". But he qualified this statement by saying:

> . . . the limit, in our opinion, is reached when the legislation effects such a curtailment of the exercise of the right of public discussion as substantially to interfere with the working of the parliamentary institutions of Canada as contemplated by the provisions of the British North America Act and the statutes of the Dominion of Canada.

He concluded:

> The legislation now under consideration manifestly places in the hands of the Chairman of the Social Credit Commission autocratic powers which, may well be thought, could if arbitrarily wielded be employed to frustrate in Alberta those rights of the Crown and the people of Canada as a whole . . . . The answer to the question concerning this Bill is that it is *ultra vires.*

Mr. Justice Cannon in a minority report agreed with the substance of the Chief Justice's remarks but made an additional point. He pointed out, as the Dominion government counsel had done in its factum and at the hearings, that "the bill does not regulate the relations of the newspaper owners with private individual members of the public . . . ". Rather, he said, it was aimed at regulating the expression of opinion by the newspapers "concerning government policies and activities". He added:

... it seems to me that the Alberta Legislature by this retrograde Bill is attempting to revive the old theory of the crime of seditious libel by enacting penalties, confiscation of space in newspapers and prohibitions for actions, which after due consideration by the Dominion Parliament, have been declared innocuous and which, therefore, every citizen in Canada can do lawfully without hindrance or fear of punishment. It is an attempt by the legislature to amend the Criminal Code in this respect .... [23]

In summary the Supreme Court Justices found the Press Act *ultra vires* by first ruling on the validity of the Alberta Social Credit Act which they ruled to be *ultra vires*. Since the Social Credit Act and its objectives were illegal—that is, the instituting of a new economic system was illegal—the means to further its goals through the control of the press were also illegal. They added *a fortiori* a further *rationale* for its being *ultra vires*. This *rationale* derived from the great liberal principles which they perceived to be essential to the operation of Canadian politics.

The press-state/journalist-politician relationship was thus explicated by the Canadian Justices. The sovereignty of the publicity system was vindicated, but not, alas, without ambiguity. [24] The questions that arise in the wake of the Press Act decision include: can the principle of freedom of the press be governed by the preamble of a statute in which the right itself is not specified? Second, are freedom of speech and press immutable rights that no legislative body, either federal or provincial, is competent to alter? Third, can the federal government prevent the criticism of a provincial legislature? These questions and others have been raised elsewhere and answers volunteered, but the answers have been inadequate. In the meantime, the journalists who operate and manage the publicity system continue to assume with the rest of us that the principle of freedom which gives them the right to organize their labor outside the supervision of the state is safe from the assaults of the kind Alberta witnessed in the midst of the Depression.

NOTES TO CHAPTER NINE

1/British common law and constitutional development are quite obviously fundamental to Canada's tradition of press freedom. The major historical discussions of British law are contained in FREDERICK SIEBERT'S *Freedom of the Press in England, 1476-1776* (Urbana, Illinois: University of Illinois Press, 1965); LAWRENCE HANSON'S *Government and the Press, 1695-1763* (Oxford: Clarendon Press, 1936); and WILLIAM WICKWAR'S *The Struggle for*

Freedom of the Press, 1819-1832 (London: George Allen and Unwin Ltd., 1928).

2/The term "publicity system" is Douglass Cater's. See *The Fourth Branch of Government* (New York: Vintage Books, Inc., 1959), p. 71. It may be taken here to mean the system by which political information and comment is distributed (the press constituting a major part of the system).

3/The rhetoric of this tradition, which is embraced by the journalist, derives from such texts as JOHN MILTON'S *Areopagitica*, JOHN STUART MILL'S *On Liberty,* some comments by Thomas Jefferson on the press (cf. *Thomas Jefferson on Democracy,* SAUL K. PADOVER, ed. (New York: Mentor Books, 1946), pp. 93-99, and many others. For contemporary discussions, a partial list would include ROGER L. BROWN, "Some Aspects of Mass Media Ideologies", *The Sociological Review Monograph 13,* ed. Paul Holmes (England: University of Keele, January 1969); DANIEL MOYNIHAN, "The Presidency and the Press", *Commentary,* Vol. 5, No. 3 (March 1971); T. PETERSON, "The Social Responsibility of the Press", *Four Theories of the Press,* ed. F.S. Siebert et al. (Urbana, Illinois: University of Illinois Press, 1963).

4/JOHN W. DAFOE, (Toronto: Ryerson Press, 1948).

5/Canada, *Report of the Special Senate Committee on Mass Media,* Vol. I (Ottawa: Queen's Printer, 1970), p. 75.

6/A case which has been compared to the Press Act arose in the same year when Quebec Premier Maurice Duplessis sponsored his celebrated "Act to Protect the Province Against Communistic Propaganda". This act exorcised civil libertarians and was the subject of a protracted debate which similarly raised the issues of disallowance and referral to the Supreme Court. It was finally ruled *ultra vires* in 1957.

7/Alberta, *Statutes,* 1937.

8/Cf. JOHN A. IRVING, *The Social Credit Movement in Alberta* (Toronto: University of Toronto Press, 1959); C.B. MACPHERSON, *Democracy in Alberta: Social Credit and the Party System* (Toronto: University of Toronto Press, 1953); J.R. MALLORY, *Social Credit and the Federal Power in Canada* (Toronto: University of Toronto Press, 1954); A.E. CARLESEN, "The Evolution of Social Credit Economic Thought", *Queen's Quarterly,* Vol. LXX, No. 3 (Autumn 1963).

9/Recorded in C.H. DOUGLAS, *The Alberta Experiment* (London: Eyre and Spottiswoode, 1937), p. 117.

10/Citations which follow from *The Journal* are recorded in the narrative.

11/DOUGLAS, *op. cit.* p. 28.

12/*Ibid.* p. 99.

13/*Ibid.* p. 115.

14/*Ibid.* p. 117.

15/For a full discussion see "The Revival of Dominion Control over the Provinces" by EUGENE FORSEY in *Politica,* Vol. V, No. 16 (June 1939); and MALLORY, *op. cit.* Chapter V.

16/FORSEY, *op.cit.* p. 106.

17/*Ibid.* p. 108.

18/The contents of the cablegram became known to *The Edmonton Journal* when the edition of the British journal *Social Credit* arrived in its offices. Aberhart had read the cable at a local meeting shortly after its arrival, but had omitted the final phrase. Subsequently, *New Age,* another British Social Credit journal, published a lengthy article explaining the rationale for the press legislation Douglas had conceived. This was what *The Journal* called "Mail Order Government". (September 10, 1937, p. 6.)

19/Alberta, *Statutes,* 1937.

20/See JOHN SAYWELL, *The Office of the Lieutenant-Governor* (Toronto: University of Toronto Press, 1957).

21/House of Commons, *Official Report of Debates,* March 30, 1937.

22/*Dominion Law Reports,* Vol. 2, 1938, pp. 106-109.

23/*D.L.R.,* p. 119.

24/The Press Act decision has been analysed in D.A. SCHMEISER'S *Civil Liberties in Canada* (Oxford, London: Oxford University Press, 1964); MARK MACGUIGAN, "Civil Liberties in Canada", *Queen's Quarterly,* Vol. LXVII, No. 2 (Summer 1965); and most recently and exhaustively, by E.A. TOLLEFSON, "Freedom of the Press" in *Contemporary Problems of Public Law In Canada,* ed. O.E. Lang; published for the College of Law, University of Saskatchewan, by the University of Toronto Press, Toronto, 1968, and reprinted in this volume.

chapter ten

Freedom of the Press*

E.A. TOLLEFSON

For almost three decades the decision of the Supreme Court of Canada in the *Alberta Press Bill* case[1] has been regarded as a signal victory for civil liberties in Canada. The case is not remembered for its *ratio* but for the sweeping dicta about how essential the communicative freedoms are in a democracy. Justified on the bases of freedom and democracy, who can oppose the decision? To attack it is to lay oneself open to the charge of advocating tyranny. Nevertheless, it is a bad decision, and bad decisions have an unfortunate tendency to beget worse decisions. A re-evaluation, even at this late date, therefore seems to be in order.

In 1935, Alberta, like the rest of Canada, was in the depths of the Depression. Traditional economic solutions did not seem to provide any hope. At times such as this a protest vote can be expected; but Alberta already had a government which had been elected on a protest vote, and which seemed to be just as incapable of doing anything about the situation as the two old-line parties. Not only had the United Farmers of Alberta, in office since 1921, been buffetted by the storms of the Depression, but the party leader had been charged with seduction and forced by circumstances to step down while the case was before the court. Into this atmosphere of despair came Major C.H. Douglas and his theory of social credit, according to which the country did not have to depend upon the machinations of international financiers in order to establish a state of prosperity, but could print money and extend credit on the basis of the unused capacity of the country's people and industries to produce wanted goods and services. People did not completely understand the theory of social credit, but they were assured by Major Douglas's prophet, William Aberhart, that they did not have to understand. Using the homely comparision of electricity he said:

> You don't have to know all about Social Credit before you vote for it; you don't have to understand electricity to use it, for you know

*Reprinted by permission of the author from *Contemporary Problems of Public Law in Canada,* edited by O.E. Lang, ©University of Toronto Press, 1968.

that experts have put the system in, and all you have to do is push the button and you get the light. So all you have to do about Social Credit is to cast your vote for it, and we will get the experts to put the system in.[2]

Aberhart was an evangelical preacher and teacher who had a large personal following. When he used social credit as the basis of a political party he led it to a landslide victory in its first test at the polls.

The Social Credit movement had never enjoyed a good press. Major Douglas believed that a sinister conspiracy existed between the closely knit press organization and international financial interests. When, in a last-ditch attempt to steal the thunder of Social Credit, the U.F.A. government hired Major Douglas in the spring of 1935 to be its chief reconstruction adviser, his first set of proposals included the setting up of an information service to counteract the unfavorable propaganda being directed against Social Credit theories.[3] The press continued its criticism when the Social Credit party formed the government of Alberta in the fall of 1935. In 1937, the government reacted by introducing "An Act to Ensure the Publication of Accurate News and Information". The Lieutenant-Governor, without instructions from Ottawa, reserved assent in respect of this and two other bills. By agreement between the federal and the Alberta governments these bills were referred to the Supreme Court of Canada for a determination of their constitutional validity.

The purpose of the Press Bill, as it is usually called, was described in its preamble as follows:

> Whereas it is expedient and in the public interest that the newspapers published in the Province should furnish to the people of the Province statements made by the authority of the Government of the Province as to the true and exact objects of the policy of the Government and as to the hindrances to or difficulties in achieving such objects, to the end that the people may be informed with respect thereto.
>
> Now, Therefore, His Majesty, by and with the advice and consent of the Legislative Assembly of the Province of Alberta, enacts as follows. . . .

The Bill then provided that every proprietor, editor, publisher, or manager of any newspaper published in the Province,

> . . . shall, when required so to do by the Chairman, publish in that newspaper any statement furnished by the Chairman which has for its object the correction or amplification of any statement relating to

any policy or activity of the Government of the Province published by that newspaper within the next preceding thirty-one days.[4]

Such statements were not to exceed the length of the statement corrected thereby and were to be given the same prominence as to position, type, and space as the statement corrected thereby.[5] Immunity against libel actions based on the publication of such statements was afforded to the proprietor, editor, publisher, manager, or printer of the newspaper publishing the same, and to the employees of any such person, and to any persons who might subsequently publish such statements.[6]

This provision bears a striking similarity to a provision which has existed in France since 1881, and which is known as "the right of reply". By this provision the director of a French newspaper or periodical is bound to insert within three days of receipt any corrections communicated to him by a public official with regard to acts, carried out in exercise of his office, which have been incorrectly reported by the said publication. A similar provision requires that the director insert within three days of receipt the reply of any person named or designated in the publication. Fines and imprisonment may be imposed if the reply is not inserted or if the reply is not given the same prominence as the original article.[7]

The second substantive provision of the Bill required newspapers to divulge their sources of information when required to do so by the chairman:

> 4. Every person who is the proprietor, editor, publisher, or manager of any newspaper, shall upon being required so to do by the Chairman in writing, within twenty-four hours after the delivery of such requirement at the office or usual place of business of any of the following persons, namely, the proprietor, editor, publisher or manager of the newspaper, make a return in writing setting out every source from which any information emanated, as to any statement contained in any issue of the newspaper published within sixty days of the making of the requirement and the names, addresses and occupations of all persons by whom such information was furnished to the newspaper, and the name and address of the writer of any editorial, article or news item contained in any such issue of the newspaper as aforesaid.

The principal penalty was set out in s.6:

> 6. In the case the proprietor, editor, publisher or manager of any newspaper has been guilty of any contravention of any of the provisions of this Act the Lieutenant-Governor in Council, upon the

recommendation of the Chairman, may by order prohibit,—

(a) the publication of such newspaper either for a definite time or until further order;

(b) the publication in any newspaper of anything written by any person specified in the order;

(c) the publication of any information emanating from any person or source specified in the order.

Contravention of the provisions of the legislation would also constitute an offence punishable by a fine not to exceed $500 (or $1,000 in the case of a person contravening an order in council passed pursuant to s.6).[8] The "Chairman", who was to act as watchdog on the press, was none other than the chairman of the "Board" established under The Alberta Social Credit Act.[9]

Newspapermen across Canada banded together to oppose the Press Bill. In the Supreme Court of Canada, two factums were filed by newspaper interests: one factum was filed by the *Edmonton Journal, Calgary Herald, Lethbridge Herald,* Edmonton *Bulletin,* Calgary *Albertan,* Medicine Hat *News,* and the Alberta division of the Canadian Weekly Newspaper Association; a second factum, containing similar arguments, was filed by the Canadian Press, Canadian Daily Newspapers Association, and Canadian Weekly Newspapers Association. Both factums cited a number of reasons why the Bill should be found to be beyond the powers assigned to the provincial legislatures by the B.N.A. Act: (1) the Bill was *ultra vires* because it was part of an over-all scheme which was *ultra vires;* (2) it did not deal with a matter of a purely local and private nature for newspapers disseminate news beyond provincial boundaries; (3) newspapers fall within the scope of s.92(10): "Other works and undertakings connecting the province with any other province or provinces or extending beyond the limits of the province"; (4) the Bill properly fell within the sphere of the criminal law: sedition, criminal libel, and the spreading of false news were said to cover the same area; (5) it was *ultra vires* as it related to newspapers which were dominion companies; and (6) it constituted a delegation of the judicial function to the Lieutenant-Governor in Council and the chairman of the Board, contrary to the provisions of ss.96, 99, and 100 of the B.N.A. Act.

The factum filed by the federal government advanced the same arguments as were contained in the factums of newspaper interests, with the exception that no reliance was placed at this stage on the arguments respecting dominion companies and delegation of the judicial function.[10]

The government of British Columbia also filed a factum but it submitted no argument. The factum submitted by the Attorney-General of Alberta maintained that newspapers were like other businesses and therefore were subject to restrictions which might be imposed on their operation by the provincial government, and that the Bill was analogous to The Alberta Libel and Slander Act insofar as jurisdiction was concerned.

The Supreme Court judges were unanimous in finding that all three bills referred to them were *ultra vires*. The majority felt that the Press Bill was *ultra vires* as forming a part of a scheme of legislation which was beyond the powers of the provincial legislature. Duff C.J.C., delivering the judgment for himself and Davis J., stated the reason for the decision in the following manner:

> We now turn to Bill No. 9.
>
> This Bill contains two substantive provisions. Both of them impose duties upon newspapers published in Alberta which they are required to perform on the demand of "the Chairman," who is, by the interpretation clause, the Chairman of "the Board constituted by section 3 of *The Alberta Social Credit Act.*"
>
> The Board, upon the acts of whose Chairman the operation of this statute depends, is, in point of law, a non-existent body (there is, in a word, no "board" in existence "constituted by section 3 of *The Alberta Social Credit Act*") and both of the substantive sections, sections 3 and 4, are, therefore, inoperative. The same, indeed, may be said of sections 6 and 7, which are the enactments creating sanctions. It appears to us, furthermore, that this Bill is a part of the general scheme of Social Credit legislation, the basis of which is *The Alberta Social Credit Act;* the Bill presupposes, as a condition of its operation, that *The Alberta Social Credit Act* is validly enacted; and, since that Act is *ultra vires,* the ancillary and dependent legislation must fall with it.[11]

Hudson J. concurred with the opinion expressed by the Chief Justice on this point,[12] and Kerwin and Crocket JJ. found the Bill to be *ultra vires* on the same basis.[13] Cannon J. spent some time showing that the Press Bill was a necessary part of the new Social Credit economic order, suggesting that "credit" comes from the Latin word *credere,* to believe, and that belief in the government plan necessarily involved control of the sources of information. But after expanding on this dubious etymological approach, Cannon J. came to no conclusion at all on whether the Bill was *ultra vires* of the province because of its relationship to the total Social Credit scheme; rather he concluded that the legislation was *ultra vires* because it invaded the domain of criminal law.[14]

This *ratio decidendi* is remarkable in several ways. In the first place, it depends upon a finding of invalidity of a statute not referred to the Court.

No question of the validity of The Alberta Social Credit Act was referred to the Court, but the Court nevertheless found it to be *ultra vires.* The effect of a finding of invalidity in such circumstances is open to question. A decision on a question referred to the Court is theoretically only an opinion, but the Supreme Court Act of the day provided that "The opinion of the Court upon any such reference, although advisory only, shall, for all purposes of appeal to His Majesty in Council, be treated as a final judgment of the said Court between the parties".[15] The words "any such reference" clearly refer to "Important questions of law or fact . . . which may be referred by the Governor in Council to the Supreme Court for hearing and consideration . . .".[16] This statement of the right of the Governor in Council to refer important questions to the Supreme Court is immediately followed by subsection 2 of s.55, which opens: "2. When any such reference is made to the Court it shall be the duty of the Court to hear and consider it, and to answer each question so referred . . .". The result is that while the opinion has the status of a final judgment insofar as the questions referred to the court are concerned, lesser weight must be attributed to collateral findings.

Having concluded that The Alberta Social Credit Act was *ultra vires,* the Court had no difficulty in finding that this Act was central to the whole range of economic legislation passed by the Alberta legislature in order to implement the theories of "social credit". The Court affirmed that because the central Act was *ultra vires,* "the ancillary and dependent legislation must fall with it".[17]

But is such a conclusion correct? A preliminary objection is that ancillary legislation should not be found *ultra vires* on the basis of its relationship to a central act unless the determination of the invalidity of the central act is *res judicata.* In the *Press Bill* case, the finding with respect to The Alberta Social Credit Act was at most little more than *dicta.* A second objection is that ancillary or dependent legislation should not automatically become *ultra vires* upon a finding that the central act is *ultra vires* unless in pith and substance the ancillary or dependent legislation is itself in relation to a matter outside the jurisdiction of the legislative body which enacted it. Being dependent upon the existence of another act, the legislation may be denuded of any practical effect as the result of a finding that the principal act is *ultra vires,* but this is quite a different thing from saying that the legislative body in question did not possess the power to pass this legislation. Even if the ancillary legislation is clearly part of a scheme of legislation which is *ultra vires* in its ultimate goal or effect, why should the ancillary legislation be struck down if, viewed by itself, it is clearly *intra vires?* There must be many grand legislative schemes which are composed of many individual statutes, each contributing something to the ultimate goal. If the ultimate goal is *ultra vires,* is it sensible that each statute of the scheme should also be declared *ultra vires* regardless of its individual jurisdictional merits? Assuming for a moment that otherwise valid statutes are to be declared *ultra vires* by association, could the legislative body in question validly re-enact these statutes once the courts had destroyed the over-all scheme by a finding of *ultra vires?* Suppose that, following the decision of the Supreme Court, the Alberta legislature had re-enacted the Press Bill, investing the Attorney-General of Alberta with the powers which had been given in the original Bill to the chairman of the Social Credit Board.[18] Would the new bill have been found *ultra vires?* The question of the validity of the Press Bill viewed independently of The Alberta Social Credit Act was left open by all members of the Court other than Cannon J.[19] If the legislation would be *intra vires* if re-enacted as an independent statute, what is the point of declaring it to be *ultra vires* in the first place?

This leaves a factual question of whether the Press Bill formed part of the scheme of Social Credit economic legislation. Certainly it was dependent upon The Alberta Social Credit Act, but this by itself is innocuous. Yet apart from reference to this dependency, the majority of the members of the Court were singularly reticent about their reasons for finding that the Press Bill formed part of the general scheme of Social Credit legislation. Only Cannon J., who in the end did not rely on this argument, suggested any other reason for concluding that the Press Bill formed a necessary part of the scheme to provide new credit, saying that "It is, therefore essential to control the sources of information of the people of Alberta, in order to keep them immune from any vacillation in their absolute faith in the plan of the government".[20] It may be asked why the Press Bill should have been identified with legislation which was *ultra vires* when some of the *intra vires* legislation of the Social Credit government was also causing public concern and evoking bitter editorial comment. Certainly there was nothing in the Press Bill itself which would identify it as part of the *ultra vires* economic plans of the government, apart from the fact that the chairman of the Social Credit Board was the *persona designata* to act as watchdog on the press.

Thus the *ratio decidendi* of the majority is open to serious question. What of Canon J.'s alternative *ratio:* namely that the Press Bill was *ultra vires* as being legislation falling within s.91(27), Criminal Law and Criminal Procedure? Cannon J. gave two reasons for his finding that the Press Bill invaded the "domain of criminal law".[21] The first reason was that the Criminal Code, in dealing with what constituted seditious words and publications, provided an exception with respect to bona fide criticism of the government:

> 133-A. No one shall be deemed to have a seditious intention only because he intends in good faith,—

(*a*) to show that His Majesty has been misled or mistaken in his measures; or

(*b*) to point out errors or defects in the government or constitution of the United Kingdom, or of any part of it, or of Canada or any province thereof, or in either House of Parliament of the United Kingdom or of Canada, or in any legislature, or in the administration of justice; or to excite His Majesty's subjects to attempt to procure, by lawful means, the alteration of any matter of state; or

(*c*) to point out, in order to their removal, matters which are producing or have a tendency to produce feelings of hatred and ill-will between different classes of His Majesty's subjects.[22]

His Lordship stated that the Press Bill was an attempt by the legislature of Alberta to amend the Criminal Code in this respect and to deny the advantage of the above section to Alberta newspaper publishers. Cannon J. fortified his argument that the impugned provision encroached on the federal power to repress sedition by reference to the historical fact that prior to Fox's Libel Act, 1792,[23] criticism of the government was punishable in the United Kingdom as a criminal libel.

His Lordship's judgment on this point is open to some serious objections. No doubt the Parliament of the United Kingdom could make criticism of the government a crime; but, being unhampered by the doctrine of *ultra vires,* it can declare anything to be a crime. The question is whether the Canadian federal government could make it a crime to criticize a provincial government. A strong argument could be advanced that such legislation was a colorable attempt to encroach on the exclusive jurisdiction of the provincial legislatures under 92(1), "The Amendment from Time to Time, notwithstanding anything in this Act, of the Constitution of the Province, except as regards the Office of Lieutenant-Governor"; 92(13), "Property and Civil Rights in the Province"; or 92(16), "Generally all Matters of a merely local or private Nature in the Province". Certainly the provinces have an acknowledged jurisdiction in relation to libel, which would seem to indicate that the provinces have a *prima facie* jurisdiction in relation to the publication of falsehoods and half-truths—the very mischief which the Press Bill was intended to remedy. Even Duff C.J.C. and Davies J. recognized that "there is a very wide field in which the provinces undoubtedly are invested with legislative authority over newspapers . . .".[24]

It would appear, therefore, that at best the federal government, by virtue of its power to repress sedition and punish criminal libel, may regulate only certain aspects of public discussion; and so long as the impugned enactment can be found to have a provincial aspect, the enactment should be valid and enforceable, unless its operation prevents the enforcement of federal legislation in the same field.[25] If the Press Bill had a provincial aspect (a question which Cannon J. did not consider), the Bill should not have been found invalid. It did not prevent the enforcement of the provisions of the Criminal Code, for s.133-A of the Code, which was relied upon by Cannon J., did not impose any penalty, but, instead, it declared an exemption from criminal liability. The fact that an act is not criminally culpable (because of either the silence of the Code or an express exemption contained therein) does not preclude the impositon of a provincial penalty for a provincial purpose.[26] This was made clear by the Supreme Court in the *Breathalyser* case,[27] in which provincial legislation requiring a driver of a motor vehicle to give a sample of his breath on the request of a police officer, was held not to conflict with s.224(4) of the Criminal Code, which provides that no person is required to give a sample of blood, urine, breath, or other bodily substance for chemical analysis for the purposes of a prosecution for drunken or impaired driving. The Court held that the provincial enactment related to the provincial purpose of regulating highway traffic and was *intra vires* and enforceable even though the evidence so gained could be used in a prosecution under the Code for drunken or impaired driving.

The second reason given by Cannon J. for finding the Press Bill *ultra vires* as being in relation to criminal law was that freedom of discussion of all matters affecting the state is the foundation of a democracy, and as such it is the birthright of all Canadians and can be curtailed only by the Parliament of Canada:

> Under the British system, which is ours, no political party can erect a prohibitory barrier to prevent the electors from getting information concerning the policy of the government. Freedom of discussion is essential to enlighten public opinion in a democratic state; it cannot be curtailed without affecting the right of the people to be informed through sources independent of the government concerning matters of public interest. There must be an untrammelled publication of the news and political opinions of the political parties contending for ascendancy. As stated in the preamble to *The British North America Act,* our constitution is and will remain, unless radically changed, "similar in principle to that of the United Kingdom". At the time of Confederation, the United Kingdom was a democracy. Democracy cannot be maintained without its foundation: free public opinion and free discussion throughout the nation of all matters affecting the State within the limits set by the criminal code and the common law. Every inhabitant in Alberta is also a citizen of the Dominion. The province may deal with his property and civil rights of a local and private nature within the province; but the province cannot interfere with

his status as a Canadian citizen and his fundamental right to express freely his untrammelled opinion about government policies and discuss matters of public concern. The mandatory and prohibitory provisions of the Press Bill are, in my opinion, *ultra vires* of the provincial legislature. They interfere with the free working of the political organization of the Dominion. They have a tendency to nullify the political rights of the inhabitants of Alberta, as citizens of Canada, and cannot be considered as dealing with matters purely private and local in that province. The federal parliament is the sole authority to curtail, if deemed expedient and in the public interest, the freedom of the press in discussing public affairs and the equal rights in that respect of all citizens throughout the Dominion. These subjects were matters of criminal law before Confederation, have been recognized by Parliament as criminal matters and have been expressly dealt with by the criminal code. No province has the power to reduce in that province the political rights of its citizens as compared with those enjoyed by the citizens of other provinces of Canada. Moreover, citizens outside the province of Alberta have a vital interest in having full information and comment, favourable and unfavourable, regarding the policy of the Alberta government and concerning events in that province which would, in the ordinary course, be the subject of Alberta newspapers' news items and articles.[28]

The *Press Bill* case now is remembered chiefly for Cannon J.'s eloquent words about the preamble of the B.N.A. Act and for similar dicta in the judgment of Duff C.J.C. and Davies J. that it was *ultra vires* of the provinces to abrogate or suppress "free public discussion of public affairs . . . the breath of life for parliamentary institutions".[29]

The arguments based upon the preamble and upon our democratic heritage are, however, not entirely convincing. The preamble declares that the constitution of the Dominion is to be "similar in principle to that of the United Kingdom". As can be seen from the above quotation from his judgment, Cannon J., noting that at the time of Confederation the United Kingdom was a democracy, concluded that the British North America Act guaranteed the foundation of democracy, namely, "free public opinion and free discussion throughout the nation of all matters affecting the State within the limits set by the criminal code and the common law". He went on to say that "The federal parliament is the sole authority to curtail, if deemed expedient and in the public interest, the freedom of the press in discussing public affairs and the equal rights in that respect of all citizens throughout the Dominion".

There is an antinomy in these two statements. If free public opinion and free discussion are the foundation of democracy, and democracy is protected by the constitution, then neither the provincial legislatures nor the federal parliament should be able to curtail this right—that is, our constitutional position with respect to freedom of speech and the press would then be analogous to that in the United States.[30] Duff C.J.C and Davies J. appear to have recognized the contradiction inasmuch as their judgment makes no reference to the power of Parliament to restrict freedom of discussion but only to its power "to legislate for the protection of this right".[31] It was not necessary in this case to decide whether the federal government had the power to curtail the right.

But, it is submitted, the basic premise of the argument regarding the preamble is wrong. Freedom of discussion was not a constitutional fact in the United Kingdom in 1867. Freedom of discussion was a condition which existed in the law at that time, but a condition which was subject to the constitutional fact of supremacy of Parliament.[32] If any conclusion is to be drawn from the statement in the preamble that the Canadian constitution is to be similar in principle to that of the United Kingdom it is that the full range of legislative powers have been distributed by the British North America Act. It follows that Parliament is supreme within its sphere of jurisdiction, and it must also follow that the provincial legislatures are supreme in their spheres of jurisdiction. Therefore, since the United Kingdom Parliament could restrict discussion of public affairs, that power must exist somewhere in Canada.[33]

In concluding that the provincial legislatures lacked such authority, Cannon J. said that the Press Bill interfered with the free working of the political organization of the Dominion and would have "the tendency to nullify the political rights of the inhabitants of Alberta, as citizens of Canada"—a power which, he said, no province possesses. His conclusion is, of course, correct insofar as debate relative to federal parliamentary institutions, federal elections, and federal issues is concerned. But since the provincial legislatures are also supreme within their own spheres of jurisdiction—supreme to the point that they can amend their own constitutions if they are so minded[34]—surely they can lay down rules restricting debate in relation to provincial politics in the same way that the Parliament of the United Kingdom can. The fact that the provincial legislatures may discriminate against particular classes of persons is established by *Cunningham* v. *Tomey Homma*,[35] in which the Privy Council held that naturalization did not confer suffrage in provincial elections. This was a privilege which could be extended or withheld at the will of the provincial legislatures.

If the provincial legislature can disfranchise a Canadian citizen who would have the franchise federally and in other provinces, it would seem to follow that the legislature could restrict public discussion of political matters falling within provincial jurisdiction and enforce its statutory provisions by the imposition of punishment, by fine, penalty, or imprisonment.[36] This would appear to be the indirect effect of the Press Bill. Section 3, which required the publication of a statement of amplification or rectification, only applied to statements relating "to any policy or activity of the Government of the Province" which had appeared within the next preceding thirty-one days in a newspaper published in Alberta. All the factors involved in s.3 were provincial in nature. On the other hand, s.4, which required the revelation of a newspaper's sources of information, was somewhat more difficult to justify, for, literally, it was not restricted to newspapers published in Alberta or to statements about the policy or activity of the government of Alberta (or matters over which that government had exclusive jurisdiction). If the Court read the words "newspaper" and "statement" in s.4 as connoting the same legislative intention as the terms used in s.3, that is, as meaning "newspaper published in the Province" and "statement relating to any policy or activity of the Government of the Province," then there would appear to be no question of the section's validity.[37] Otherwise, s.4 would appear to have been in excess of provincial jurisdiction. However, even if that was the case, s.4 was quite severable from the remainder of the Press Bill, and its excision in no way would have rendered the Bill incomplete or inoperative.

The conclusion to be drawn from the above discussion is that the reasoning in the *Press Bill* case is of doubtful validity. It can at this time perhaps be queried whether certain members of the Court regarded not only the Bill but the Alberta government of the day with extreme distaste, which led them to use emotionally charged terms such as "freedom," "Democracy," and "parliamentary institutions" in place of the colorless language of precedent and reason which normally characterizes judgments of superior courts.

Certainly the Alberta government felt that the decision on the three referred bills, and the decision on the Press Bill in particular, had been motivated by policy considerations. For the Alberta government, therefore, it became a matter of political principle that the decision of the Supreme Court with respect to the three bills and the Court's decision (which was handed down the same day) on the federal power of disallowance, should be appealed to the court of last resort—the Judicial Committee of the Privy Council. Actually, counsel for the province of Alberta were of two minds as to the most expedient way of effecting the purpose of the Press Bill. O.M. Biggar, K.C., chief counsel for the Attorney-General of Alberta in these cases, recommended that instead of appealing the decision the government give serious consideration to preparing a fresh press bill giving power, for example, to the Attorney-General instead of the chairman of the Social

Credit Board, thus making the bill clearly independent of the Social Credit Act.[38]

Counsel also submitted that the appeal on the referred bills would be seriously prejudiced in the eyes of the Privy Council if coupled with an appeal against the decision of the Supreme Court on the disallowance question. Cyril Radcliffe, K.C.,[39] who was retained by the province of Alberta to argue the cases before the Privy Council, felt so strongly on this issue that he refused to present the appeal on disallowance, and urged the provincial government to withdraw the appeal before the hearing because he was convinced "that an attempt to argue this appeal, which has only political considerations to support it will have the most undesirable effect upon the arguments and consideration of the Province's appeal in the other case".[40] As a result of Radcliffe's advice, the Alberta government withdrew the appeal on the disallowance question and proceeded only with respect to the three referred bills.

Prior to the hearing of the appeal, The Alberta Social Credit Act was repealed. Counsel for the Attorney-General of Alberta therefore argued that the Press Bill could not be held *ultra vires* on the grounds of its connection with the general legislative scheme of which The Alberta Social Credit Act was the basis, because the latter Act was no longer in existence.[41] Much to the surprise of counsel for all parties[42] the Judicial Committee itself raised the question whether the appeal on the Credit Regulation Bill and the Press Bill should be heard at all because, in view of the repeal of The Alberta Social Credit Act, neither bill could be made operative without amendment. It was pointed out by their Lordships that it was not the Committee's practice to express an opinion on a matter which was of academic interest only.[43] The matter was left at that until the second day of the hearing, at which time their Lordships returned to this point. They asked for an expression of opinion not only from counsel for the Attorney-General of Alberta, but also from Aimé Geoffrion, K.C., counsel for the Attorney-General of Canada and J.L. Ralston, K.C., counsel for the Alberta newspapers. Mr. Geoffrion indicated that he had communicated with Ottawa as to the position he should take if the suggestion made by their Lordships at the previous day's sitting came up again; and acting on instructions he had received he intimated a preference for having the reference with regard to the Press Bill go on. Mr. Ralston, in his turn, also pressed the Committee to have the questions involved finally disposed of. However, after a short adjournment, the Committee announced that in view of the academic character of the question it could hear no argument on the Credit Regulation Bill or the Press Bill.[44] The appeal therefore proceeded only with respect to the Bank Taxation Bill.

In view of the express wishes of the parties concerned and the fundamental importance of the issue, it is a pity that the Privy Council could not have relaxed its rules of practice so that a definitive ruling could have been given in this case. Cases of this nature do not often arise, and the result is that we frequently must go for decades in a state of uncertainty about matters basic to our constitution. Freedom of the press, if involved in a case before the court at all, is usually only a collateral issue, and therefore it has failed to receive the serious consideration by the courts which it would otherwise require. The issue has arisen in this way in two cases before the Supreme Court of Canada, *Saumur* v. *Quebec and the A.-G. for Quebec*,[45] and *Switzman* v. *Elbling and the A.-G. for Quebec*.[46]

In the former case, the constitutionality of a by-law of the City of Quebec, forbidding the distribution in the streets of the city of "any book, pamphlet, booklet, circular, or tract whatever without having previously obtained for so doing the written permission of the Chief of Police", was challenged by a member of the Jehovah's Witnesses sect. The action was dismissed by the trial judge and by the majority of the Court of Appeal. In the Supreme Court of Canada the appellant (plaintiff) won, five judges finding the by-law to be *ultra vires* and four finding it to be *intra vires*. Of the majority, Rand, Kellock, and Locke JJ. approved and applied the statements found in the judgments of Duff C.J.C., and Davies and Cannon JJ. in the *Press Bill* case that the provincial legislatures could not restrict the discussion of public affairs—Rand and Kellock JJ. reserving the question whether the federal parliament had such power.[47] Estey J. made no reference to freedom of speech or the press but based his judgment instead on freedom of religion, which he said was a subject-matter falling outside "civil rights within the province" and within the federal power to pass laws for the "peace, order and good government of Canada".[48] Kerwin J., who had also sat on the *Press Bill* case, expressly disagreed with the sweeping statement of Duff C.J.C., and Davies and Cannon JJ., and stated that freedom of the press is a civil right in the province.[49] He based his judgment in the *Saumur* case on a conflict between the by-law and a binding pre-Confederation statute guaranteeing "the exercise and enjoyment of Religious Profession and Worship without discrimination or preference . . .".[50] Of the minority judges, Rinfret C.J.C. and Taschereau J. made no reference to freedom of the press, but they found freedom of religion to be a civil right within the province.[51] Cartwright and Fauteux JJ. found that the by-law was valid as falling within provincial jurisdiction in relation to the use of highways and police regulation to control conditions likely to cause public disorder. They expressed the view that "freedom of the press is not a separate subject matter committed exclusively to either Parliament or the Legislature", and that "If the subject matter of a Provincial enactment falls within the class of subjects enumerated in s.92 of the *British North America Act* such enactment does not . . . cease to be *intra vires* of the legislature by reason of the fact that it has the effect of cutting down the freedom of the press".[52] They expressly disagreed with the view put forth by Cannon J. in the *Press Bill* case that the federal parliament by legislation had indicated what publications were criminal and therefore by implication had declared all other publications to be lawful and consequently beyond provincial jurisdiction.[53]

In *Switzman* v. *Elbling and the A.-G. for Quebec* the Supreme Court of Canada considered the validity of a Quebec statute, An Act Respecting Communistic Propaganda,[54] and found it to be *ultra vires.* Sections 3 and 12 of the Act read:

> 3. It shall be illegal for any person, who possesses or occupies a house within the Province, to use it or allow any person to make use of it to propagate communism or bolshevism by any means whatsoever.

> 12. It shall be unlawful to print, to publish in any manner whatsoever or to distribute in the Province any newspaper, periodical, pamphlet, circular, document or writing whatsoever propagating or tending to propagate communism or bolshevism.

Infringement of s.3 could result in the Attorney-General ordering that the house be closed, and infringement of s.12 could result in imprisonment. Only three of the nine judges relied on the argument that freedom of discussion of public matters was beyond the jurisdictional authority of the provincial government.[55] The other five judges in the majority made no mention of the freedom of the press aspect of the case.[56] It is doubtful therefore whether the case can be cited as holding that provincial legislatures are precluded from restricting public discussion of provincial matters.

The judgments in the Supreme Court on the issue of constitutional authority in relation to the press do not provide much comfort for those who like to find certainty in the law. While uncertainty is a great boon to those who rejoice in academic speculation, the issue in this case is far from being purely academic. As was declared by Duff C.J.C., and Davies and Cannon JJ., the idea of thought-control by the government is abhorrent to us. But we seem to regard with equanimity the possibility of thought-control by the press itself. The famous British publisher, the late Lord Beaverbrook, when asked by the Royal Commission on the Press (1947-1949) what was his main purpose in running his papers, replied: "I run the paper purely for the purpose of making propaganda, and with no other motive."[57] Probably very few Canadian publishers are motivated in the same way as was Lord Beaverbrook—at least they would be unwilling to admit that they are; but whether a story is consciously or unconsciously biased, its effect is the same—the reader does not get a balanced and accurate account. It may be suggested that the reader may counteract the effect of this bias by reference to other sources—but radio and television, because of the evanescent character of such communications, are not an adequate substitute, and in many areas alternative daily newspapers are not available at all. The problem has national implications with the increasing concentration of ownership in the hands of a few large interests and because of the monopoly position of the Canadian Press wire service.

The United Kingdom, which was looked to in the *Press Bill* case as the bastion of freedom and the model for our constitution, has been sufficiently worried about the apparent failure of the press to fulfil its function of keeping the citizenry informed that it has appointed two royal commissions on the press since World War II. The Royal Commission of 1947-1949 concluded that the British press was inferior to none,[58] but found that the popular papers (as distinct from the quality papers) frequently were satisfied with only a rough approximation of the truth[59] and generally catered "to the lowest common denominator of taste and interest".[60] In assessing the reasons for the shortcomings of the British press the Royal Commission concluded: "Such of the shortcomings of the Press as are not attributable to excessive bias, competition for higher circulations, or the hazards inherent in collecting and publishing news at high speed, seem to us to be attributable very largely to the inadequate standard of education in the profession of journalism".[61] To overcome these weaknesses the Royal Commission recommended the establishment of a general council of the press, composed of proprietors, editors, other journalists and laymen. The council would be completely independent of the government of the day and would not be a creature of statute, but by the volition of the constituents of the press itself would be given the powers to curb unprofessional conduct on the part of British journalists.[62] The council was also to be charged with responsibility for scrutinizing changes in the ownership, control, and growth of press undertakings and giving wide publicity to authoritative information on these matters.[63]

The report of the Royal Commission was not enthusiastically received by the press, and it was over four years before the General Council of the Press was established—even then, all lay representation was excluded from the Council. The Council had indifferent success in its attempts to upgrade the British press, and was almost completely inactive in the economic field.[64] In the period 1948-1961 the three leading newspaper chains in Britain increased their percentage of circulation of daily newspapers from 45 per cent to 67 per cent.[65] The second Royal Commission on the Press, which reported in 1962, found that concentration of ownership carried with it the potential danger that variety of opinion might be stifled. To prevent this from occurring, the Royal Commission recommended that the press be given a time limit within which to reconstitute the General Council of the Press in accordance with the recommendations of the first Royal Commission, and to invest it with the necessary authority and financial capacity to carry out its objectives to the fullest degree. If the press failed to comply with this request, the Royal Commission said that the case for a statutory body with definite powers and the right to levy the industry was a clear one.[66] In addition, the second Royal Commission recommended the introduction of legislation designed to prevent mergers of press enterprises which in the opinion of a special press amalgamations tribunal were contrary to the public interest.[67]

Pursuant to the recommendations of the second Royal Commission, the General Council of the Press was reconstituted voluntarily by the press so as to include lay representation,[68] and the Government passed the Monopolies and Mergers Act, 1965.[69] Section 8 of that Act declares unlawful and void any transfer of a newspaper or of newspaper assets to a newspaper proprietor whose newspapers have an average circulation per day of publication amounting, with that of the newspaper concerned, to five hundred thousand or more copies, unless the transfer is made with the written consent of the Board of Trade given after the Board has received a report from the Monopolies Commission.[70] The Commission shall report to the Board whether or not the transfer may be expected to operate against the public interest, taking into account all matters which appear in the particular circumstances to be relevant and having regard (amongst other things) to the need for accurate presentation of news and free expression of opinion.[71]

The primary submission of this paper is that the *Press Bill* case cannot be relied upon as authority for any rule relating to jurisdiction over the press. While it would be practically convenient for the federal government to have exclusive jurisdiction over the press because of the national nature of some publications and the boundless nature of news itself, it cannot be stated with any degree of confidence that the constitution so provides. It seems more likely that the jurisdiction over the press is divided between the federal and provincial governments.

To those who suggest that there is nothing to worry about, the British experience may be cited as evidence that the press is either unable or unwilling to rectify its own shortcomings without some form of governmental regulation. Perhaps it is time that Canadians re-examined their century-old clichés about freedom of the press, with emphasis not on freedom of the press itself but on the goal to which that freedom is directed—an enlightened public. The task of the legislator and the lawyer alike is to consider what measures will best facilitate the attainment of this goal within the framework of the Canadian constitution.

NOTES TO CHAPTER TEN

1/ *In the Matter of Those Bills Passed by the Legislative Assembly of the Province of Alberta at the 1937 (Third Session) thereof, entitled respectively: "An Act Respecting the Taxation of Banks"; "An Act to Amend and Consolidate the Credit of Alberta Regulations Act"; and "An Act to Ensure the Publication of Accurate News and Information"*, [1938] S.C.R.100.

2/Quoted in C.B. MACPHERSON, *Democracy in Alberta*, 2nd ed. (Toronto: University of Toronto Press, 1962), at 152.

3/J.R. MALLORY, *Social Credit and the Federal Power in Canada* (Toronto: University of Toronto Press, 1954), at 65.

4/Alberta, 1937 (Third Session), Bill 9, s. 3(1).

5/ *Ibid.* s. 3(4).

6/ *Ibid.* s. 5.

7/"Act concerning the Freedom of the Press of 29 July 1881", articles 12 and 13; Draft Act Regulating the Press, 1945, articles 65-72. For translation of text of these Acts see *Freedom of Information* (United Nations Department of Social Affairs, 1950), II, at 31, 52-53. For discussion of this aspect of French press law see ZECHARIAH CHAFEE, JR., *Government and Mass Communications* (Chicago: University of Chicago Press, 1947), I, at 147-58. For the right of reply under the German Press Law of 1874 see CHAFEE, at 158-60.

8/ *Supra* note 4, s. 7.

9/ *Ibid.* s. 2(a). The Alberta Social Credit Act was enacted in 1937 (first session), c. 10.

10/These two arguments were added to the factum of the federal government when the case was appealed to the Privy Council. The factum and case of the federal government are a gold mine of information about Social Credit.

11/[1938] S.C.R. 100, at 132.

12/ *Ibid.* at 162-63.

13/ *Ibid.* at 161-62.

14/ *Ibid.* at 143-45.

15/R.S.C. 1927, c. 35, s. 55(6).

16/ *Ibid.* s. 55(1).

17/ *Supra* note 11, *per* Duff C.J.C. and Davies J.

18/See *infra*. This course of action was suggested by O.M. Biggar K.C., senior counsel in the case for the Attorney-General of Alberta to J.J. Frawley, K.C., of the Alberta Attorney-General's Department in a letter dated March 4, 1938 (the day the judgment was delivered). Letter in files of Attorney-General for Alberta.

19/*Supra* note 11, at 134-35 *per* Duff C.J.C. and Davies J.; at 163 *per* Hudson J. Although they do not say so explicitly, this also appears to have been left open implicitly by Kerwin and Crockett JJ. especially at 161-62. See also Kerwin J.'s statement in *Saumur* v. *Quebec and the A.-G. for Quebec.* [1953] 2.S.C.R.299, at 324. See *infra* for discussion of this case.

20/*Ibid.* at 144.

21/*Ibid.* 144-46. It is questionable whether in fact there is a "domain of criminal law". Lord Atkin, in *Proprietory Articles of Trade Association* v. *A.-G. for Canada,* [1931] A.C. 310, stated at 324: "Criminal law connotes only the quality of such acts or omissions as are prohibited under appropriate penal provisions by authority of the State. The criminal quality of an act cannot be discerned by intuition; nor can it be discovered by reference to any standard but one: Is the act prohibited with penal consequences? Morality and criminality are far from co-extensive; nor is the sphere of criminality necessarily part of a more extensive field covered by morality—unless the moral code necessarily disapproves all acts prohibited by the State, in which case the argument moves in a circle. It appears to their Lordships to be of little value to seek to confine crimes to a category of acts which by their very nature belong to the domain of 'criminal jurisprudence'; for the domain of criminal jurisprudence can only be ascertained by examining what acts at any particular period are declared by the State to be crimes, and the only common nature they will be found to possess is that they are prohibited by the State and that those who commit them are punished". For a statement to the same effect, see *Lord's Day Alliance of Canada* v. *A.-G. for British Columbia,* [1959] S.C.R. 497, at 508-509, *per* Rand J., delivering the judgment for himself, Cartwright, Martland, and Judson JJ.

22/R.S.C. 1927, c. 36, as amended by S.C. 1930, c. 11, which introduced this provision as s. 133A.

23/32 Geo. III, c. 60. For a discussion of the law of criminal libel for this period see SIR JAMES FITZJAMES STEPHEN, *History of the Criminal Law of England* (London: Macmillan, 1883),II, Ch. 24.

24/*Supra* note 11, at 134.

25/On this point see *Re Section 92(4) of The Vehicles Act, Statutes of Saskatchewan, 1957, c. 93,* [1958] S.C.R. 608; *O'Grady* v. *Sparling,* [1960]

S.C.R. 804; *Stephens* v. *The Queen,* [1960] S.C.R. 823; *Smith* v. *The Queen,* [1960] S.C.R. 776; *Mann* v. *The Queen,* [1966] S.C.R. 238. For a most instructive commentary on the problem of legislative paramountcy see Laskin, "Occupying the Field: Paramountcy in Penal Legislation" (1936), 41 *Can. Bar Rev.* 234.

It is interesting that Cannon J. did not refer to the then s. 136 of the Criminal Code on the spreading of false news: "136. Everyone is guilty of an indictable offence and liable to one year's imprisonment who wilfully and knowingly publishes any false news or tale whereby injury or mischief is or is likely to be occasioned to any public interest". The Press Bill would appear to have covered this situation plus situations in which (a) the news was not false but only incomplete, (b) false news was not published knowingly or (c) no injury or mischief was or was likely to be occasioned to a public interest.

26/This is implicit in the cases cited in notes 25 and 27. See also comment of Cartwright and Fauteux JJ. in *Saumur* v. *Quebec and the A.-G. for Quebec, supra* note 19, at 385-86. See *infra.*

27/*Re Section 92(4) of The Vehicles Act, Statutes of Saskatchewan, 1957, c. 93,* [1958] S.C.R. 608. See comment on this case by the author in (1958), 23 *Sask. Bar Rev. 78* and (1959), 2 *Can. Bar J.* 103.

28/*Supra* note 11, at 145-46.

29/*Ibid.* at 133.

30/The First Amendment to the Constitution of the United States of America provides: "Congress shall make no law respecting an establishment of religion, or prohibiting the free exercise thereof; or abridging the freedom of speech, or of the press; or the right of the people peaceably to assemble, and to petition the Government for a redress of grievances". By virtue of the Fourteenth Amendment the same guarantee is provided with respect to state law: " . . . No state shall make or enforce any law which shall abridge the privileges or immunities of citizens of the United States; nor shall any State deprive any person of life, liberty, or property, without due process of law; nor deny to any person within its jurisdiction the equal protection of the law". It has been held that the due process clause precludes the states from legislating in such a way as to deprive a citizen of the United States of any of the liberties set out in the first eight amendments to the constitution. As to the fourteenth amendment and the press see *Near* v. *Minnesota,* 283 U.S. 697(1931).

31/*Supra* note 11, at 133. Doubts as to whether the federal government has authority to curtail or restrict some of the so-called basic freedoms have been expressed in *Saumur* v. *Quebec and the A.-G. for Quebec, supra* note

19, at 329 (*per* Rand J.), and at 354-56 (*per* Kellock J.); and in *Switzman* v. *Elbling and the A.-G. for Quebec*, [1957] S.C.R. 285, at 328 (*per* Abbott J.).

32/See A.V. DICEY, *The Law of the Constitution*, 10th ed. (London: Macmillan, 1959), Ch. 6. This section has remained virtually unchanged since the 3rd ed. of 1889. See also Chapter 1, "The Nature of Parliamentary Sovereignty".

33/There is weighty authority for the proposition that the full range of domestic legislative authority was distributed between the provinces and the Dominion by the B.N.A. Act. See in particular *A.-G. for Ontario* v. *A.-G. for Canada*, [1912] A.C. 571, at 581 and *Saumur* v. *Quebec and the A.-G. for Quebec, supra* note 19, at 324, *per* Kerwin J.

34/See s. 92(1) of the B.N.A. Act.

35/[1903] A.C. 151.

36/See s. 92(15) of the B.N.A. Act.

37/Judges in civil cases can compel a party or witness to disclose the sources of his information: *Wismer* v. *Maclean-Hunter Publishing Co. Ltd. and Fraser (No.2)*, [1954] 1 D.L.R. 501 (B.C.C.A.); *McConachy* v. *Times Publishers Ltd. et al.* (1964), 49 D.L.R. (2d) 349 (B.C.C.A.). This point has recently been reaffirmed in Great Britain in *A-G.* v. *Mulholland; A.-G* v. *Foster*, [1963] 2 W.L.R. 658, and *A.-G.* v. *Clough*, [1963] 2 W.L.R. 343. The provincial legislatures would appear to have jurisdiction under either s. 92(13) (Civil Rights in the Province) or 92(14) (Procedure in Civil Matters).

38/See *supra* Note 18.

39/Later Lord Radcliffe.

40/Memorandum of Cyril Radcliff, Lincoln's Inn, June 3, 1938, files of the Attorney-General for Alberta. The reference on the disallowance question is reported in [1938] S.C.R. 71.

41/Reported in argument, *A.-G. for Alberta* v. *A.-G. for Canada*, [1939] A.C. 117, at 121.

42/Letter J.J. Frawley, K.C. (in collaboration with O.M. Biggar, K.C.) to the Honourable William Aberhart, Attorney-General for Alberta, July 8, 1938; files of the Attorney-General for Alberta.

43/*Ibid.*

44/*Ibid.* The report of the argument in [1939] A.C. 117 does not indicate either the delay or the fact that counsel for the Attorney-General of Canada and for the Alberta newspapers also wished the matter to be considered and finally disposed of. Neither is the account in *The Times* of London, July 8, 1938, clear. J.J. Frawley says in his letter to the Honourable Mr. Aberhart that the account of J.L. Ralston's representations were "incompletely set out" in *The Times* report.

45/[1953] 2 S.C.R. 299.

46/[1957] S.C.R. 285.

47/On the question of the federal government's power to restrict freedom of discussion of public affairs, see *supra* note 31.

48/[1953] 2 S.C.R. 299, at 359.

49/*Ibid.* at 324.

50/(1852), Can. 14 & 15 Vict., c. 175.

51/[1953] 2 S.C.R. 299, at 318-20.

52/*Ibid.* at 386.

53/*Ibid.* at 385-86.

54/R.S.Q. 1941, c. 52.

55/These judges were Rand, Kellock, and Abbott JJ.

56/The other majority judges were Kerwin C.J.C., Locke, Cartwright, Fauteux, and Nolan JJ. Taschereau J. dissented on the ground that the legislation related to the regulation of property and the suppression of conditions likely to favor the development of crime—*Bédard* v. *Dawson,* [1923] S.C.R. 681 followed.

57/*Royal Commission on the Press 1947-1949 Report* (London: H.M.S.O. Cmd. 7700), at 25.

58/*Ibid.* at 149.

59/*Ibid.* at 150.

60/*Ibid.* at 152.

61/*Ibid.* at 153.

62/*Ibid.* at Ch. 17.

63/*Ibid.* at 174.

64/*Royal Commission on the Press 1961-1962 Report* (London: H.M.S.O. Cmd. 1811), at 101.

65/*Ibid.* at 15.

66/*Ibid.* at 102.

67/*Ibid.* at 105-11.

68/The new constitution was adopted July 1, 1963, and the first meeting of the new Council, complete with lay representatives, took place January 14, 1964.

Under the new constitution the Council's name was changed from "The General Council of the Press" to "The Press Council". The first lay chairman of the Press Council was the well-known law lord, Lord Devlin. See *The Press and the People*—the annual report of the Press Council, particularly the 10th and 11th annual reports covering the years 1962-1964.

69/13 Eliz. II (1965), c. 50.

70/*Ibid.* s. 8(1).

71/*Ibid.* s. 8(3).

chapter eleven

The Claim to Secrecy of News Sources: A Journalistic Privilege?*

PETER J. GOLDSWORTHY

INTRODUCTION: The recent Report of the Special Senate Committee on Mass Media[1] declines to recommend any modification of the common law position denying the claim by newsmen to maintain, before official bodies, secrecy of news source.[2] The case for recognition of the claim has been argued stridently by the mass media, and recent cases have once again stimulated the controversy: in the United States, important news media have been confronted by governmental demands that they release, in the course of judicial proceedings, unpublished notes, files, films and other material relating to certain political organizations; in Canada, journalists have, in some well-publicized cases, kept silent when questioned as to the identity of the sources of their information.[3]

Generally there has been a lack of legislative and judicial response to the newsmen's claim, apart from several states of the United States where legislative action has been taken.[4] It is clear that recognition of a privilege for newsmen must proceed from the legislature; the common law is set against a privilege,[5] although the common law always upheld a discretion in the judge to aid the reluctant journalist. This was an illustration of the principle, expressed by Wigmore, that there should be no general privilege of confidential communications. "The investigation of facts, for reaching the truth in the administration of justice, would be intolerably obstructed by such a general privilege."[6]

It has been urged, with perhaps undue romanticism, that newsmen today have a new role and deserve a special treatment to which members of other occupational groups are not entitled. The massive growth and increased public influence of traditional media (newspaper, magazines) in this century, together with the gargantuan development of radio and television, has inspired the emergence of a myth of the newsman as guardian of democratic freedoms; he is seen as the public watchdog against official and bureaucratic

*Reprinted from the *Osgoode Hall Law Journal,* Vol. 9, No. 1. 1971, pp. 157-177, with the permission of the publisher and the author.

abuse of power. A measure of the change in status and public position of the newsman is the dignity, now accorded the profession of journalists, of "the fourth estate". It is therefore urged that the newsman in this quasi-public role should be entitled to preserve secrecy of source before official bodies demanding information from him. Newsmen fear professional emasculation; they fear lest their function and efficiency as gatherers of news for the information of the public be impeded by compulsory disclosure of sources of information.

It is customary to commence an examination of a claim to privilege by quoting Wigmore. Wigmore named four conditions which he considered to be essential prerequisites to the recognition of a professional privilege:

(1) the communications must originate in a *confidence* that they will not be disclosed;

(2) this element of *confidentiality* must be essential to the full and satisfactory maintenance of the relation between the parties;

(3) the *relation* must be one which in the opinion of the community ought to be sedulously *fostered;*

(4) the *injury* that would inure to the relation by the disclosure of the communications must be *greater than the benefit* thereby gained for the correct disposal of litigation.[7]

Wigmore opposed the creation of any privilege in favour of journalists.[8] However, it has been urged that newsmen do meet the four conditions. First, there is no doubt that the relationship between newsman and informant is confidential; secondly, the informant often relies on an express or implied promise of confidentiality maintained by the newsman; thirdly, it is argued that the public has a vital interest in the maintenance of a satisfactory relationship between the newsman and informant, because the public is vitally interested in the information yielded by the relationship; community opinion must therefore favor the privilege; lastly, it is urged that the faculty of the newsman to acquire confidential information deserves protection at the expense of judicial and other authorities to demand disclosure.[9]

The fourth condition presents the crux of the dispute: it juxtaposes the two principal interests in conflict. On the one hand, the public has an interest in the free and unrestricted flow of information and in accurate reporting; on the other hand, there is quite clearly an opposing public interest in the due administration of justice. The treatments accorded the newsman's claim to privilege in the United Kingdom, Canada and the United States will be examined to determine what weight should be accorded the various interests at play in order to reach a fair evaluation of the claim.

The United Kingdom

In 1967, the United Kingdom Law Reform Committee reported on the topic of privilege in civil proceedings.[10] The Committee discussed at length the classic privileges—against self-incrimination; in aid of litigation, settlement and conciliation; and concerning husband and wife. Then, under "confidential relationship", the Committee considered claims to privilege between priest and penitent, and doctor and patient. The Committee did not mention the claim to privilege affecting newsmen, although it did note the existence of claims by "accountants, bankers, many servants and agents".[11] In relation to the latter claims the Committee reported that the duty of non-disclosure was recognised by the courts "and given effect to by the judges so far as is consistent with the overriding claims of the interests of justice".[12] In the circumstances the Committee did not recommend the extension of a statutory privilege to these relationships. It is obvious that the Committee was influenced to its decision by the desirability of keeping the number of recognised privileges at a minimum, and by the belief that the better solution is to grant a wide discretion to courts to permit non-disclosure "where disclosure would be a breach of some ethical or social value and non-disclosure would be unlikely to result in serious injustice in the particular case in which it is claimed".[13]

The position of the privilege at common law was clarified by three cases decided in 1963[14] arising out of the Vassall spy scandal. A tribunal had been set up to investigate, in very broad terms, the circumstances in which offences under the Official Secrets Act had been committed by Vassall, an Admiralty official. Shortly after Vassall's trial a newspaper published a statement to the effect that Vassall's spying had led to Russian trawlers being in the vicinity of secret N.A.T.O. sea exercises. The reporter who wrote the passage, and acknowledged full responsibility therefore, was called by the tribunal and asked to name the source of his information. He refused to do so and, ultimately, was found guilty of contempt. In the other cases, the reporters had published statements of such a nature that a source within Admiralty was clearly indicated. Again, the reporters declined to disclose the sources of their information and were eventually found guilty of contempt.

In all the cases, the courts first decided that the questions put to the reporters were relevant. The courts then held that the journalists could claim no privilege, although in particular cases a court could hold that public policy demanded immunity for the journalist. In the *Clough* case, Parker C.J. added that the former rule of practice that in interlocutory proceedings for discovery the press would never be required to reveal the source of information had hardened into a rule of law.[15] His Lordship reasoned thus from a consideration of the wholly discretionary character of discovery, which has nothing to do with what may have to be ordered at the trial itself. In the *Mulholland* and *Foster* cases, Donovan L.J. added that disclosure will not be ordered unless the answer will serve a useful purpose in the instant proceedings, a matter wholly within the discretion of the judge.[16] Donovan L.J. also alluded to the possible existence of other considerations which might lead a judge to conclude that more harm than good would result from compelling a disclosing or punishing a refusal to answer. His Lordship declined to give any examples, but Lord Denning M.R. suggested the case where, in a libel action, the plaintiff wants the defendant newspaper to reveal the source of its information before the trial.[17] In such a case the court will not as a rule compel disclosure because it may open others to suit.

The *Foster* case provides an interesting variation. The respondent reporter in that case did not remember the source of his information. All he refused to disclose was the type of the source. Lord Denning M.R. pointed out that the question of type of source was relevant to the investigation of the tribunal encompassing possible neglect of duty by those responsible for Vassall, as knowledge of the type of source could have led to pinpointing of the actual source.[18]

These three cases relied heavily on a leading Australian decision, *McGuiness* v. *Attorney General of Victoria*.[19] There a commission, established to investigate bribery of a member of Parliament, found a journalist guilty of contempt under a statutory provision relating to its proceedings. On appeal, the High Court of Australia unanimously refused to recognise any claim to privilege by the journalist. Dixon J. spoke of "the inevitable conflict" that had to be resolved between "the necessity of discovering the truth in the interests of justice" and "the obligation of secrecy or confidence" to another person by the witness.[20] However, except for the few relations where "general policy" required the existence of a privilege, such as husband and wife, attorney and client, and, where applicable by force of statute, physician and patient, priest and penitent, the rule was inflexible that no mere obligation of honor could hinder the public policy inherent in requiring answers in the witness box.[21]

Early in English law the claim to privilege based on point of honor was dismissed. On the trial of the Duchess of Kingston,[22] a physician's claim to privilege was dismissed along with a claim by another witness based on an obligation of honor. In dismissing the first claim the Court convinced itself that while the revealing of secrets by a physician would ordinarily be counted a breach of honor and indiscreet, it was otherwise when the revelation was made in the course of a legal proceeding. The second claim was treated with less seriousness; the Court was dealing with a criminal case, and the etiquette of honor could not be observed at the same time as the Court was trying lives and liberties. This potential restriction to criminal cases was forgotten by later courts.[23]

Another line of cases demonstrates a judicial readiness to permit silence when the effect of the answer would be to disclose the name of a writer of an allegedly libellous article or of the sources he has relied upon.[24] It seems that the rule is based upon consideration of the desirability of protecting contributors from unnecessary disclosure of their names. It has been established that, as a rule of practice, in the absence of special circumstances, reporters need not disclose their sources in the context of litigation against newspapers.[25]

Canada

(a) At Common Law

Agitation in Canada has grown recently for a privilege for newsmen and their informants in respect of their communications. The matter has been highlighted by some recent cases,[26] and bills may be introduced into the Ontario legislature to give journalists the right to preserve anonymity of news source.[27] However, the Report of the Ontario Royal Commission into Civil Rights recommends that no changes be made in the common law position, on the ground "that the injury that would be done to the administration of justice" by such a privilege "far outweighs" the alleged benefits.[28] The Report notes favorably the operation of judicial discretion in this area. In addition the Canadian Senate Committee on the Mass Media has recommended that no change be made in the common law.[29]

It is worth noting that some difference exists between the various provincial jurisdictions as to the possibility of a claim to privilege in the context of litigation against a newspaper. In *Reid* v. *Telegram Publishing Co. Ltd. and Drea*,[30] an action for libel against a newspaper, the Court refused to grant discovery of the identity of the newspaper's informants on the grounds of public policy. The defences of justification, qualified privilege and fair comment had been raised by the newspaper, and the informants would have to be called at the trial to prove truth in fact and lack of malice. This view accords with the English exception, noted above,[31] to the obdurate refusal of English courts to grant an occupational privilege to journalists in respect of their sources in all cases. However, a different conclusion was reached in *McConachy* v. *Times Publishers Ltd.*,[32] another libel action against a newspaper. Both the editor and the reporter were asked to name the sources of their information for the alleged defamatory article during a discovery proceeding. The British Columbia Court of Appeal compelled both the editor and the reporter to disclose their sources, holding that the English rule had no application in British Columbia. Davey J.A. thought that it was unnecessary to consider the question of "a residual discretion to restrict cross-examination as to a newspaper's source of information",[33] because the newspaper article in question referred to information the reporter asserted he had received from other persons. The Court refused to allow the *Reid* case,[34] first, because it had been decided contrary to prior decision of the British Columbia Court of Appeal and, secondly, because judgment had been given before the decisions in *Attorney-General* v. *Clough, Attorney-General* v. *Mulholland* and *Attorney-General* v. *Foster*.[35] It is difficult to perceive any strength in the second reason given, as those English cases support the *Reid* case on the question of discovery in libel actions against newspapers. It is well to note that the *Reid* case was referred to approvingly by the Alberta Supreme Court in *Red Deer Nursing Home Ltd.* v. *Taylor*,[36] where the defendant in a libel action was a political candidate. The Alberta Supreme Court considered that the defendant should receive the same special treatment as newspapers in libel actions, and he was permitted to refuse to answer a question directed to the name of a person to whom the alleged defamatory matter was communicated. In effect, the Court sought to give a candidate in an election campaign "as much freedom of comment as would be given to a newspaper".[37]

(b) *The Constitutional Aspect*

The Bill of Rights, in section 1 (f), guarantees "freedom of the press".[38] What effect does this provision have on the existence of a privilege in favor of newsmen? The famous Alberta Press Bill case[39] has been regarded by some as establishing Dominion control over the media; by others, as providing flimsy authority for such control. For instance, Professor E.A. Tollefson says:

> While it would be practically convenient for the federal government to have exclusive jurisdiction over the press because of the national nature of some publications and the boundless nature of news itself, it cannot be stated with any degree of confidence that the constitution so provides.[40]

The Press Bill of Alberta, which provided *inter alia* that newspapers must, upon request of a government agency, disclose sources of information, was one of three bills by which the government of Alberta tried to establish the machinery of Social Credit in the province. Four of the Supreme Court justices[41] found the Press Bill *ultra vires* as part of the general scheme of legislation; it fell as ancillary and dependent legislation. The fifth justice (Cannon J.) concluded that the legislation was *ultra vires* because it invaded the sphere of the criminal law reserved to the Dominion. There is nothing in the case which affirms exclusive Dominion control of the mass media.[42]

It is apparent that some matters concerning the press are subject to provincial control.[43] At the same time, some jurisdiction over the media inheres in the Dominion. As Rand J. once pointed out, the rights of free opinion, public debate, and discussion are necessary to Parliamentary government.[44] Those powers which may yield a basis for some media control, direct or indirect, by the provinces include the constitutional categories of "Property and Civil Rights", "Matters of a merely local or private Nature", and section 92 (14) of the British North America Act. The latter provision is of particular significance in the present context, for it gives the provinces exclusive authority in relation to:

> The administration of justice in the province, including the Constitution, Maintenance and Organization of Provincial Courts, both of Civil and Criminal Jurisdiction, and including Procedure in Civil Matters in those Courts.[45]

It is probable that freedom of the press, or any of the other freedoms mentioned in the Bill of Rights, is not a class of subject which is by the B.N.A. Act given either to the provincial legislatures or to the federal Parliament. It can be a "matter" falling within a class of subject within provincial jurisdiction or a class of subject within federal jurisdiction.

The right of a province to regulate the rights and privileges of witnesses in civil proceedings would probably authorize provincial statutes granting testimonial privilege to journalists in such proceedings. Newfoundland has granted a privilege of secrecy of communication between priest and penitent.[46] This privilege is very doubtful at common law, and its validity must depend solely on the power of the Newfoundland legislature. A statutory privilege of secrecy given to newsmen would find a similar justification. In criminal proceedings, the Dominion would, it is submitted, clearly have the power to determine the rights and privileges of newsmen witnesses. To ensure uniformity in civil and criminal proceedings throughout Canada, a concerted plan of legislation would be necessary.[47]

Professor Laskin points out that:

> [T]he test of legislative power, in relation to political liberties lies not in any enactments which recognize them for particular purposes (as does, for example, provincial defamation legislation) but rather in legislation which compels obedience to them or which limits their exercise.[48]

It is obvious that a provincial statute granting a privilege of secrecy of news source to journalists in civil proceedings would involve recognition of the freedom of the press for a particular purpose.[49] That purpose, related as it is to the administration of justice within the province, may be implemented by provincial authorities. It is probably a very different matter for a province to legislate to protect the right of freedom of discussion. It may be persuasively argued that that is a matter in respect of which the federal Parliament alone has power to legislate.[50]

The United States

(a) The Statutes

The subject of claim to secrecy by newsmen has received more publicity and has provoked more discussion, and action, in the United States than elsewhere. Fifteen states now recognise a privilege of non-disclosure in favor of journalists and other newsmen in respect of their sources.[51] In 1970, New York became the fifteenth state. Congress has had before it many times bills seeking to confer a privilege of non-disclosure, but all attempts have so far proved abortive. The statutes provide, in effect, that no person connected with specified media in a capacity involving the collecting, gathering, editing or publishing of news should be required to disclose, in a legal proceeding or investigation, the source of any information obtained by him. However, the significant differences of treatment accorded the privilege by the various states require elaboration.

First, at least two statutes in their terms restrict the privilege to those connected, in the capacity described in the preceding paragraph, with newspapers.[52] The other statutes extend the privilege to those associated with other media, particularly radio and television. Note the exhaustive New York definition: "any newspaper, magazine, news agency, press association, wire service, radio or television . . . ".[53] The tendency is in fact towards an all-inclusive definition. There is no good reason for restricting the privilege to those associated with newspapers.

Secondly, at least five states[54] clearly require that the communication for which privilege is sought must have been published. Other states use ambiguous language in this connection; for example, "procured or obtained by him (the newsgatherer) for publication";[55] "used as the basis for an article he may have written, published or broadcast",[56] "coming into his possession . . . for publication or to be published".[57] One state explicitly provides a privilege in respect of material "whether published or not published".[58]

The Arkansas statute,[59] unlike those in most other states, grants a limited privilege only. The privilege is inapplicable where publication is in bad faith, with malice, and not in the public interest. The New York law contains no such qualification, although a similar provision had been incorporated in the bill unsuccessfully recommended by the New York Law Reform Commission in 1949.[60] The Louisiana statute provides for a challenge to the initial granting of a privilege to a newsman in a particular case.[61] The New Mexico statute contains a vague qualification to the privilege; it is not available if disclosure be essential to prevent injustice, and any order compelling disclosure is appealable, and subject to stay.[62]

The list of bodies before which the privilege may be claimed is, generally, exhaustive. New York, for example, refers to "any court, the legislature or other body having contempt powers",[63] and most of the existing statutes contemplate the claim of privilege in a great variety of situations. An exception to this breadth of definition is the Michigan statute which applies only in respect of criminal proceedings[64]

(b) *The Cases*
The most important judicial pronouncement on the statutory privilege is *Re Taylor,*[65] a decision of the Supreme Court of Pennsylvania. A majority of the court defined "source" in the relevant Pennsylvania statute to include not only the identity of the informant, but also documents, inanimate objects and all sources of information generally. On the facts of the case, a newspaper successfully claimed a privilege of non-production, before an investigating grand jury, of documents and tape recordings relating to an interview with a person claiming knowledge of corruption in city government. Cohen J., in a strong dissent, restricted "source" to the name of the informant, and not the information itself.

On the other hand, there is a distinct tendency for the courts to construe the statutes strictly by employing generally the rule of construction that statutes in derogation of the common law must be strictly construed. In *State* v. *Donovan*[66] a New Jersey court was asked to compel newspapers to disclose some information concerning press releases printed by them. The names of the informants were known, but not the means by which the newspapers had obtained the information. The Court held that the statute granted a privilege only in respect of the sources, not in respect of the identity of the messenger from whom the information was obtained. On the facts of the case, the identity of the messenger was crucial to the issues, because the publication of the releases in question was alleged to be an act in furtherance of conspiracy to obtain an indictment, a principal defence raised by the defendants.

Again, in *Re Howard*[67] a newspaperman had written a story which included quotations from a union official, and was called in a labor dispute case to state whether or not he had a conversation with the official on a particular day. The lower court held that as the published article referred to the source, the privilege could not be claimed; the privilege had been waived. On appeal, the claim to privilege was upheld, but on the ground that the story did not necessarily disclose the source. In *Brogan* v. *Passaic Daily News*[68] the Supreme Court of New Jersey, in a libel action against a newspaper, found that the privilege had been waived. The editor of the offending article, asked upon what information it had been based, replied that it was information obtained from a "reliable source", and the information had been later verified. The Court considered that this statement, and the fact that the editor had disclosed some of his sources of information, amounted to a waiver. To testify that alleged defamatory matter came from a "reliable source" is to waive the privilege of non-disclosure, if defences of fair comment and good faith are raised.

Some courts have adopted extremely literal interpretations of the statutes to defeat the privilege. In one case the writer who claimed the privilege wrote for a biweekly magazine, and the California statute protects only persons connected with newspapers, press associations or wire services. The claim to privilege was defeated.[69]

Where statutes conferring a privilege do not exist, the interest most frequently invoked by the courts in disallowing claims to privilege is the public interest in the due administration of justice.[70] Where the question asked of the newsman goes to the very heart of a party's case, the Court will compel an answer. Silence will not be permitted when there is a clear and direct conflict with the interests of justice. The Court would not usually compel an answer when the information, or its source, are not relevant to the principal proceeding.[71]

Where no statute is available, and it is apparent that the newsman will not succeed with arguments of irrelevance or social policy, it may still be possible in some cases for a plea of possible self-incrimination by the journalist to succeed. In *Burdick* v. *United States,*[72] a newspaper had published articles about customs frauds. The editor who wrote the articles was asked by a grand jury his sources of information for the articles, and he refused to answer on the ground that his answer might tend to incriminate him. His claim was respected. As Chafee points out,[73] the claim was probably unfounded in fact. Even after the editor was given a pardon absolving him of any crime in this connection he remained silent; he could not be forced to accept the pardon. Learned Hand J. delivered a strong contrary opinion in the lower Court[74] to the effect that a witness needs only protection, and he has protection when the means of safety, in this case a pardon, are at hand.

Attempts to persuade the Courts that newsmen have a constitutionally protected right to privilege have failed. In one of the latest cases, the Supreme Court of Oregon stated that

> [I]t would be difficult to rationalize a rule that would create special constitutional rights for those possessing credentials as news gatherers which would not conflict with the equal-privileges and equal-protection concepts also found in the Constitution. Freedom of the press is a right which belongs to the public, it is not the private preserve of those who possess the implements of publishing.[75]

But the Court went on to say that it did not hold that the Constitution forbids statutes conferring "reasonable privileges to withhold evidence". If the claimed privilege is to be found in the Constitution, its benefits could not be limited to the members of a particular class. The Court left open the possibility of legislative experimentation with definitions restricting the class of those able to claim the privilege. Generally, the courts have held that even if the claim to privilege does involve a First Amendment liberty, the public interest in the due administration of justice must prevail. But the cases tacitly acknowledge that the compelled disclosure of confidential information is, to some extent, an impairment of the freedom of the press.[76]

Evaluation

The proponents of the newsman's claim to privilege emphasize the public interest in the unrestricted flow and wide disseminatin of news information. In *Associated Press* v. *United States*,[77] Black J. insisted that "the widest possible dissemination of information from diverse and antagonistic sources is essential to the welfare of the public . . . . [A] free press is a condition of a free society".[78] It is often urged that those sources upon which the media rely to keep themselves aware of events or of opinions of which society should properly be informed would vanish if newsmen were compelled to publicize sources of information in giving evidence before courts, or legislative or administrative tribunals. The public is entitled to have available to it the full facts on any matter of public interest.

The interest in freedom of information may be defined in terms of the value accruing to society in the political, social and cultural progress of a healthy and viable community (the social interest) or in terms of its critical importance to the individual in providing the *sine qua non* of a bountiful existence as a free member of a civilized community. This latter individual interest is translatable into a profound social interest in the general well-being, in a broad sense, of the individual members of society. At times, other social interests, such as the interest in the administration of justice, conflict with the individual interest in freedom of information. When such a conflict occurs, the conflicting interests ought to be placed "on the same level" for adjustment, as Roscoe Pound insisted.[79] Otherwise, the personal preferences of the decision-maker may be influenced by the verbal symbols "social" and "individual". Thus, as Professor Julius Stone has pointed out,[80] the right of free speech has normally been conceived as a conflict between society and the individual. "Yet on a true analysis society as a whole is also deeply concerned in the preservation of the claim of individuals to freedom of speech."[81] The conflict between the claims involved in freedom of information, in its specific expression as the unimpeded flow and wide dissemination of news information, should be stated as one between the social interest in the due administration of justice and the integrity of existing institutions, and the social interest in political, social and cultural progress.

There is, undoubtedly, in freedom of information a fundamental safeguard of the democractic process and of the effective functioning of the democratic state.[82] This effective functioning is only possible if organs of opinion yield the most accurate information essential to each individual to ascertain his position *vis-à-vis* the society and his fellow citizens. At the world level, the Universal Declaration of Human Rights affirms the right to information inhering in the individual.[83] In the context of freedom in Canada, Monsieur Lépine comments:

> La liberté de l'information est un concept très vaste: il comprend le droit d'informer et d'être informé; il signifie donc pour l'individu le droit de dire et d'exprimer les faits, les événements et ses idées; le droit d'avoir accès aux idées et aux opinions des autres; il signifie le droit pour l'individu de discuter; de critiquer les faites, les événements et la conduite des autres hommes.[84]

The claim to freedom of information is rarely explicitly recognized, but oblique reference is apparent in such fundamental freedoms as speech, press association and religion. In *Stanley* v. *Georgia,* the Supreme Court of the United States recently affirmed that "this right to receive information and ideas, regardless of their social worth . . . is fundamental to our free society".[85] In the context of the Leviathan state, with its immense powers remote from the influence or control of the individual, the right to freedom of information is crucial. The interests that seek to disrupt or displace freedom of information should be overwhelming before granting recognition.

But is the free flow of information in fact restricted by the absence of a privilege of secrecy in favor of newsmen and their informants? It has not been reliably demonstrated that the absence of such a privilege hinders freedom of information; or, more to the point, that the creation of such a privilege increases the information gained by reporters. It has been suggested that "the interference with the flow of information . . . is imperceptible or non-existent".[86] Reference has been made to the superiority of information found in *The New York Times*,[87] although until 1970 the State of New York did not have a privilege statute.[88] Again, it is said that better news reporting is not guaranteed by a statute for two reasons. First, the newsman will not refrain from publishing confidential information out of fear that he might later be cited for contempt for failing to reveal his informant. Second, even though no statute exists, the newsman will not reveal his informant when judicially ordered to do so.[89] However, further research into this question beyond the scope of this paper is obviously necessary.

A countervailing interest may, at times, be found in the public need to ensure the integrity and authority of legislative, judicial, and administrative bodies. The number of privileges recognized at common law was severely limited. It was no doubt considered that only overriding social policy could justify silence by a witness in legal proceedings, for otherwise the integrity of the court of law as an impartial and accurate arbiter would be eroded. As has been noted, this interest in the administration of justice is that most frequently enlisted by courts to justify refusal to permit silence by newsmen. It may be noted that this same interest plays some part in the refusal of the English and Canadian courts to compel newspapermen to answer questions directed to source in discovery proceedings in the course of litigation against newspapers: the courts will not permit their procedures to be used by plaintiffs as a device for finding other defendants.[90]

Another interest that might be weighed against this interest in the freedom of information is the maintenance of law and order. This is related to, but distinct from, the interest in the integrity of institutions. As distinct from the latter interest, it is more specifically concerned with disclosure by newsmen in criminal proceedings; or, in civil proceedings, information relating to criminal activities. At times, this interest has been suppressed in the face of overriding public policy, as in the refusal of the law to compel a spouse to testify against the other spouse. The privilege against self-incrimination was originally inspired by public policy considerations but has been weakened by statute; generally, an answer must be given to a question, although it cannot later be used against the witness.[91] In this case the public policy inherent in the privilege against self-incrimination is not of such a magnitude as to require the total suppression of information contrary to the interest in law and order.

A number of individual interests range themselves against these public interests in the administration of justice, and law and order. First, the informant often has an interest in keeping his identity hidden, whether for reasons of personal safety, or economic security, or social position. But it cannot be said that in every case such an interest exists. Should a newsman be allowed to be the arbiter of the existence of the interest? It has been said that the privilege, where it exists, belongs to the newsman.[92] The cases on waiver of the privilege suggest this. It has been said that "[T]he informant's protection . . . is purely derivative; he has not recourse of any kind if the reporter elects to reveal his identity".[93] This "rule" is anomalous. As Professor Cross says, "It is of the essence of a privilege that it may be waived by the person who enjoys it."[94] If the privilege belongs to the newsman, the informant has no protection beyond an obligation of honor. The American statutes[95] already discussed adopt ambiguous language, providing that no person "shall be compelled" or "shall be required" to disclose. If the social interest to be protected is freedom of information, in the dissemination of news, surely the only person able to waive the privilege should be the informant. If it is purely a matter in the discretion of the journalist, then it is arguable that the confidence of informants would not be encouraged any more than it is now when no privilege exists. On the other hand, it is arguable that the confidence of informants will be guaranteed because they know that their confidants need not disobey the law to preserve the confidence, and hence the danger of disclosure is certainly minimized. But it is apparent that the *maximum* protection of informants will be achieved only if the privilege belongs to the informant. Further, as has been noted, there is sometimes a danger of implied waiver of privilege in the testimony given by the newsman which can best be avoided by granting the privilege to the informant.[96]

It has been suggested that the newsman is entitled to claim a professional or economic interest in gathering news information that deserves protection. In most cases where the argument has been made, it has been roundly dismissed.[97] The courts emphasize that this interest cannot prevail against the public interest in the due administration of justice. The claim has usually been framed in terms of forfeiture of estate and, as such, is clearly untenable because the newsman's answer would not result in forfeiture *by law*.[98] However, the argument has been successful in encouraging a judicial leniency in some cases.[99]

Any rule which seeks to strike a balance between the interests at play should be carefully considered. Precision in the definition of terms should be sought: Key terms such as "source" should be carefully defined and the class of those benefiting should be defined in the most exact terms possible. In this way, the effect of judicial discretion on the question of the legitimacy of the claimed privilege is minimized. But a judicial discretion should be retained to deal with certain exceptional cases which, it is submitted, may not be entitled to the privilege, although *prima facie* within the terms of the statute. For example, the Arkansas limit in the privilege is desirable: The privilege should not, for reasons of public policy, be claimable where publication consequential on the obtaining of secret information is in bad faith, malicious and not in the public interest.[100] Another desirable limitation on the privilege derives from the public interest in the general security: A newsman should not be allowed to remain silent when the source of the information he is seeking to hide bears on a subject of national security. A limitation as to information relating to the details of any proceeding required to be secret under state or federal law is in the public interest. However, it is submitted that any further limitation compelling an answer simply because the newsman is the only source available and the trial cannot be concluded without his testimony, is unreasonable. The effect of such a limitation would be to vest too large a discretion in the judge sufficient to enable the conservative judiciary to nullify the privilege in most cases.

As suggested above, the privilege should belong to the informant, not to the newsman. Just as in the attorney-client relationship it is the client who enjoys the privilege,[101] in the present situation the informant enjoys the privilege in the same sense. The newsman should not have a power of waiver. If the chief interest to be protected is, as is urged, the public interest in the unrestricted flow and wide dissemination of information, the strongest protection will be provided only if the right of waiver belongs to the informant. If the newsman may waive, the argument for statutory protection is weakened, if not destroyed. For where, prior to the statute, the informant relied on an express or implied promise by the newsman not to reveal, he would now, after the statute, rely on an express or implied promise by the newsman not to waive the privilege. In other words, the principal justification for a privilege statute—to encourage informants by giving a guarantee of privilege upon which the state will renege only in exceptional circumstances and which cannot be waived by anyone other than the informant—would be destroyed. Finally, the term "privilege" is inaccurate unless the informant has the right of waiver, for the historical connotation of a legal privilege includes a power in the person who has made the confidential communication to prevent disclosure.[102]

It is important that the terms of a privilege statute be as precise as possible. First, the category of newsman entitled to refuse to answer must be unambiguous. It is submitted that all newsmen should be included; there is no valid reason for the exclusion of, say, reporters for underground or student newspapers. The New York statute[103] contains broad definitions of "professional journalist" and "newscaster". In the modern age there is, again, no valid reason for excluding the latter from the benefit of a privilege statute which extends beyond the written press to radio and television.

As the circumstances of *Re Taylor* [104] suggest, the term "source" should be defined with greater accuracy. That case extended the statutory protection to material compiled by the newspaper and which was, in a broad sense, a source. A possible distinction might be desirable between news obtained from a source, in the sense of an informant, and news obtained without the aid of any informant but by reporter "scouting" and "probing". If the interest mainly protected is the public interest in the continued flow of information, then, logically, only cases in which information has been obtained from an informant on a promise of confidentiality, express or implied, ought to come within the protection of a statute granting a privilege. For example, suppose a newsman writes a story on the activities of some criminal group, from bootleggers to drug-takers to gangsters, after having infiltrated the group in disguise. Assuming he has not committed a crime in the course of gathering the information, should the newsman be compelled to answer questions directed to a disclosure of the sources of his information? One can say that the public interest in freedom of information is at stake in this situation, but, if so, a change of emphasis is then necessary, for there is no informant who is relying on an express or implied promise of non-disclosure. It then must be argued that newsmen will be less zealous about embarking on such fact-finding activities if disclosure is forced because, for instance, they fear reprisals from resentful members of the group they have been investigating or that it will, in the future, be more difficult to infiltrate such groups. But it is clear that the traditional argument that newsmen must protect their "leaks", or they will "dry up", is weak in this type of case.

It is therefore suggested that only the source, *as informant*, ought to receive protection. As the dissenting opinion in *Re Taylor* said, "It is the name of the informant and not the information itself which is protected".[105] In *Re Taylor* itself the informant was already known, yet the Court protected the material associated with that informant. What possible reason can be adduced for continuing protection when the name of the informant is known? In such a case the public interest in the administration of justice, in the correct disposal of litigation, is not confronted with the public interest in the free flow of information. The criterion for ascertaining the relevance of the latter interest must be the possibility of the intimidation of future informants. Such a possibility is non-existent in a case like *Re Taylor*. The criterion upon which all information and material ought to be tested for qualification to privilege is whether the tendency of the information and material is to disclose the informant. Once the informant is known all claims to privilege or information and material connected with the information ought to fall. Thus, the Maryland Court of Appeals has intimated that it would not uphold a newsman's claim to privilege in respect of the details of the information when he had revealed the name of the source.[106] The Maryland statute in question protects only "the source of any news or information" and not the "news or information".[107]

A final suggestion relates to the model law prepared by the Harvard Students Legislation Research Bureau.[108] The model extends protection to a wide variety of newsmen, and establishes procedures for challenge to the protection by any "body, officer, person or party". With a similar intent, the Louisiana statute[109] provides that the persons seeking the information may apply for an order revoking the privilege. The application must state "the reason why the disclosure is essential to the protection of the public interest". Revocation of the privilege may only be granted when "disclosure is essential to the public interest". These types of procedural safeguards are desirable.

Conclusion

The principal trends in the major common law countries in relation to the newsman's claim to secrecy of news source have been defined. In the result, it appears that a persuasive case can be made for the legal recognition of the claim, subject to limitations in the best interests of public policy. While it is not yet certain, because of a lack of empirical data, that freedom of information is protected and advanced by giving a privilege to newsmen or their informants, some part at least of the newsman's fear of emasculation occasioned by the absence of the privilege may be justified. It is considered that the matter should no longer be left entirely to judicial discretion as it is in the United Kingdom and Canada. Further, it is not sufficient to dismiss the claim by saying, as did the Canadian Senate Committee on Mass Media,[110] that the traditional privileged relations, such as attorney and client, are not "analogous to that between newsman and informant".[111] To do so is to rely on narrow categories and definitions, and to fail to take account of changing social, political and cultural conditions. If it is objected that, unlike the usual privileged relationship, the privilege in this case may be claimed by the newsman, a statute could provide in unequivocal terms that the privilege belongs to the informant and may be waived by him alone. If some American statutes have seen fit to repose the privilege in the newsman alone, it does not follow that Canada should slavishly adopt this philosophy. If it is objected that, unlike the traditional privileged relationship, this claim is made in respect of any information, whether a confidential communication or not, a simple statutory provision could restrict the privilege to traditional concepts. Finally, it is not sufficient to dismiss the claim by pleading, as did the Canadian Senate Committee, that there is a problem of definition; who is, and who is not, entitled to the privilege? Again, the necessity for precise definition of terms, discussed above, is apparent and would solve this alleged problem. The Report of the Canadian Senate Committee is, on the point of privilege, unconvincing in its reasons for refusing to recommend a change in the law. The shocking flippancy of the Committee in saying that if jail terms imposed on newsmen were short, most newsmen would find the experience "refreshing, educational and possibly even profitable"[112] must cast doubt on the seriousness with which the newsman's claim has been considered.

A statute should ideally set forth the privilege as precisely as possible. The U.S. experience has taught that interpretation will be aided by thoughtful and careful definition of terms. A statute should be liberal in its application, granting the privilege to all members of news media who gather or edit the news; the privilege should be claimable before any bodies having contempt powers.

Some restriction of the privilege is nevertheless desirable. Even where there is a *prima facie* entitlement to the privilege the availability of the privilege should be conditioned by reference to "the public interest".[113] It is considered that this concept of the public interest should be restricted to clearly defined cases to avoid the possibility of judicial emasculation of the privilege in cases where no serious public interest is involved. The interests of the national security would, of course, be one criterion upon which to determine the availability of the privilege. The privilege should likewise be inapplicable where the publication of the information sought to be privileged is in bad faith, with malice and not in the public interest. However, it should be made clear that the concept of public interest does not extend to cases where the newsman is the only available source of the information and without his testimony the proceedings, whether before legislative, judicial, or administrative bodies, cannot be successfully concluded without his testimony. To impose such a limitation would be tantamount to returning the claim to secrecy to the untrammelled discretion of the judge.

Two trends in the United States should be avoided in Canada by careful drafting in any new statute. First, the privilege of secrecy ought to be restricted to the name of the informant and any material tending to disclose the identity of that informant. The news or information should not in itself be privileged. Secondly, the privilege should, by clear definition, be granted to the informant, not to the newsman. The legal conception of an occupational privilege would seem to require that the informant alone be entitled to the right of waiver; and, logically, the public interest in freedom of information is best served, if it is served at all, by the granting of the privilege to the informant who will alone have the power to reveal or not to reveal, subject of course to the tentative limitations on the availability of the privilege outlined in the preceding paragraph.

NOTES TO CHAPTER ELEVEN

1/Canada, *Report of the Special Senate Committee on Mass Media,* Vol. I (Ottawa: Queen's Printer, 1970) 105-06 [hereinafter the Davey Committee].

2/The main concern of this paper will be with the claim to privilege in judicial proceedings, but it is acknowledged that legislative bodies and tribunals may also be involved. For a classic illustration of the claim before a legislative body, see the Deutsch Case, reported *New York Times,* May 19, 1945 at 8;91 Congressional Record, Appdx. 2554 May 28, 1945.

3/On March 18, 1969, a Canadian Broadcasting Corporation television journalist, John Smith, was cited for contempt of court for having refused to reveal the identity of a confidential source of information. Smith had apparently interviewed a young man claiming to be a member of the Front de Libération du Québec (F.L.Q.). See *Memoire de la Fédération Professionelle des Journalistes du Québec au Comité Spécial du Senat sur les moyens de communications de masse,* le 15 avril 1970 at 3. Bills have been presented to the Ontario Legislature by members of the New Democratic Party in order to give newspaper reporters the right to preserve anonymity of source: see *Toronto Daily Star,* Oct. 8, 1970 at 6. Recently, two reporters refused to identify their sources before a Commission of Inquiry in Toronto (the "Duke Inquiry"). The Commissioner decided not to take action against the reporters because the information the reporters could provide was obtained from other witnesses: see *Toronto Daily Star,* Oct. 9, 1970 at 4. See also *Report, supra* note 1 at 105, for reference to the Smith case.

4/See, for a recent discussion, GOLDSTEIN, "Newsmen and their Confidential Sources", *The New Republic* (March 21, 1970), at 13. A good bibliography on this topic is *Freedom of the Press* (Carbondale: Southern Illinois University Press, 1968). Useful notes and articles include P. CARTER, *The Journalist, his Informant and Testimonial Privilege* (1960), 35 N.Y.U.L. Rev. 1111; *Notes,* (1958-59), 72 Harv. L. Rev. 768; (1956), 35 Neb. L. Rev. 562; (1950), 36 Va. L. Rev. 61.

5/Apart from the attorney-client relationship (see *Wigmore on Evidence* [McNaughton Revision] (Boston: Little, Brown, 1961) s. 2282 at 541 [hereinafter *Wigmore*]), which has been privileged for centuries and is now recognized by statute in many jurisdictions, some legislatures have extended privileged protection of other confidential relationships. These include physician-patient, priest-penitent, psychologist-patient, and other relationships (see *Id.* s. 2286 at 536). Most of the moves to establish occupational privileges outside the attorney-client privilege have been in the United States. In Canada, Newfoundland recognizes a priest-penitent privilege by state (*Evidence Act* R.S.N. 1952, c. 120 s. 6.). But in England, the trend against the granting of privilege is more pronounced: some old privileges were abolished by the Civil Evidence Act 1968 c. 64, s. 16 (U.K.). On the physician-patient and priest-penitent privileges, see NOKES, *Professional Privilege* (1950), 66 L.Q.R. 88 at 94.

6/WIGMORE, *A Student's Textbook on the Law of Evidence* (Chicago: Foundation Press, 1935) s. 386 at 391.

7/VIII *Wigmore,* s. 2285 at 527. The conditions were quoted, with little discussion, in the Report *supra* note 1 at 106.

8/*Id.* s. 2286, n. 9.

9/See, for example, the views of Dr. F.S. Siebert quoted in School of Journalism, University of Missouri, *Reporters' Privilege Worldwide* (Freedom of Information Center Publication No. 116, February 1964) 4. This pamphlet should be consulted as an excellent résumé of the position, particularly for its journalistic publications references. It also gives a brief survey of the position in countries other than Great Britain, Canada and the United States; *id.* at 5-6, mentioning, *inter alia,* cases in Norway (secrecy of source permissible if there had not been a breach of official secrecy) and Puerto Rico (privilege available). Austria gives a right of professional secrecy to the journalist.

10/Law Reform Committee (U.K.), *Sixteenth Report* (London: H.M.S.O., 1967).

11/*Id.* para. 54 at 23. It is curious that no news media appear in the list of organizations and individuals which submitted evidence to the Committee (Annex 1, at 25).

12/*Id.* para. 54 at 23.

13/*Id.* para. 1 at 3.

14/*Attorney-General* v. *Clough,* [1963] 1 Q.B. 773, [1963] 1 All E.R. 420 (Q.B.D.); *Attorney-General* v. *Mulholland,* [1963] 2 Q.B. 477, [1963] 1 All E.R. 767 (C.A.); *Attorney-General* v. *Foster,* [1963] 2 Q.B. 477, [1963] 1 All

E.R. 767 (C.A.); Discussion of these cases will be found in Tapper, *Freedom and Privilege* (1963), 26 M.L.R. 571; Gottesman, *Letter from London* (1963), 18 Record of Assn. Bar of City of N.Y. 371.

15/[1963] 1 Q.B. 773 at 790, [1963] 1 All E.R. 420 at 426.

16/*Attorney-General* v. *Foster* [1963] 2 Q.B. 477 at 492, [1963] 1 All E.R. 767 at 772-773.

17/*Id.* at 490, [1963] 1 All E.R. at 771.

18/*Id.* at 488, [1963] 1 All E.R. at 770.

19/(1940), 63 C.L.R. 73, 14 A.L.J. 38. This case appears to state the present position in Australia in relation to the claimed privilege. See G. SAWER, *A Guide to Australian Law for Journalists, Authors, Printers and Publishers* (Melbourne: Melbourne University Press, 1968). See also *Re Buchanan* (1964), 65 S.R. (N.S.W.) 9 (Full Court of N.S.W.) 69-70.

20/(1940), 63 C.L.R. 73 at 92-105.

21/The relationships of doctor and patient and priest and penitent are the subjects of statutory privilege in certain parts of the British Commonwealth, such as New Zealand, Victoria, Tasmania, Newfoundland and British Honduras, and in some states of the United States. See *Report, supra* note 10, para. 41. at 17.

22/(1776), 20 Howell St. Tr. R. 335.

23/See *O'Brennan* v. *Tully* (1935), 69 I.L.T. 115 where a newspaper editor refused to reveal the name of a correspondent with the newspaper and was found guilty of contempt. A report in *The Times,* 20th Feb. 1889, at 8, cols. 3-6 reports a case during the proceedings of the Parnell Commission, when *The Times* editor refused to disclose the names of the writers of certain articles, and was compelled to answer the specific questions put to him.

It seems, however, that English courts are reluctant to compel newsmen to reveal their sources, and will do so only, as the "Vassall cases" indicate, when overwhelming considerations of public policy or justice so dictate. A judge will rarely, if ever, compel a clergyman to reveal the details of a penitential conversation, although the privilege of the confessional is in theory denied. See *Wilson* v. *Rastall* (1792), 4 T.R. 759; 100 E.R. 1283 and *R.* v. *Hay* (1860), 2 F. & F. 4, 175 E.R. 933.

24/See *Lyle-Samuel* v. *Odhams Ltd.,* [1920] 1 K.B. 135; and *South Suburban Co-Operative Society Ltd.* v. *Orum,* [1937] 2 K.B. 690, and cases referred therein.

25/*Georgius* v. *Vice Chancellor of Oxford University Press,* [1949] 1 K.B. 729.

26/See *e.g.,* the Smith case discussed *supra* note 3.

27/See a report in the *Toronto Daily Star,* Oct. 8, 1970, at 4.

28/See *Royal Commission Into Civil Rights* (Report Number One) Vol. 2 (Toronto: Queen's Printer, 1968) 826.

29/*Report of the Special Senate Committee on Mass Media, supra* note 1.

30/(1961), 28 D.L.R. (2d) 6 (H.C. of Ont.).

31/*Supra* note 15.

32/(1965), 49 D.L.R. (2d) 349, 50 W.W.R. 389 (B.C.C.A.).

33/*Id.* at 352, 50 W.W.R. at 391.

34/*Reid* v. *Telegram Publishing Co. Ltd.* and *Drea, supra* note 30.

35/*Supra* note 14 for the references to the three cases.

36/(1969), 1 D.L.R. (3d) 491, (1969) 67 W.W.R. 1 (Alta. S.C.)

37/*Id.* at 500, 67 W.W.R. at 13.

38/Canadian Bill of Rights, S.C. 1960, c. 44 s. 1(f); see WALTER S. TARNOPOLSKY, *The Canadian Bill of Rights* (Toronto: Carswell Co., 1966) 27-32, 122-38.

39/*Re Alberta Legislation,* [1938] 2 D.L.R. 81, [1938] S.C.R. 100.

40/E.A. TOLLEFSON, "Freedom of the Press", *Contemporary Problems of Public Law in Canada,* 49, ed. O.E. Lang (Toronto: University of Toronto Press, 1968). For background and details and a good discussion of the *Alberta Press Bill,* Tollefson's essay is a good source.

41/Duff, C.J.C., Hudson, Kerwin, Crocket JJ.

42/The statements of their Lordships which suggest Dominion control must be read in the context in which they were delivered, viz., a concern that "the mandatory and prohibitory provisions of the Press Bill . . . [interfere] with the free working of the political organization of the Dominion" (Cannon J. *supra* note 39, [1938] 2 D.L.R. at 119, [1938] S.C.R. at 146), and the need for a parliament working under the influence of public opinion and public discussion (Duff C.J.C. *supra* note 39, [1938] 2 D.L.R. at 108-109, [1938] S.C.R. at 134-135). Obviously, these broad statements were inspired by a fear that the character of the provincial press regulation in question was such that the working of parliamentary institutions was gravely threatened.

43/See, *e.g.,* the opinion of Duff C.J.C., *supra* note 39, [1938] 2 D.L.R. at 108, [1938] S.C.R. at 134, that "there is a very wide field in which the provinces undoubtedly are invested with legislative authority over newspapers".

44/*Switzman* v. *Ebling,* 7 D.L.R. (2d) 337, [1957] S.C.R. 285.

45/British North America Act, 30 & 31 Vict. c. 3, s. 92(14); s. 92(13) "property and civil rights"; s. 92(16) "local matters in the province".

The Claim to Secrecy of News Sources/217

46/ *The Evidence Act,* R.S.N. 1952, c. 120, s. 6.

47/As Kerwin C.J.C. said in *Klein* v. *Bell,* [1955] 2 D.L.R. 513 at 518, [1955] S.C.R. 309 at 315. Canada, of course, could only provide with reference to all proceedings over which it had legislative authority and the provincial legislature with reference to proceedings over which it had such authority.

48/LASKIN, *An Inquiry Into the Diefenbaker Bill of Rights* (1959), 37 Can. Bar Rev. 120.

49/DUFF, C.J.C. in *Re Alberta Statutes, supra* note 39, [1938] 2 D.L.R. at 107, [1938] S.C.R. at 133.

50/As Professor Laskin indicates, (*supra* note 48 at 116) *Saumur* v. *Quebec and Attorney-General of Quebec* [1953] 4 D.L.R. 641, [1953] 2 S.C.R. 299 supports a contention for provincial power of political freedoms, including freedom of the press, but an analysis of the judgements shows that there is no clear majority in favor of an exclusive competence. Three of the judges (Rinfret, C.J.C., Taschereau and Kerwin JJ.) considered that the political freedoms (in this case, freedom of religion) came within Section 92 (13) of the B.N.A. Act. Four judges (Rand, Kellock, Estey and Locke JJ.) thought that the political freedoms were not within provincial competence. The two remaining judges (Cartwright and Fauteux JJ.) thought that both province and Dominion could deal with political freedom in certain respects. So only four judges deny any provincial competence in respect of the political freedoms. But note the cases invalidating provincial legislation compelling Sunday observance: *Hamilton Street Railway case* [1903] A.C. 524; *Henry Birks & Sons (Montreal) Ltd.* v. *Montreal and Attorney-General of Quebec,* [1955] 5 D.L.R. 321, [1955] S.C.R. 799.

It is a question of classification. In the above cases, the question is whether the provincial law is best described as one with respect to store closing hours (then competence) or with respect to religious observance (then incompetence).

51/The statutes are:

Ala. Code Ann. tit. 7 § 370 (West 1958)

Ariz. Rev. Stat. Ann. tit. 12 § 2237 (West Supp. 1970)

Ark. Stat. Ann. tit. 43 § 917 (West 1964)

Cal. Evidence Code § 1070 (West 1966)

Ind. Sta. Ann. tit. 2 § 1733 (West 1966)

Ky. Rev. Stat. § 421.100 (West 1963)

La. Rev. Stat. § § 45:1451 to 45:1454 (West 1965)

Md. Ann. Code Art. 35, § 2 (West 1965)

Michigan Compiled Laws, § 767.5a (West 1968)

Mont. Rev. Code Ann. tit. 93 ch.601.2 (West 1964)

N.J. Stat. Ann. § 2A : 84A-21 : 84A - 29 (West 1969)

N.M. Stat. Ann. § 20-1-12.1 (1953, Supp. 1967)

N.Y. Civil Rights Law § 79(b) (effective May 12, 1970)

Ohio Rev. Code Ann. § 2739.12 (West 1966)

P. Stat. Ann. tit. 28 § 330 (West 1969)

It appears that, in the absence of statute, no privilege of this kind exists in any state of the United States. In the absence of statute, the matter is left to judicial discretion. A recent decision (*infra* note 74) indicates constitutional difficulties of equal protection in the way of judicial creation of a privilege in favor of particular newsmen. The statutes are discussed in numerous excellent articles. See, Note, *The Right of a Newsman to Refrain from Divulging the Source of His Information* (1950), 36 Va. L. Rev. 61; and other articles cited, *supra* note 3. See also: Note, *Privilege of Newspapermen to Withhold Sources of Information from the Court* (1935), 45 Yale L.J. 357; Comment, *Confidentiality of News Sources Under the First Amendment* (1959), 1 Stan. L. Rev. 541.

52/Arkansas (includes radio, but not T.V.) and New Jersey, *supra* note 51. The privilege granted to radio and T.V. newsmen is qualified under the Pennsylvania statute - *supra* note 51, § 330(b).

53/*Supra* note 51.

54/Alabama, Kentucky, California, Maryland and New Jersey, *supra* note 51. Arkansas is a doubtful sixth: see, *infra* note 56.

55/Arizona, *supra* note 51.

56/Arkansas, *supra* note 51.

57/New York, *supra* note 51.

58/Indiana, *supra* note 51.

59/*Supra* note 51.

60/See New York Law Revision Commission, Leg. Doc. No.65(A), App. A (1949).

61/*Supra* note 51.

62/*Supra* note 51. The factors to be considered by New Mexico Courts include: . . . the nature of the proceeding, the merits of the claim or defense, the adequacy of the remedy otherwise available, the relevancy of the source, and the possibility of establishing by other means that which the source is offered as tending to prove.

63/*Supra* note 51.

64/*Supra* note 51.

65/(1963), 412 Pa. 32, 7 A.L.R. (3d) 580. The cases are collected and discussed in Annotation, *Privilege of Newspaper or Magazine and Persons Connected therewith not to disclose communications to or information acquired by such a person,* 7 A.L.R. (3d) 591. This note supersedes one in 102 A.L.R. 171.

66/(1943), 129 N.J.L. 478, 30 A.2d 421.

67/(1955), 136 Cal. App. (2d) 816, 289 P.2d 537 (District Ct. of App.).

68/(1956), 22 N.J. 139, 123 A.2d 473.

69/*Cepeda* v. *Cohane* (1964), 233 Fed. Supp. 465 (D.C.N.Y.).

70/See, for instance, *Re Goodfader's Appeal* (1961), 45 Hawaii 317, 37 P.2d 472; *People ex rel. Mooney* v. *New York County* (1936), 269 N.Y. 291, 199 N.E. 415, 102 A.L.R. 769; *People* v. *Durrant* (1897), 116 Cal. 179, 48 P.75; *Garland* v. *Torre* (1958) 259 Fed. 2d 545, cert. den. 358 U.S. 910.

71/*Rosenberg* v. *Carroll,* 99 F. Supp. 629.

72/(1915), 236 U.S. 79.

73/Z. CHAFEE, *Government and Mass Communications* (Hamden, Conn.: Archon Books, 1967), 497.

74/*United States* v. *Burdick* (1914), 211 Fed. Rep. 492.

75/*State* v. *Buchanan* (1968), 436 P. 2d 729: 250 Or. 244 (S. Ct. of Oregon); cert, den. 392 U.S. 905. See also *Murphy* v. *Colorado* (1961), 365 U.S. 843, cert. denied (S. Ct. of Col.). For evaluation of the constitutional aspect see J. GUEST AND A. STANZLER, *The Constitutional Argument for Newsmen Concealing their Sources* (1969-70), 64 N.W.U.L. Rev. 18.

76/See, *e.g., Re Goodfader's Appeal, supra* note 70, a leading case on the law of the subject where no statute exists and see *Garland* v. *Torre, supra* note 70.

For a discussion of the *Buchanan case, supra* note 75, see J.E. Beaver, *The Newsman's Code, The Claim of Privilege and Everyman's Right to Evidence* (1969), Oregon L. Rev. 243 at 258, the author concludes that the claim to privilege based on the First Amendment is rightly rejected, for otherwise the courts would be faced with "the task of determining who was in fact a newsgatherer entitled to the privilege".

77/(1944), 326 U.S. 1.

78/*Id.* at 20.

79/Pound, *Survey of Social Interests* (1943), 57 Harv. L. Rev. 2.

80/JULIUS STONE, *Social Dimensions of Law and Justice* (Stanford: Stanford Univ. Press, 1966) at 182.

81/*Id.*

82/As Stone points out, *id.* at 348, there is a "special value for political progress attaching to wide public discussion stimulated by the press".

83/G.A. Res. 217 A., U.N. Doc A/810 (1948) art. 19. This document is probably not a legal instrument possessing international normative validity—see J. BRIERLY, *The Law of Nations,* 6th ed. (Oxford: Clarendon, 1963), 294. It should be noted that, historically, freedom of information has been recognized as having limits. See, generally C. ANTIEAU, *Rights of our Fathers* (Vienna, Va.: Coiner Publications, 1968). See also B. DE SPINOZA, *Tractatus - Theologico - Politicus* (1670) *The Chief Works,* Vol. 1, Ch. XX (R.H.M. Elwes translation). A modern echo of this limitation is found in the Arkansas privilege statute, *supra* note 51. Other limitations proceed from the nature of the information, *e.g.,* defamatory matter, or as in the Wisconsin statute which prohibits the publication of the names of child victims of sex crimes (*see State* v. *Evjue* (1948), 253 Wis. 146, 33 N.W. (2d) 305), and from the social or political situation, *e.g.,* wartime. See *Re Drummond Wren* [1945] O.R. 778, 4 D.L.R. 674 (Ont. H.C.) on judicial application of Charter provisions on human rights as indicative of public policy.

84/LÉPINE, *La Liberté de l'information dans le droit Canadien* (1968), 14 McGill L.J. 733. Freedom of information has, says Lépine, been developed by dicta in the Supreme Court of Canada. Lépine thinks this freedom is best protected by the courts, rather than by the Parliament or the provincial legislatures. The writer does not comment directly on our problem.

85/(1969), 394 U.S. 564.

86/Note, *Compulsory Disclosure of a Newsman's Source: A Compromise Proposal* (1959), 54 N.W.U.L. Rev. 243.

87/R. SEMETA, *Journalist's Testimonial Privilege* (1960), 9 Clev. Mar. L. Rev. 311, but see criticism of this kind of evidence as "meaningless" in Guest and Stanzler, *supra* note 75 at 43.

88/*Supra* note 51.

89/See *Note,* 36 Va. L. Rev., *supra* note 4 at 82, but see Guest and Stanzler, *supra* note 75 at 56.

90/See cases cited *supra* notes 14, 27.

91/See, *e.g., Canada Evidence Act,* R.S.C. 1952, c. 307, as am. by S.C. 1952-53 c. 2, ss. 4(1) and 5.

92/Several States of the United States which have privilege statutes clearly grant the privilege to the newsman, *e.g.,* New Jersey, *supra* note 51. It has been held that the Indiana statute grants the privilege to the reporter and can only be claimed by him. See *Lipps* v. *State* (1970), 258 N.E. 2d 622. Note also the *Report of the Canadian Senate Committee, supra* note 1 at 105-06. But see *Pais* v. *Pais* [1970] 3 All E.R. 491 (Baker J., P.D. & A.).

93/R. WEINBERG, *Confidential and other Privileged Communications* (Dobbs Ferry, N.Y.: Oceana Publications, 1967), 40.

94/*Supra* note 6 at 225.

95/*Supra* note 51.

96/On implied waiver, see *Brogan* v. *Passaic Daily News, supra* note 68.

97/See, *e.g., Plunkett* v. *Hamilton* (1911), 136 Ga. 72, 70 S.E. 781; and see *Note,* 36 Va. L. Rev. *supra* note 4 at 68-69. Similarly, claims to privilege based on a code of professional ethics have been dismissed. See *e.g., Re Wayne* (1914), 4 Hawaii Dist. F. 475.

98/*Plunkett* v. *Hamilton* (1911), 136 Ga. 72, 70 S.E. 781.

99/See unreported case discussed *Note,* 36 Va. L. Rev. *supra* note 4 at 69.

100/*Supra* note 51.

101/The basis for the attorney-client privilege is the benefit of the public; it is the privilege of the client and of the public; *per* Riddell J. in *U.S.A.* v. *Mammoth Oil Co.,* [1925] 2 D.L.R. 966, 56 O.L.R. 635. See also *Canary* v. *Vested Estates Ltd.,* [1930] 3 D.L.R. 989, [1930] 1 W.W.R. 996, 43 B.C.R. 1. So, too, the physician-patient privilege is said to rest on the need to promote public health - see *Wigmore, supra* note 5, § 2380(a). See *Pais* v. *Pais, supra* note 92.

102/The "informer" privilege is exceptional. There, the recipient, rather than the communicant, possesses the privilege. This is of course due to the special position of the State as recipient. The privilege is not absolute; it is unavailable where disclosure is necessary to show the innocence of an accused - see *R.* v. *Blain* (1960), 33 C.R. 217, 31 W.W.R. 693, 127 C.C.C. 267 (Sask. C.A.).

103/*Supra* note 51.

104/*Supra* note 65.

105/*Supra* note 65 at 589, *per* Cohen J.

106/*State* v. *Sheridan* (1967), 248 Md 320, 236 A.2d 18.

107/*Supra* note 51.

108/D'ALEMBERTE, *Journalists Under The Axe: Protection of Confidential Sources of Information* (1968-69), 6 Harv. Journal on Legis. 307. See 327-330 for a tabular breakdown and analysis of the U.S. statutes. At 341, "An Act to Protect Confidential Sources of Information" appears. S. 3 of the draft statute specifies "Procedure For Divestiture of Privilege".

109/*Supra* note 51, § 1453. See also the New Mexico statute, *supra* note 51, which makes any order for disclosure appealable, and subject to stay of proceedings.

110/*Supra* note 1.

111/*Id.* at 107.

112/*Id.* at 107.

113/See *supra* note 108. See s. 2 of the draft statute there referred to.

PART
FOUR

Bibliography

chapter twelve

Studies in Journalism: An Introductory Bibliography

PETER JOHANSEN

Journalism is an underdeveloped area of study in Canada. This is not because Canadians lack interest in communication. As one commentator has written, the size of Canada has meant that "communications have always meant more to us than to most countries".[1] Furthermore, public policy has repeatedly focussed on communication. As early as the 1870s, Sir John A. Macdonald developed the Canadian Pacific Railway to establish an east-west communication link which would diminish the strong natural pulls to the south. Government investigators from Aird to Davey have analyzed various aspects of communications. It is probably no coincidence that Alexander Graham Bell, Harold Innis, Marshall McLuhan and the world's first domestic satellite are all Canadian.[2]

Despite all this, there has been little academic writing about journalism. The reasons are many and they include foremost the lack of interest of university and college administrators in developing departments of journalism. Until recently there were only two such departments in Canada and it is only within the last year that these two have offered graduate courses.

From time to time, sociologists, political scientists and economists have contributed to journalism studies, but they have not extended widely our knowledge of Canadian journalism because their professional backgrounds have led them to a variety of concerns of which journalism research was only one waystation. Furthermore, many have been more interested in communications in a broad sense than in journalism specifically.[3]

The bibliography which follows is nothing more than an introduction to journalism studies. It might be seen as an attempt to reconcile the lack of serious writing on journalism in this country with the need to establish a reading program for undergraduates designed to give them a strong understanding of the way the profession is practised here. It is organized into seven categories.

First are *General Works About Journalism*. Some titles in this section survey the mass media generally, but the criterion for inclusion has been a strong emphasis on the news—as opposed to entertainment—media. Also included are books on the theory of mass communication and collections of readings about journalism not cited elsewhere. *The Journalism Tradition* which follows is divided into three subcategories: "Philosophical Statements about Journalism" are classic writings on the role of the press in democratic society; "The History of Journalism" includes both historical surveys and studies on major journalists of the past, and it is organized into British, American and Canadian titles; "Current Journalistic Practices" includes studies which are concerned with definitions of news and styles of writing and editing.

The next category, *Studies About Contemporary Journalists,* includes a number of titles concerned with today's individual newsmen; some are anecdotal, while others are analyses of the journalist's role and performance by social scientists. *Studies About Media,* by contrast, deals with journalists in groups—the media within which they work and the content of news in such institutions as newspapers.

In the category entitled *The Impact of Society Upon the Media,* consideration is given to the mechanisms by which society influences the news process both formally (through the courts, for example) and informally (through such means as manipulation by publicity-seekers). *The Impact of the Media Upon Society,* which follows, contains two kinds of studies—those which analyze the effects of the news media upon individual members of the audience, and others that treat the effects of the news media on society as a whole. Finally, *Issues in Journalism* embraces normative questions currently debated by practitioners and students of journalism. Among these are the desirability of objectivity in news writing and issues raised by new journalism and adversary journalism.

It is unlikely that any two journalism scholars could agree on the relative worth of every title in the field, and on which ones ought to be included in a listing such as this. Because it is designed to encourage an understanding of Canadian journalism, I have favored books and articles from this country; in some cases, perhaps, the standards of excellence imposed for native works is less rigorous than for titles from Britain and the United States. Even so, large gaps exist in the Canadian literature, and these have been filled by including some of the most seminal writing from these other countries. Inclusion of some British and American sources is a requirement in any case since journalism in Canada is part and parcel of the Anglo-American tradition.[4]

The user should supplement this bibliography by turning to other sources readily available. There are good bibliographies in many of the works listed below. Some are exhaustive in particular areas of journalism study.

A second guide to additional reading is the growing number of academic and professional periodicals related to journalism. Among the best are *Journalism Quarterly, Public Opinion Quarterly, Journal of Broadcasting, Columbia Journalism Review, More, Editor and Publisher, Broadcaster* and *Content*. The last two are Canadian.

Finally, the student should consider specialized bibliographies such as *Mass Communication: A Research Bibliography*, by Donald A. Hansen and J. Herschel Parsons (Santa Barbara, Calif.: Glendessary Press, 1968); *Reference Books in the Mass Media*, by Eleanor Blum (Urbana: University of Illinois Press, 1962); *Journalism Abstracts* (School of Journalism, University of Minnesota, Minneapolis, Minn. 55455); *Bibliography: Some Canadian Writings on the Mass Media*, by Helene Cantin (Ottawa: Canadian Radio-Television Commission, 1974); *Aspen Handbook on the Media: Research, Publications, Organizations*, by William L. Rivers and William T. Slater (Palo Alto, Ca.: Aspen Program on Communications and Society, 1973); *Freedom of the Press: An Annotated Bibliography*, by Ralph E. McCoy (Carbondale: Southern Illinois University Press, 1968); and "Canadian Communications: A Resource Guide", by Victor Paddy and Vincent F. Sacco in *Communications in Canadian Society*, 2nd revised edition, edited by Benjamin D. Singer (Toronto: Copp Clark, 1975).

NOTES TO CHAPTER TWELVE

1/JOHN A. IRVING, *The Mass Media in Canada* (Toronto: Ryerson Press, 1962), pp.234-235.

2/A similar comment is made by D.F. THEALL, in "Review Symposium: The Impact of Communications Technology", Communication Research I (1974), p.332.

3/Harold Innis provides a clear example of both these points. Although he distinguished himself in communication studies, he also made significant contributions to his principal field, Canadian economic history. His communications writings, moreover, were not so much concerned with issues of journalism as with the impact of communication technology on society; he was the mentor of Marshall McLuhan, who parlayed technological impact into the catch phrase, "the medium is the message".

4/This point is made in a historical context by W.H. KESTERTON, *A History of Journalism in Canada* (Toronto: McClelland and Stewart, 1967), Chapter 1.

I/General Works About Journalism

ARONSON, JAMES. *Packaging the News: A Critical Survey of Press, Radio, TV.* New York: International Little New World Paperbacks, 1971.

COHEN, STANLEY, AND JOCK YOUNG, eds. *The Manufacture of News: A Reader.* Beverly Hills, Ca.: Sage, 1973.

Canada. *Special Senate Committee on Mass Media, Report* (3 vols.). Ottawa: Queen's Printer, 1970.

DEFLEUR, MELVIN L. *Theories of Mass Communication,* 2nd ed. New York: David McKay Co., 1970.

DEXTER, LEWIS A., AND DAVID M. WHITE, eds. *People, Society, and Mass Communications.* New York: Free Press, 1964.

HAMLIN, D.L.B., ed. *The Press and the Public.* Toronto: University of Toronto Press, 1962.

HUTTENG, JOHN L., AND ROY PAUL NELSON. *The Fourth Estate: An Informal Appraisal of the News and Opinion Media.* New York: Harper and Row, 1971.

IRVING, JOHN A. *Mass Media in Canada.* Toronto: Ryerson Press, 1962.

KESTERTON, W.J. "Journalism", *Canadian Annual Review,* ed. John Saywell. Toronto: University of Toronto Press, 1960-1964.

————. "Mass Media", in *Canadian Annual Review,* ed. John Saywell. Toronto: University of Toronto Press, 1965-1969.

KIRSCHNER, ALLEN AND LINDA KIRSCHNER, eds. *Journalism: Readings in the Mass Media.* New York: Odyssey Press, 1971.

LEROY, DAVID J., AND CHRISTOPHER H. STERLING, eds. *Mass News: Practices, Controversies and Alternatives.* Englewood Cliffs, N.J.: Prentice-Hall, 1973.

LIEBLING, J.J. *The Press.* New York: Ballantine, 1961.

MACDONALD, DICK, ed. *The Media Game.* Montreal: Content Publishing, 1972.

MACDOUGALL, A. KENT, ed. *The Press: A Critical Look from the Inside.* Princeton: Dow Jones, 1972.

MCQUAIL, DENIS. *Towards a Sociology of Mass Communications.* London: Collier-Macmillan, 1969.

MERRILL, JOHN C., AND RALPH L. LOWENSTEIN. *Media, Messages and Men.* New York: David McKay, 1971.

RIVERS, WILLIAM L., THEODORE PETERSON AND JAY W. JENSEN. *The Mass Media and Modern Society,* 2nd ed. San Francisco: Rinehart, 1971.

————, AND WILBUR SCHRAMM. *Responsibility in Mass Communication,* 2nd ed. New York: Harper and Row, 1969.

SINGER, BENJAMIN. *Communications in Canadian Society,* 2nd rev. ed. Toronto: Copp Clark, 1975.

WRIGHT, CHARLES R. *Mass Communication: A Sociological Perspective,* 2nd ed. New York: Random House, 1975.

II/The Journalism Tradition

A. Philosophical Statements About Journalism

Commission on Freedom of the Press, *A Free and Responsible Press.* Chicago: University of Chicago Press, 1947.

Great Britain, Royal Commission on the Press, 1947-1949. *Report.* London: HMSO, 1949.

Great Britain, Royal Commission on the Press, 1961-1962. *Report.* London: HMSO, 1962.

LEVY, LEONARD W. *Legacy of Suppression: Freedom of Speech and Press in Early American History.* Cambridge, Mass.: Harvard University Press, 1960.

MILL, JAMES. "Liberty of the Press", *Essays on Government Jurisprudence, Liberty of the Press and Law of Nations [1825].* New York: Augustus M. Kelley, 1967.

MILL, JOHN STUART. *On Liberty.* New York: The Liberal Arts Press, 1956.

MILTON, JOHN. *Areopagitica.* Oxford: Clarendon Press, 1932.

MOTT, FRANK LUTHER, AND RALPH D. CASEY. *Interpretations of Journalism.* New York: Crofts, 1937.

SIEBERT, FRED S., THEODORE PETERSON AND WILBUR SCHRAMM. *Four Theories of the Press.* Urbana: University of Illinois Press, 1956.

B. The History of Journalism

(i) Great Britain

HAMMOND, W.L. *C.P. Scott of the Manchester Guardian.* London: Bell, 1934.

HANSON, LAWRENCE. *Government and the Press, 1695-1763.* Oxford: Clarendon Press, 1936.

HOLLIS, PATRICIA. *The Pauper Press.* London: Oxford University Press, 1970.

HYAMS, EDWARD. *The New Statesman.* London: New Statesman and Nation

Publishing Co., 1963.

MORRISON, STANLEY. *The English Newspaper.* Cambridge: University Press, 1932.

SIEBERT, FREDERICK. *Freedom of the Press in England, 1476-1776.* Urbana: University of Illinois Press, 1965.

The Times, *The History of The Times* (4 vols.). London: Times Publishing Co., 1935.

WICKWAR, WILLIAM. *The Struggle for Freedom of the Press, 1819-1832.* London: George Allen and Unwin Ltd., 1928.

WILLIAMS, FRANCIS. *Dangerous Estate: The Anatomy of Newspapers.* New York: Macmillan, 1958.

(ii) United States

BODE, CARL. *Mencken.* Carbondale: Southern Illinois University Press, 1969.

EMERY, EDWIN. *The Press and America: An Interpretative History of the Mass Media,* 3rd ed. Englewood Cliffs, N.J.: Prentice-Hall, 1972.

HUGHES, HELEN MACGILL. *News and the Human Interest Story.* New York: Greenwood Press, 1968.

KOBLER, JOHN. *Luce, His Time, Life, and Fortune.* Garden City: Doubleday, 1968.

LEE, ALFRED MCCLUNG. *The Daily Newspaper in America: The Evolution of a Social Instrument.* New York: Macmillan, 1937.

MOTT, FRANK LUTHER. *American Journalism,* 3rd ed. New York: Macmillan, 1962.

SNYDER, LOUIS L., AND RICHARD B. MORRIS, eds. *A Treasury of Great Reporting.* New York: Simon and Schuster, 1962.

STEFFENS, LINCOLN. *The Autobiography of Lincoln Steffens.* New York: Harcourt, Brace, 1931.

SWADOS, HARVEY, ed. *Years of Conscience: The Muckrakers.* Cleveland, Ohio: Meridian, 1962.

SWANBERG, W.A. *Citizen Hearst.* New York: Bantam, 1967.

———. *Luce and His Empire.* New York: Bantam, 1967.

———. *Pulitzer.* New York: Scribner's, 1967.

(iii) Canada

BOWMAN, CHARLES A. *Ottawa Editor: The Memoirs of Charles A. Bowman.*

Sidney, B.C.: Gray's, 1966.

BRAULT, LUCIEN, *et al. A Century of Reporting: National Press Club Anthology.* Toronto: Clarke Irwin, 1967.

BRUCE, CHARLES TORY. *News and the Southams.* Toronto: Macmillan, 1968.

CARELESS, J.M.S. *Brown of the Globe.* Toronto: Macmillan, 1963.

CHALMERS, FLOYD S. *A Gentleman of the Press.* Toronto: Doubleday, 1969.

COOK, RAMSAY. *The Politics of John W. Dafoe and the "Free Press".* Toronto: University of Toronto Press, 1963.

DONNELLY, MURRAY S. *Dafoe of the "Free Press".* Toronto: Macmillan, 1968.

FAUCHER, ALBERT. *A Tradition Lives: The Story of "The Gazette".* Montreal: The Gazette, 1953.

FERGUSON, C.V. *John W. Dafoe.* Toronto: Ryerson Press, 1948.

FORD, ARTHUR. *As the World Wags On.* Toronto: Ryerson Press, 1950.

GRANATSTEIN, J.L., ed. *Forum: Canadian Life and Letters, 1920-70; Selections From The Canadian Forum.* Toronto: University of Toronto Press, 1972.

GREENAWAY, ROY. *The News Game.* Toronto: Clarke Irwin, 1966.

HARKNESS, ROSS. *J.E. Atkinson of the "Star".* Toronto: University of Toronto Press, 1963.

KESTERTON, W.H. *A History of Journalism in Canada.* Toronto: McClelland and Stewart, 1967.

KILBOURN, WILLIAM. *The Firebrand.* Toronto: Clarke Irwin, 1960.

MACEWAN, GRANT. *Eye Opener Bob: The Story of Bob Edwards.* Edmonton: Institute of Applied Art, Ltd., 1957.

MACGILLIVRAY, GEORGE B. *A History of Fort William and Port Arthur Newspapers From 1875.* Toronto: Bryant, 1968.

POULTON, RON. *The Paper Tyrant: John Ross Robertson of the "Toronto Telegram".* Toronto: Clarke Irwin, 1971.

SMITH, I. NORMAN. *The Journal Men.* Toronto: McClelland and Stewart, 1974.

STEELE, FRANK. *Prairie Editor.* Toronto: Ryerson Press, 1961.

C. Current Journalistic Practices

ADAM, G. STUART. "The Journalistic Imagination", in this volume.

BASTIAN, GEORGE C., LELAND D. CASE AND FLOYD K. BASKETTE. *Editing the Day's News,* 4th ed. New York: Macmillan, 1956.

BIRD, ROGER. "Journalism, Fiction, and Other Alliances", in this volume.

CHARNLEY, MITCHELL V. *Reporting,* 2nd ed. Toronto: Holt, Rinehart and Winston, Inc., 1966.

FANG, IRVING E. *Television News.* New York: Hastings House, 1968.

GREEN, MAURY. *Television News: Anatomy and Process.* Belmont, Ca.: Wadsworth Publishing, 1969.

HOHENBERG, JOHN. *The Professional Journalist,* 3rd ed. New York: Holt, Rinehart and Winston, 1973.

MACDOUGALL, CURTIS D. *Interpretative Reporting,* 6th ed. New York: Macmillan, 1972.

MEYER, PHILIP. *Precision Journalism.* Bloomington: Indiana University Press, 1973.

THAYER, R., JR., *et al. The Media Primer.* Toronto: Methuen, 1970.

WILSON, PHYLLIS. "The Nature of News", in this volume.

III/ Studies About Contemporary Journalists

BAMBRICK, KENNETH. "Summary of Survey Results: Canadian Broadcast News Staffs, 1968-70". *Journalism Quarterly* 48 (1971), 757-760.

BERNSTEIN, CARL AND BOB WOODWARD. *All the President's Men.* New York: Simon and Schuster, 1974.

BLACK, HAWLEY L. "French and English Canadian Political Journalists: A Comparative Study". M.A. Thesis, McGill University, 1968.

BRADDON, RUSSELL. *Roy Thomson of Fleet Street.* Toronto: Collins, 1965.

BREED, WARREN. "Newspaper Opinion Leaders and Processes of Standardization". *Journalism Quarterly* 32 (1955), 277-328.

CAREY, JAMES W. "The Communications Revolution and the Professional Communicator", *The Sociological Review Monograph,* No. 13, ed. Paul Holmes. Keele: University of Keele, 1969.

CATER, DOUGLASS. *The Fourth Branch of Government.* Boston: Houghton-Mifflin, 1959.

COHEN, BERNARD C. *The Press and Foreign Policy.* Princeton: Princeton University Press, 1963.

CROUSE, TIMOTHY. *The Boys on the Bus.* New York: Random House, 1973.

DEMPSON, PETER. *Assignment Ottawa: Seventeen Years in the Press Gallery.* Toronto: General Publishing, 1968.

DONOHEW, LEWIS. "Newspaper Gatekeepers and Forces in the News Channel".

Public Opinion Quarterly 31 (1967), 61-68.

DONOHUE, GEORGE A., PHILLIP J. TICHENOR, AND CLARICE N. OLIEN. "Gatekeeping: Mass Media Systems and Information Control", *Current Perspectives in Mass Communication Research,* eds. F. Gerald Kline and Phillip J. Tichenor. Beverly Hills, Ca: Sage, 1972.

DUNN, DELMER D. *Public Officials and the Press.* Reading, Mass.: Addison-Wesley, 1969.

GIEBER, WALTER. "News Is What Newspapermen Make It", *People, Society and Mass Communications,* eds. Lewis Anthony Dexter and David Manning White. New York: Free Press, 1964.

GILBERT, MARCEL. "L'information gouvernementale et les courrieristes parlementaires au Québec". *Revue Canadienne de Science Politique* 4 (1971), 26-51.

GREY, DAVID L. *The Supreme Court and the News Media.* Evanston: Northwestern University Press, 1968.

HALLORAN, JAMES D., PHILIP ELLIOTT AND GRAHAM MURDOCK. *Demonstrations and Communication: A Case Study.* Harmondsworth, Middlesex, England: Penguin Books Ltd., 1970.

JONES, FRANK. "The Watchdogs on Parliament Hill", *A Media Mosaic,* ed. Walt McDayter. Toronto: Holt, Rinehart and Winston, 1971.

KENDRICK, ALEXANDER. *Prime Time: The Life of Edward R. Morrow.* Boston: Little, Brown, 1969.

NIMMO, DAN D. *Newsgathering in Washington.* Englewood Cliffs, N.J.: Prentice-Hall, 1964.

OLIEN, CLARICE N., GEORGE A. DONOHUE AND PHILLIP J. TICHENOR. "The Community Editor's Power and the Reporting of Conflict". *Journalism Quarterly* 45 (1968), 243-252.

POOL, ITHIEL DESOLA AND IRWIN SHULMAN. "Newsmen's Fantasies, Audiences and Newswriting". *Public Opinion Quarterly* 23 (1959), 145-148.

RIVERS, WILLIAM L. *The Opinion Makers: The Washington Press Corps.* Boston: Beacon Press, 1965.

ROSTEN, LEO. *The Washington Correspondents.* New York: Harcourt, Brace and Company, 1937.

RUBIN, DAVID M. AND STEPHEN LANDERS. "National Exposure and Local Cover-Up: A Case Study". *Columbia Journalism Review* (Summer, 1969), 17-22.

SEYMOUR-URE, COLIN. *The Press, Politics and the Public.* London: Methuen, 1968.

SNIDER, PAUL B. " 'Mr. Gates' Revisited: A 1966 Version of the 1949 Case Study". *Journalism Quarterly* 44 (1967), 419-427.

TAYLOR, CHARLES. *Reporter in Red China.* London: Random House, 1966.

TUNSTALL, JEREMY. *The Westminster Lobby Correspondents.* London: Routledge and K. Paul, 1970.

WESTELL, ANTHONY. "Reporting the Nation's Business", in this volume.

WHITE, DAVID M. "The 'Gate Keeper': A Case Study in the Selection of News". *Journalism Quarterly* 27 (1950), 383-390.

WILSON, C. EDWARD. "Why Canadian Newsmen leave Their Papers". *Journalism Quarterly* 43 (1966), 769-772.

WORTHINGTON, PETER. "Foreign Affairs: The Irrelevant Beat", *A Media Mosaic,* ed. Walt McDayter. Toronto: Holt, Rinehart and Winston, 1971.

ZOLF, LARRY. *Dance of the Dialectic.* Toronto: James Lewis and Samuel, 1973.

IV/ Studies About Media

ADLER, RUTH. *A Day in the Life of The New York Times.* Philadelphia: J.B. Lippincott, 1971.

ALLARD, T.J. "Canadian Private Broadcasting". *Gazette* 15 (1969), 145-149.

ARGYRIS, CHRIS. *Behind the Front Page.* San Francisco: Jossey-Bass, 1974.

BAGDIKIAN, BEN H. *The Information Machines.* New York: Harper Colophon, 1971.

BARRETT, MARVIN, ed. *Survey of Broadcast Journalism 1968-1969; 1969-70; 1970-71.* New York: Grosset and Dunlap, 1969, 1970, 1971.

BEATTIE, EARLE J. "Canadian Mass Media: Development and Economic Structure". *Gazette* 15 (1969), 125-137.

BOWERS, DAVID R. "A Report on Activity by Publishers in Directing Newsroom Decisions". *Journalism Quarterly* 44 (1967), 43-52.

BREED, WARREN. "Social Control in the Newsroom: A Functional Analysis". *Social Forces* 33 (1955), 326-335.

BROWN, ROGER L. "Some Aspects of Mass Media Ideologies", *The Sociological Review Monograph,* No. 13, ed. Paul Holmes. Keele: University of Keele, 1969.

BRUCE, JEAN. "A Content Analysis of Thirty Canadian Daily Newspapers Published During the Period January 1 - March 31, 1965, with a Comparative Study of Newspapers Published in 1960 and 1965". Research report prepared for the Royal Commission on Bilingualism and Biculturalism. Ottawa: Public

Archives, 1966.

CAMPBELL, ROBERT AND RUSSELL HUNT. "Oil, logs, minerals, ships, buses, and the media". *Content* (September, 1973), 2-12.

Canadian Broadcasting Corporation. *Annual Report.* Ottawa: CBC, 1936.

CLARKSON, STEPHEN. "Policy and Media: Communicating the Liberal Platform in the 1971 Ontario Election Campaign". Paper presented to the 46th Annual Meeting of the Canadian Political Science Association, Toronto, June 3, 1974.

CUMMING, CARMAN. "The Canadian Press: A Force for Consensus?" in this volume.

EPSTEIN, EDWARD JAY. *News From Nowhere: Television and the News.* New York: Random House, 1973.

FRIENDLY, FRED W. *Due to Circumstances Beyond Our Control.* New York: Random House, 1967.

GORDON, DONALD R. "National News in Canadian Newspapers". Research report prepared for the Royal Commission on Bilingualism and Biculturalism. Ottawa: Public Archives, 1965.

The Last Post, "An Anatomy of the *Time* Canada Lobby and How It Controls What is Published", *Canada: A Sociological Profile,* ed. W.E. Mann. Toronto: Copp Clark, 1971.

LITVACK, ISAIAH AND CHRISTOPHER MAULE. *Cultural Sovereignty: The Time and Reader's Digest Case in Canada.* Toronto: Burns and MacEachern, 1974.

MCNAUGHT, CARLTON W. *Canada Gets the News.* Toronto: Ryerson Press, 1940.

MERRILL, JOHN C. *The Elite Press.* New York: Pitman, 1968. Chap.8.

MERRILL, JOHN C., CARTER R. BRYAN AND MARVIN ALISKY. "Canada", *The Foreign Press.* Baton Rouge, La.: Louisiana State University Press, 1970.

MOUSSEAU, MONIQUE. "Analyse des nouvelles télévisées". Documents de la Commission Royale sur le Bilinguisme et le Biculturalisme, no. 8. Ottawa: Information Canada, 1970.

NICHOLS, M.E. *(CP) The Story of the Canadian Press.* Toronto: Ryerson Press, 1948.

NIXON, RAYMOND B., AND TAE-YOUL HAHN. "Concentration of Press Ownership: A Comparison of 32 Countries". *Journalism Quarterly* 48 (1971), 5-16.

PHILPOT, FRANK ALLEN. "The Making of a Newscast", *Media Casebook,* eds. Peter M. Sandman, David M. Rubin and David B. Sachsman. Englewood Cliffs, N.J.: Prentice-Hall, 1972.

PRINCE, VINCENT. "La presse canadienne-française". *Gazette* 15 (1969), 93-103.

PURCELL, GILLIS. "The Canadian Press (CP)". *Gazette* 15 (1969), 151-158.

QUALTER, T.H., AND K.A. MACKIRDY. "The Press of Ontario and the Election", *Papers on the 1962 Election,* ed. John Meisel. Toronto: University of Toronto Press, 1964.

RAY, IVOR. "Telecommunication and the Transmission of News", *Communication in the Space Age,* UNESCO, (Paris, 1968), 51-57.

ROSS, LINE AND MONIQUE MOUSSEAU. "Analyse du contenu des nouvelles nationales à la télévision canadienne". Rapport de recherche, Commission Royale sur le Bilinguisme et le Biculturalisme. Ottawa: Archives Publiques, 1967.

SCANLON, T. JOSEPH. "Canada Sees the World through U.S. Eyes: One Case Study in Cultural Domination". *Canadian Forum* (September, 1974), 34-39.

SEYMOUR-URE, COLIN K. "An Inquiry into the Position and Workings of the Parliamentary Press Gallery in Ottawa". M.A. Thesis, Carleton University, 1962.

SINGER, BENJAMIN D. "Violence, Protest and War in Television News: The U.S. and Canada Compared". *Public Opinion Quarterly* 34 (1970-71), 611-616.

SMYTHE, DALLAS W. "Time, Market and Space Factors in Communications Economics". *Journalism Quarterly* 39 (1962), 3-14.

TALESE, GAY. *The Kingdom and the Power.* New York: World Publishing, 1969.

TUNSTALL, JEREMY. *Journalists at Work.* Beverly Hills, Ca.: Sage, 1971.

WILSON, C. EDWARD. "News Staff Hiring Practices of Canadian Dailies". *Journalism Quarterly* 48 (1971), 755-757.

WINSOR, HUGH. "Is the Canadian Press Doing its Job?" *The Globe and Mail,* July 4, 1972.

V/ The Impact of Society Upon the Media

ADAM, G. STUART. "The Sovereignty of the Publicity System: The Case of the Alberta Press Act", in this volume.

ATKEY, RONALD G. "The Law of the Press in Canada". *Gazette* 15 (1969), 105-124, 185-200. Reprinted in this volume.

BLACK, EDWIN R. "Canadian Public Policy and the Mass Media". *Canadian Journal of Economics* 1 (1968), 368-379.

Canada. *Broadcasting Act.* Statutes of Canada, Chap.25, 1967-68 (as amended Chap.1. 1970).

Canada. Canadian Radio-Television Commission. *Annual Report.* Ottawa: Information Canada, 1968-.

Canada. Canadian Radio-Television Commission. "Report of the Special Committee on 'Air of Death' ". Ottawa: CRTC, 9 July, 1970.

Fédération Professionnelle des Journalistes du Québec, "Yes, Virginia, There is a Dossier Z". *Content* (May, 1971), 5-11.

GOLDSWORTHY, PETER. "The Claim to Secrecy of News Sources: A Journalistic Privilege". *Osgoode Hall Law Journal,* Vol. 9, No. 1., 1971, 157-177. Reprinted in this volume.

HAGGART, RON. "The Strange Case of the All-Alike Letters", *Politics: Canada,* 3rd ed., ed. Paul W. Fox. Toronto: McGraw-Hill, 1970.

———. "The Brilliant Campaign to Make Public Opinion", *Politics: Canada,* 3rd ed., ed. Paul W. Fox. Toronto: McGraw-Hill, 1970.

KNOLL, STEVE. "Sponsor Rules in ABC Docus", *Media Casebook,* eds. Peter M. Sandman, David M. Rubin and David B. Sachsman. Englewood Cliffs, N.J.: Prentice-Hall, 1972.

LEPINE, NORMAND. "La liberté de l'information dans le droit canadien". *McGill Law Journal* 14 (1968), 733-756.

MINIFIE, JAMES MACDONALD. "Mass Media and Their Control", *Canadian Society: Pluralism, Change, and Conflict,* ed. Richard J. Ossenberg. Scarborough: Prentice-Hall of Canada, 1971.

PARKER, GRAHAM E., ed. *Collision Course: Free Press and the Courts.* Toronto: Ryerson Press, 1966.

ROBINETTE, J.J. *Libel, Defamation, Contempt of Court and the Right of the People to be Informed.* Toronto: Thomson Newspapers, 1962.

ROURKE, FRANCIS E. *Secrecy and Publicity.* Baltimore: Johns Hopkins Press, 1961.

RUSSELL, PETER H. *Leading Constitutional Decisions.* Toronto: McClelland and Stewart, 1965. Part 5.

SCANLON, T. JOSEPH. "How Government Uses the Media", in this volume.

SCHIFF, MARVIN. "On Being in a Prickly Position". *Content* (January, 1972), 2-4.

TOLLEFSON, E.A. "Freedom of the Press", *Contemporary Problems of Public Law in Canada,* ed. O.E. Lang. Toronto: University of Toronto Press, 1968. Reprinted in this volume.

WINSOR, HUGH. "A Power Elite Gets Its Way in Kitchener". *The Globe and*

Mail, February 7, 1972.

———. "How Kitchener's Renewal Scheme was Kept off the Record". *The Globe and Mail,* February 8, 1972.

VI/ The Impact of the Media Upon Society

ATKIN, CHARLES K. "How Imbalanced Campaign Coverage Affects Audience Exposure Patterns". *Journalism Quarterly* 48 (1971), 235-244.

BAKER, ROBERT K. AND SANDRA J. BALL, eds. *Violence and the Mass Media: A Staff Report to the National Commission on the Causes and Prevention of Violence.* Washington: U.S. Government Printing Office, 1969.

BAUER, RAYMOND A. "The Obstinate Audience: The Influence Process from the Social View of Communication", *The Process and Effects of Mass Communication,* rev. ed., eds. Wilbur Schramm and Donald F. Roberts. Urbana: University of Illinois Press, 1971.

BEATTIE, EARLE J. "In Canada's Centennial Year, Influence of U.S. Mass Media Probed". *Journalism Quarterly* 44 (1967), 667-672.

BERELSON, BERNARD. "Communications and Public Opinion", *Mass Communications* 2nd ed., ed. Wilbur Schramm. Urbana: University of Illinois Press, 1960.

———. "What Missing the Newspaper Means", *The Process and Effects of Mass Communication,* ed. Wilbur Schramm. Urbana: University of Illinois Press, 1954.

BOGART, LEO, AND F.E. ORENSTEIN. "Mass Media and Community Identity in an Interurban Setting". *Journalism Quarterly* 42 (1965), 179-188.

CAMERON, ANDREW D., AND JOHN A. HANNIGAN. "Mass Communications in a Canadian City", *Communications in Canadian Society,* 2nd rev. ed., ed. Benjamin D. Singer. Toronto: Copp Clark, 1975.

CIRINO, ROBERT. *Don't Blame the People: How the News Media Use Bias, Distortion and Censorship to Manipulate Public Opinion.* New York: Random House, 1971.

COOPER, EUNICE AND MARIE JAHODA. "The Evasion of Propaganda". *The Journal of Psychology* 23 (1947), 15-25.

DAVIDSON, W. PHILLIPS. "On the Effects of Communication". *Public Opinion Quarterly* 23 (1959), 343-360.

DION, LEON. "The Impact of Radio-Canada on French-Canadian Society". *Exchange* 1 (December, 1961).

EDELSTEIN, ALEX S., AND OTTO N. LARSEN. "The Weekly Press' Contribution to a Sense of Urban Community". *Journalism Quarterly* 37 (1960), 489-498.

ELKIN, FREDERICK. "Communications Media and Identity Formation in Canada", *Communications in Canadian Society,* 2nd rev. ed., ed. Benjamin D. Singer. Toronto: Copp Clark, 1975.

FATHI, ASGHAR. "The Diffusion of a 'Happy' News Event". *Journalism Quarterly* 50 (1973), 271-277.

GREENBERG, BRADLEY S. "Mass Communication Behaviors of the Urban Poor", *Why Aren't We Getting Through?: The Urban Communications Crisis,* ed. Edmund M. Midura. Washington: Acropolis Books, 1971.

————, AND EDWIN B. PARKER, eds. *The Kennedy Assassination and the American Public.* Stanford: Stanford University Press, 1965.

HYMAN, HERBERT AND PAUL SHEATSLEY. "Some Reasons Why Information Campaigns Fail". *Public Opinion Quarterly* 11 (1947), 412-423.

KATZ, ELIHU AND PAUL LAZARSFELD. *Personal Influence.* New York: The Macmillan Company, 1964.

KIRWIN, W.J. "The Utilization of a Community Newspaper by Community Leaders". Thesis, University of Calgary, 1970.

KLAPPER, JOSEPH T. *The Effects of Mass Communication.* Glencoe, Illinois: Free Press, 1960.

LANE, ROBERT E., AND DAVID O. SEARS. *Public Opinion.* Englewood Cliffs, N.J.: Prentice-Hall, 1964.

LANG, KURT AND GLADYS ENGEL LANG. "The Unique Perspective of Television and Its Effect: A Pilot Study", *The Process and Effects of Mass Communication,* Rev. ed., eds. Wilbur Schramm and Donald F. Roberts. Urbana: University of Illinois Press, 1971.

LAUTENS, TREVOR. "When the Newspapers Had to Stop". *Saturday Night* (May, 1970), 33-35.

LAZARSFELD, PAUL F., AND HERBERT MENZEL. "Mass Media and Personal Influence", *The Science of Human Communication,* ed. Wilbur Schramm. New York: Basic Books, 1963.

LEMIEUX, VINCENT. "Election in the Constituency of Levis", *Papers on the 1962 Election,* ed. John Meisel. Toronto: University of Toronto Press, 1964.

LIPPMANN, WALTER. *Public Opinion.* New York: The Free Press, 1922.

MCCOMBS, MAXWELL E., AND DONALD L. SHAW. "The Agenda-Setting Function of Mass Media". *Public Opinion Quarterly* 36 (1973), 176-187.

————. "A Progress Report on Agenda-Setting Research". Paper presented to Association for Education in Journalism, San Diego, August 18-21, 1974.

MCNEIL, ROBERT. *The People Machine: The Influence of Television on American Politics.* New York: Harper & Row, 1968.

PALETZ, DAVID L., REGGY REICHERT AND BARBARA MCINTYRE. "How the Media Support Local Governmental Authority". *Public Opinion Quarterly* 35 (1971), 80-92.

PORTER, JOHN. *The Vertical Mosaic.* Toronto: University of Toronto Press, 1964.

ROBINSON, JOHN P. "Mass Communication and Information Diffusion", *Current Perspectives in Mass Communication Research,* eds. F. Gerald Kline and Phillip J. Tichenor. Beverly Hills, Ca.: Sage, 1972.

SCANLON, T. JOSEPH. "The Not So Mass Media: The Role of Individuals in Mass Communication", in this volume.

————, and ROMAN R. MARCH. "Canadian Experiment Indicates Change of Knowledge a Result of Broadcasts". *Radio Television News Directors Association Bulletin,* 21, 6-7 (1967), 15-16, 19.

SEARS, DAVID O., AND JOHNATHAN L. FREEDMAN. "Selective Exposure to Information: A Critical Review". *Public Opinion Quarterly* 31 (1967), 194-213.

SEYMOUR-URE, COLIN. *The Political Impact of the Mass Media.* London: Constable, 1974.

WEISS, WALTER. "Effects of the Mass Media of Communication", *Handbook of Social Psychology,* Vol. 5, eds. Gardner Lindzey and Elliot Aronson. Boston: Addison-Wesley, 1970.

WIRTH, LOUIS. "Consensus and Mass Communication". *American Sociological Review* 13 (1948), 1-15.

VII/ Issues in Journalism

BOORSTIN, DANIEL J. *The Image: A Guide to Pseudo-Events in America.* New York: Harper, 1961.

ELLUL, JACQUES. *The Political Illusion.* New York: Alfred A. Knopf, 1967.

FIELDS, JAMES E. "Press Access: Rationale and Response". *Freedom of Information Report* (no.296). Columbia, Mo.: School of Journalism, University of Missouri, 1973.

FULFORD, ROBERT. "The Built-in Bias of the Press", *Reporting the News,* ed. Louis M. Lyons. Cambridge, Mass.: Harvard University Press, 1965.

GERALD, J. EDWARD. *The Social Responsibility of the Press.* Minneapolis: University of Minnesota Press, 1963.

GILLMOR, DONALD M. *Free Press and Fair Trial.* Washington: Public Affairs Press, 1966.

GLESSING, ROBERT J. *The Underground Press in America.* Don Mills, Ont.: Fitzhenry and Whiteside, 1971.

GROSS, GERALD, ed. *The Responsibility of the Press.* New York: Simon and Schuster, 1966.

HOHENBERG, JOHN. *The News Media: A Journalist Looks at His Profession.* New York: Holt, Rinehart and Winston, 1968.

HOLMGREN, ROD, AND WILLIAM NORTON, eds. *The Mass Media Book.* Englewood Cliffs, N.J.: Prentice-Hall, 1972.

HONDERICH, BELAND H. "We Need a Press Council", *Politics: Canada* 3rd ed., ed. Paul W. Fox. Toronto: McGraw-Hill, 1970.

KRIEGHBAUM, HILLIER. *Pressures on the Press.* New York: Crowell, 1972.

LEVY, H. PHILLIP. *The Press Council.* London: Macmillan, 1967.

MCDAYTER, WALT. "The Myth of Objectivity", *A Media Mosaic,* ed. Walt McDayter. Toronto: Holt, Rinehart and Winston, 1971.

MACDOUGALL, CURTIS D. *Newsroom Problems and Policies.* New York: Dover, 1963.

Ontario Press Council. *Annual Report 1972-73.* Ottawa: Ontario Press Council, 1974.

POOL, ITHIEL DE SOLA. "Newsmen and Statesmen: Adversaries or Cronies?", *Aspen Notebook on Government and the Media,* eds. William L. Rivers and Michael J. Nyhan. New York: Praeger, 1973.

RESTON, JAMES. *The Artillery of the Press: Its Influence on American Foreign Policy.* New York: Harper and Row, 1967.

RIVERS, WILLIAM L. *The Adversaries.* Boston: Beacon Press, 1970.

RUCKER, BRYCE W. *The First Freedom.* Carbondale: Southern Illinois University Press, 1968.

SCANLON, T. JOSEPH, ed. *Cases For Discussion.* Ottawa: Carleton University School of Journalism, 1968.

SMALL, WILLIAM. *To Kill a Messenger.* New York: Hastings House, 1970.

WARNOCK, JOHN W. "All the News It Pays to Print", *Close the 49th Parallel, etc.,* ed. Ian Lumsden. Toronto: University of Toronto Press, 1970.

WAYS, MAX. "What's Wrong with News? It Isn't New Enough". *Fortune* (October, 1969), 110-113, 155-161.

WOLFE, TOM. *The New Journalism.* New York: Harper and Row, 1973.

THE CONTRIBUTORS

G. Stuart Adam is an associate professor and director of the School of Journalism at Carleton University, Ottawa. Formerly a reporter and deskman at the *Toronto Star* and editorial writer at *The Ottawa Journal,* he holds an M.A. in Canadian Studies from Carleton University and is currently completing doctoral studies in Political Science at Queen's University.

Ronald Atkey practices law in Toronto with the firm of Osler, Hoskin and Harcourt. Formerly, he taught law at the University of Western Ontario and Osgoode Hall. From 1972-74 he was member of Parliament for Toronto St. Paul's.

Roger Bird is an associate professor in the School of Journalism at Carleton University. He has worked as a reporter and deskman for *The Montreal Gazette, The Financial Times of Canada* and *The Ottawa Journal.* He holds a Ph.D. in literature and for a number of years taught in the English Department at Sir George Williams University in Montreal.

Carman Cumming is an associate professor in the School of Journalism at Carleton University, having joined the faculty in 1969 after many years as a correspondent and editor with Canadian Press in Toronto, New York and Ottawa. He holds a B.A. (Toronto) and B.J. (Carleton) and was a Southam Fellow at the University of Toronto in 1965-66.

Peter J. Goldsworthy was a teaching fellow at Osgoode Hall Law School in 1970-71, and is now teaching in Australia at the University of Sydney. He holds an L.L.B. (Sydney) and an L.L.M. (Va.)

Peter Johansen is an assistant professor in the School of Journalism at Carleton University. A former reporter at *The Ottawa Citizen,* he is currently completing doctoral studies in Communication at Stanford University.

T. Joseph Scanlon is an associate professor and former director of the School of Journalism at Carleton University. Prior to joining the school's faculty, he was a reporter with the *Toronto Star* and *The Toronto Telegram* and his assignments included stints in Ottawa and Washington for the *Star.* He holds an M.A. in Political Science from Queen's University and specializes in communications research problems.

E. A. Tollefson is the Director of Programs and Law Information in the Department of Justice in Ottawa. Before joining the federal government, he was on the faculty of law at the University of Saskatchewan. He earned a B.A. and L.L.B. at Saskatchewan and B.C.L. at Oxford.

Anthony Westell is an associate professor in the School of Journalism at Carleton University. A winner of several awards for journalism, he was most recently Ottawa editor and columnist for the *Toronto Star,* a post he assumed after many years as an editorial writer, reporter and editor with both the *Star* and *The Globe and Mail.*

Phyllis Wilson is an associate professor in the School of Journalism at Carleton University. She has spent a career as a reporter at *The Ottawa Journal* and *The Citizen.* She holds a B.A. degree from Queen's University.

ACKNOWLEDGMENTS

Grateful acknowledgment is made for permission to quote:

1/Excerpts from *From Max Weber: Essays in Sociology,* H. H. GERTH AND C. WRIGHT MILLS, eds. Copyright © 1946, Oxford University Press. Reprinted by permission of Oxford University Press.

2/Excerpts from *News and the Human Interest Story* by HELEN MACGILL HUGHES, Greenwood Press edition; Copyright © 1940 by the University of Chicago Press. Reprinted by permission of Greenwood Press, Inc.

3/Excerpts from "How the Tories Hold Power in Ontario" by RON HAGGART, in *Saturday Night,* January 1972. Reprinted by permission of the author and *Saturday Night.*

4/Excerpt from *Miami and the Siege of Chicago* by NORMAN MAILER. Copyright © 1968 by Norman Mailer. Reprinted by permission of George Weidenfeld and Nicolson Limited.

5/Excerpts from "On Chuck Hughes Dying Young" by BARNARD COLLIER in *Esquire,* February 1972. Reprinted by permission of *Esquire* Magazine © 1972 by Esquire, Inc.

6/Excerpt from *News: A Consumer's Guide* by IVAN AND CAROL DOIG. Copyright © 1972 by Prentice-Hall, Inc., Englewood Cliffs, N. J. Reprinted by permission of Prentice-Hall, Inc.

7/Excerpt from an address to Lovejoy Convocation, Colby College, May 5, 1975, by ERWIN D. CANHAM. Reprinted from the *Columbia Journalism Review,* November/December 1972. Copyright © 1972 *Columbia Journalism Review.* Reprinted by permission of the author and *Columbia Journalism Review.*